Contents

Such are the two ways of the photograph. The choice is mine: to subject its spectacle to the civilized code of perfect illusions, or to confront in it the wakening of intractable reality.

Roland Barthes
Camera Lucida

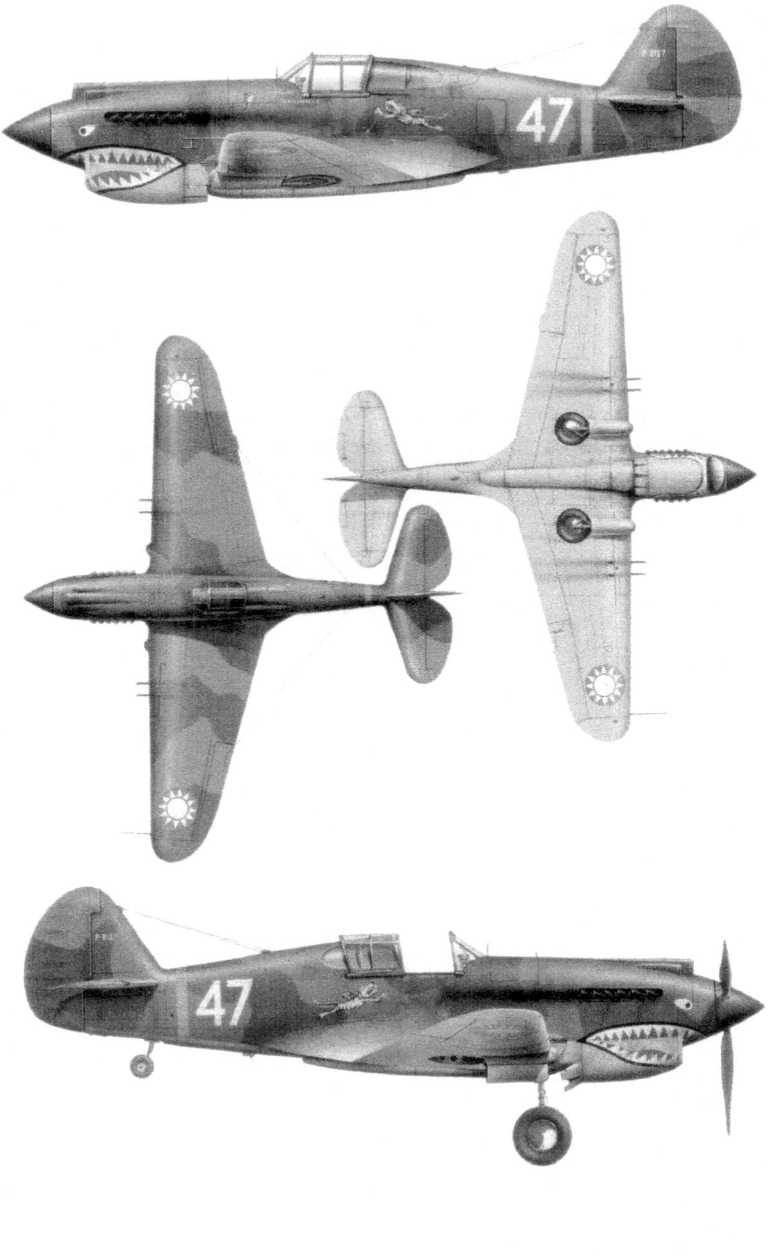
47
47

Prologue

My father was an amateur photographer in his youth, developing his film and making prints in a damp, earthen-floored cellar darkroom in his childhood home in Syracuse, New York. He stored his negatives in a glass Heinz mustard jar, which his twin brother occasionally raided to make "stink bombs" by rolling up the inflammable nitrate-based films and lighting them on fire.

Whether they had been burned up or simply lost, none of the pictures existed by the time I began to hear stories about them. Among the missing photographs were some depicting objects that had also been lost. My father had made a model of a Curtiss P-40 fighter during the opening years of the Second World War. It had enjoyed a brief moment of celebrity during the summer of 1942, only a few months after the raid of Tokyo by Jimmy Doolittle's squadron of bombers. One of the Doolittle raiders, a Lieutenant Thomas C. Griffin, attended a fund-raising event in Syracuse, and appeared in a photograph in the *Syracuse Herald-Journal* newspaper holding the model. My father would often end his story about his famous model with a lamentation: "I wish I still had a picture of that airplane to show you."

The Curtiss P-40 was his favorite airplane. Its form was celebrated in countless instances of iconography in our household. There were paintings and photographs and three-dimensional models of various kinds. The gaping red mouth with flashing white teeth painted on the front cowl-

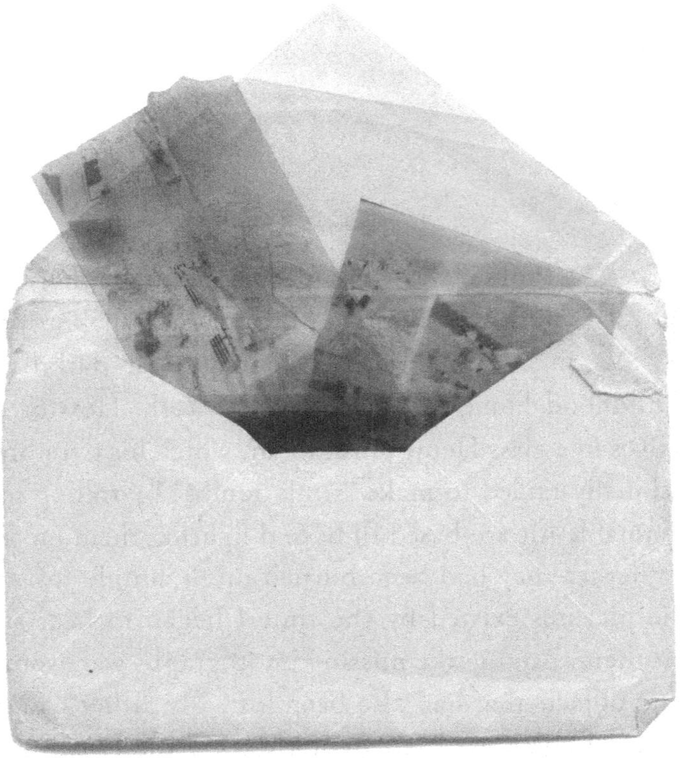

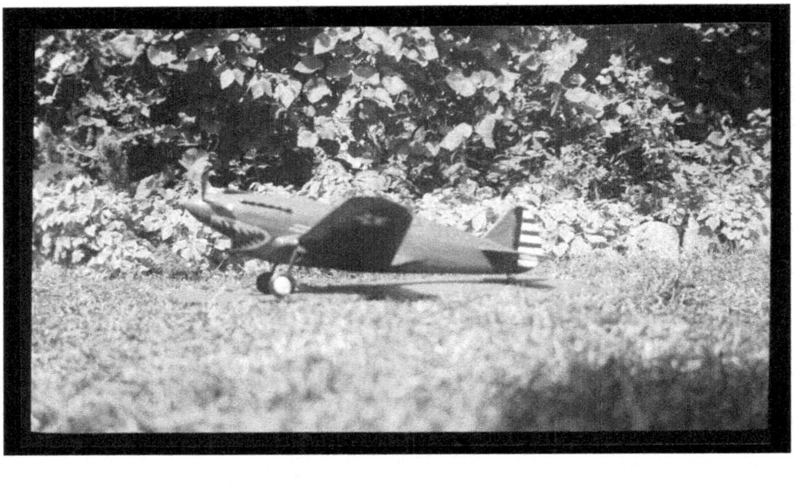

ing transformed the aircraft into a magnificent creature called a "Flying Tiger." As a child, I had no knowledge of the military history or utility of this design. But it somehow connected me back through my father's youth during the heroic times of the Great Depression and Second World War to the very spiritual foundations of the world.

Many years after I first learned about the burned negatives, an envelope containing thirteen surviving frames was discovered in a drawer in my grandmother's house. Among these were three frames containing images of the P-40 model. My father was thrilled to find them, but the images fell short of what I had always imagined them to have been. They could not compare with the fantastic ideas I had conjured of the famous lost model airplane from the stories I had been told. The enchanted power of all the Flying Tiger iconography of my youth was displaced by the cold monochromatic reality of the photographs.

Recently I tracked down the newspaper story in the Tuesday, July 28, 1942 *Syracuse Herald Journal*, and there, spread across four columns, was the photograph of Lieutenant Griffin holding the same model. An element of oral family history was thus verified and normalized by the undeniable evidence of a few photographs that had lain dormant for decades.

Although the subjects of the found photographs did not live up to expectations inspired by the stories and the aeronautical iconography of our household, aspects of some of the photographs held a different kind of power. My father had photographed his model of the P-40 Flying Tiger against a backdrop of grape vines cultivated by his parents to supply grapes for wine making and leaves for wrapping dolmades, a

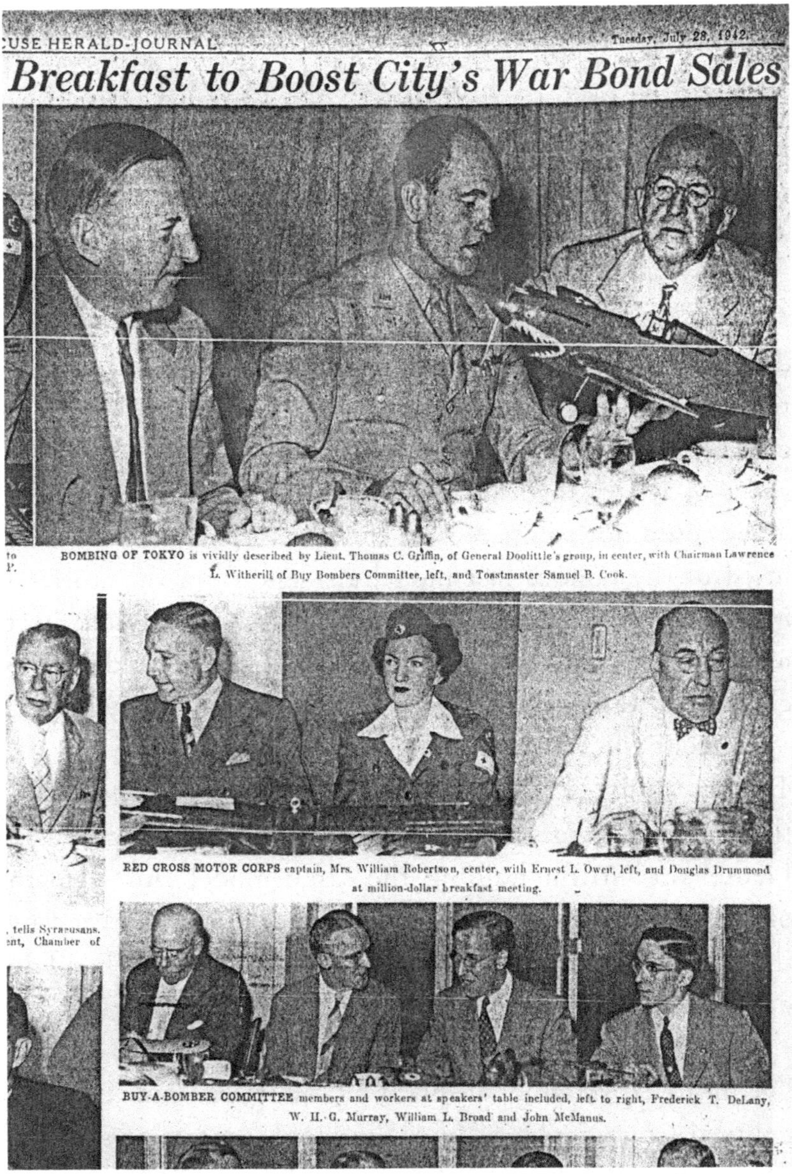

USE HERALD-JOURNAL Tuesday, July 28, 1942.

Breakfast to Boost City's War Bond Sales

to P.

BOMBING OF TOKYO is vividly described by Lieut. Thomas C. Griffin, of General Doolittle's group, in center, with Chairman Lawrence L. Witherill of Buy Bombers Committee, left, and Toastmaster Samuel B. Cook.

RED CROSS MOTOR CORPS captain, Mrs. William Robertson, center, with Ernest L. Owen, left, and Douglas Drummond at million-dollar breakfast meeting.

, tells Syracusans. ent, Chamber of

BUY-A-BOMBER COMMITTEE members and workers at speakers' table included, left to right, Frederick T. DeLany, W. H. G. Murray, William L. Broad and John McManus.

A picture story appearing in the July 28, 1942 Syracuse Herald Journal *featured a large photograph of Lieutenant Thomas C. Griffin holding one of my father's model airplanes. Griffin had flown on Jimmy Doolittle's famous bombing mission over Tokyo a few months prior.*

culinary staple in their Greek immigrant household. While the object of my father's photographic gaze was the model airplane, he accidentally focused his camera instead on the grape vines. This sharp backdrop to the blurry image of his model inadvertently opens a window into a trove of parallel stories that were not part of the official oral canon of our family, but that have unfolded in the background of my life.

During the spring 2015 semester I taught a new elective course at the Rochester Institute of Technology (RIT). It was the first course in aerial photography ever offered by RIT's School of Photographic Arts & Sciences, and it was made possible by a revolution in the technology of remotely-controlled flying platforms called drones, or Unmanned Aerial Vehicles (UAVs). It was also my first real opportunity, after

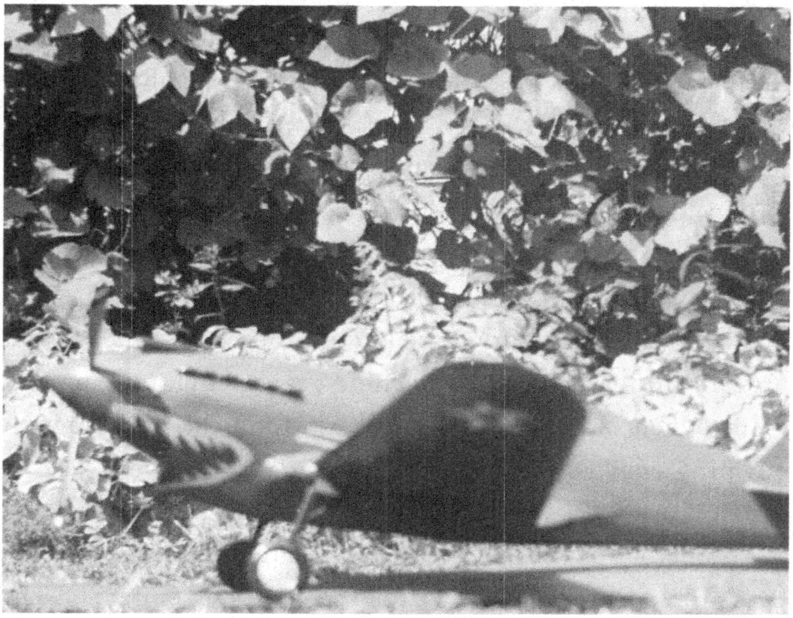

My father photographed his model of the Curtiss P-40, but focused on the grape arbor in the background.

more than three decades of teaching, to invite my students into the world of aeronautical experience and aerial seeing I had inherited and inhabited since my earliest childhood.

We studied the history of aviation for the first month of the semester, beginning with the hot-air balloon ascents of the Montgolfier brothers in France in the late eighteenth century. We read the first descriptions of what the world looked like from an aerial viewpoint, and the accounts of the first successful attempts to make aerial photographs from balloons filled with hydrogen gas. We traced the history of airborne photography from that time to the present, through the revolution in powered flight at the beginning of the twentieth century and then out into space.

During the first class, by way of proving my credentials to teach this new course, I presented a slide show of photographs from our family album chronicling four generations of involvement with aviation and aerial photography. The first pictures I showed were a few of my father's surviving darkroom negatives, including the picture of the P-40 against the backdrop of the grape arbor. Each picture in the slide show contributed to a narrative of continuous development of technology and visual sophistication beginning with my father's rudimentary models and proceeding forward and upward through all the intervening years to that present moment, when our class would embark upon the next stage of our progressive march into the future.

But five weeks into the semester, a tragic event altered the trajectory of the course, and ultimately the path of many lives, including my own. After the semester ended I went back through the collection of photographs and images I had shown the students. Other, perhaps more important, stories emerge from the background. The elements in the original story rearranged themselves into new patterns that I had never before seen. So while many of the details recounted in this book remain the same as when I first shared them with my students, the story itself is entirely new.

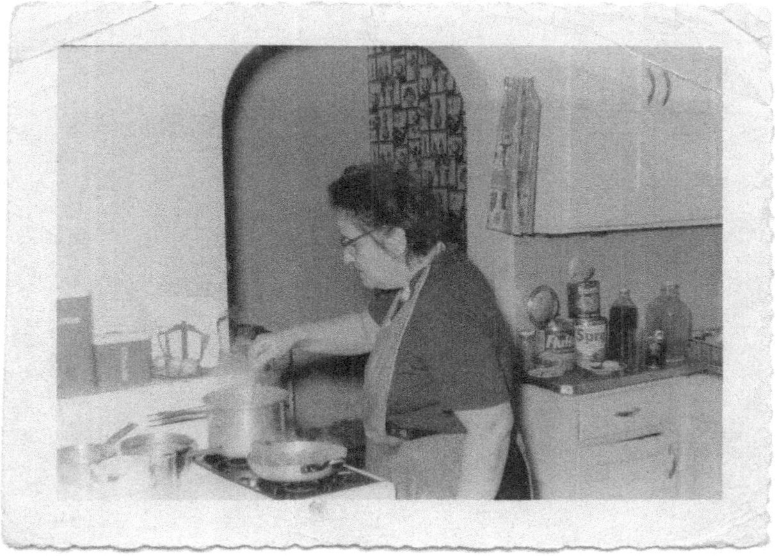

My grandmother Dimitra cooking dolmades in her kitchen sometime in the 1950s. The grape leaves came from her backyard grape arbor.

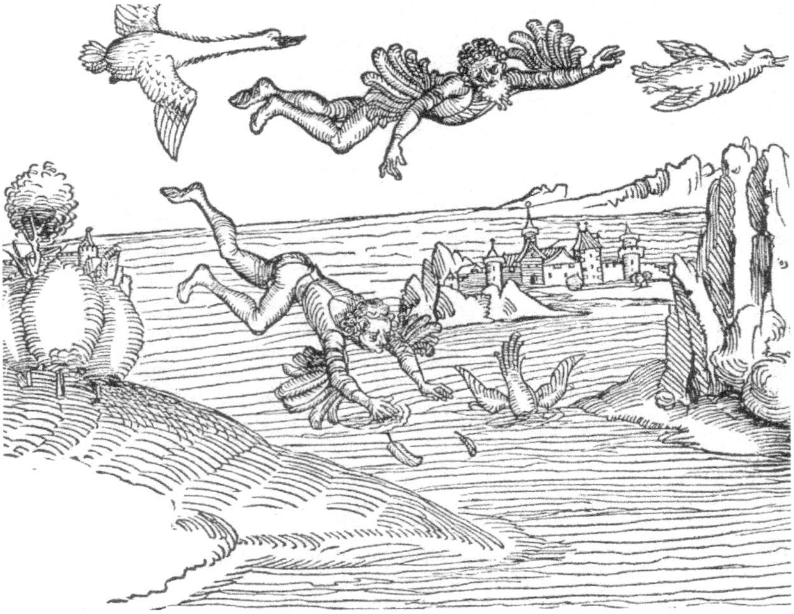

1

THIS WOODCUT by Albrecht Dürer of Icarus falling into the sea while his father Daedalus watches from above appeared in my first childhood picture book about flight. Icarus had not heeded his father's warning to fly low, not getting too close to the Sun, which Daedalus feared might melt the wax used to secure the feathers to his son's wings. I remember hoping it might have been possible for Icarus to swim to shore, which looked in the woodcut very close to where he would have fallen, and thus not suffer the terrible ordeal of drowning.

My hope that Icarus could have been spared from drowning must have come from the knowledge that my father's twin brother, after whom I was named, had drowned only a few years before I was born, when his boat capsized not far from shore in one of the small lakes in the Adirondack Mountains. No details of the accident beyond these simple facts were ever told. My father could not talk about it without being overcome by emotion and falling silent. I learned as a child not to ask. It was enough to know that a terrible tragedy had befallen my father at a time before I existed, and that he was always carrying this loss silently within his memory.

Three other people in my father's family lived through this tragedy: his older brother, their mother, and her older brother. I somehow knew I was not welcome to ask any of them about my uncle's death or even about his life. My father suggested by his silence that it was not necessary for me to know anything more than the few simple facts he was willing to disclose.

As a result, the time between my uncle's drowning and my own birth is a void in the fabric of space and time that troubled me greatly as a child, and still challenges me today. There would never be a way to reach backward and make physical contact with the person whose name I shared, who had been closer to my father than anyone else in the world could ever be. This was my first encounter with the forever unknowable unknown, and I have eventually accepted the fact that perhaps all of the most important things in life are those which can never be known. Perhaps this acceptance might be a key to some kind of freedom.

But as a child I could not help wanting to know. I tried to extrapolate knowledge from the physical remnants of a

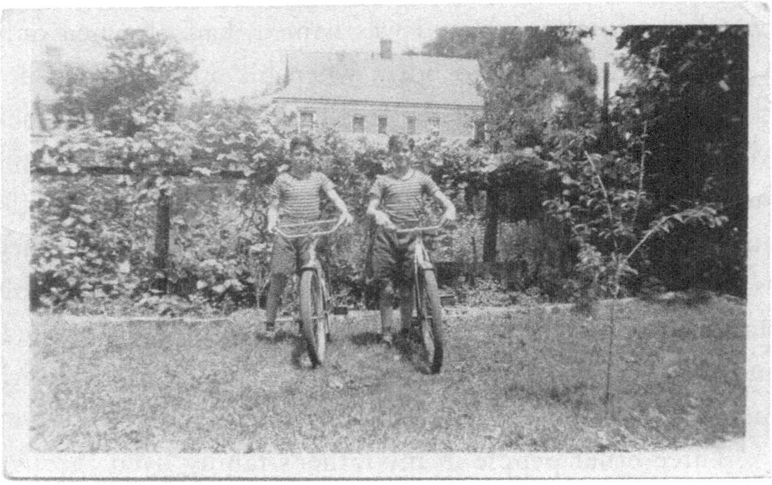

Frank J. Cost and Emil J. Cost were twins born on March 13, 1927 in Syracuse, New York, and like their bicycles in this photograph from around 1938, they were not identical.

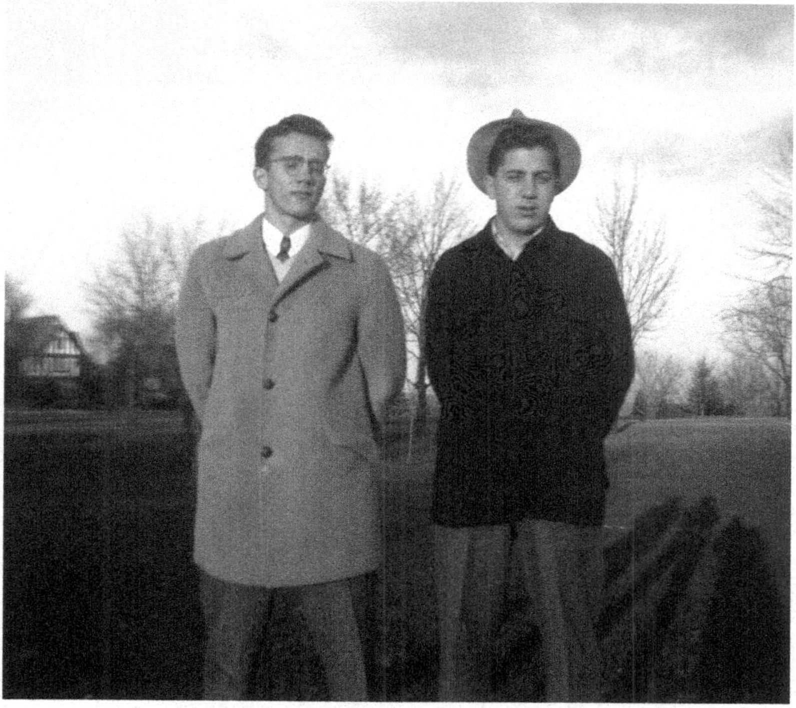

Emil and Frank sometime in the mid 1940s.

world I knew my uncle to have inhabited. My grandmother had carried my father and his brother together in her womb. They were fraternal twins, so there was little I could learn from studying my father's features. The few photographs we have of the twins together show clearly that they were as different as any two brothers who are not identical twins. As hard as I tried to imagine my father and his brother together, one of the twins was clear and corporeal, while the other was a mere trace of an outline. I would try to color in the outline with information gleaned from the few photographs we had of my father's missing twin. But there was no color, sound, motion, or bodily warmth in my renderings.

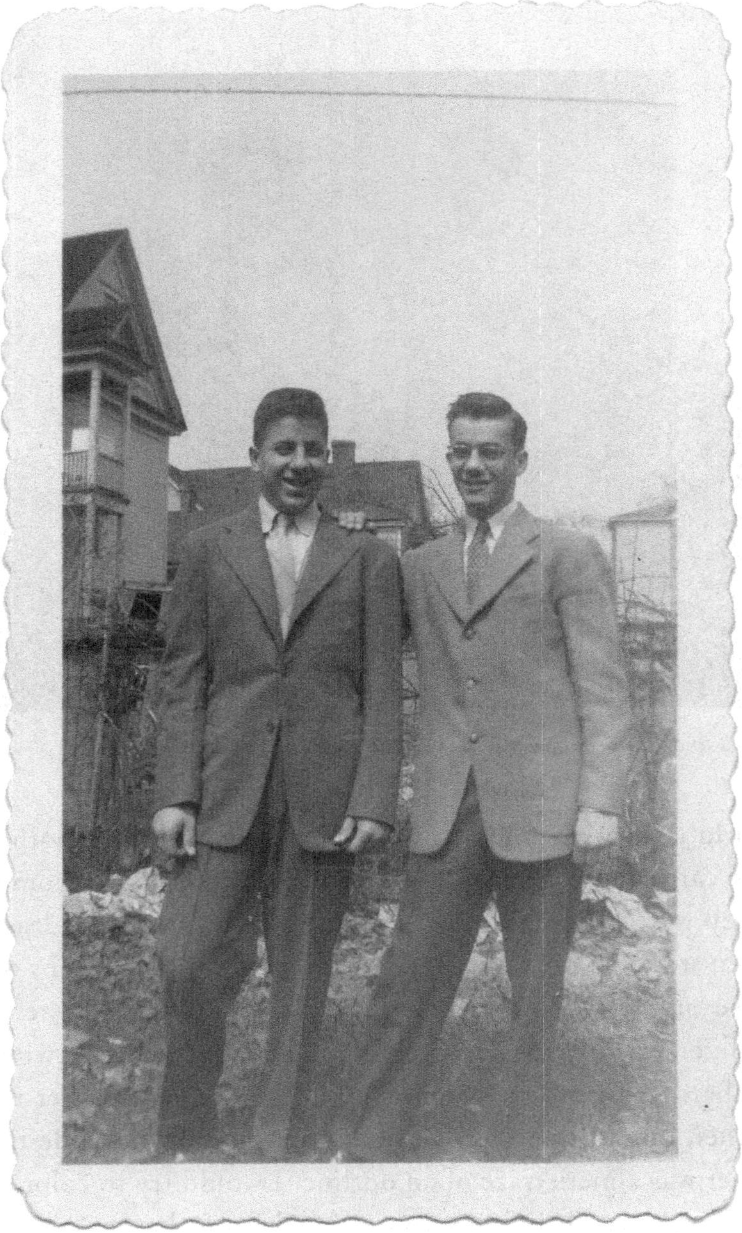

Frank and Emil age 17 on April 9 (Greek Orthodox Palm Sunday), 1944.

Nonetheless, I was able to receive two significant messages from the photographs: my uncle had indeed existed, and his relaxed and kindly demeanor seemed to suggest we would have shared an affection for one another, had he survived.

My father's reluctance to talk about his brother outside of the safe confines of a small canonical repertoire of familiar stories, along with my learned reluctance to ask questions that tested those boundaries, have left me dependent upon the photographs alone when I have wished to know more than what was originally disclosed. Fortunately, the few surviving photographs provide enough of a visceral sense of the indelible reality of my uncle's life to enable me sometimes to imagine a viewpoint and listen for a voice that could have been his. In this way the missing person of my uncle became a guide, directing my attention back to the people who were still living, and clarifying my vision of the family into which I fell in late November 1954.

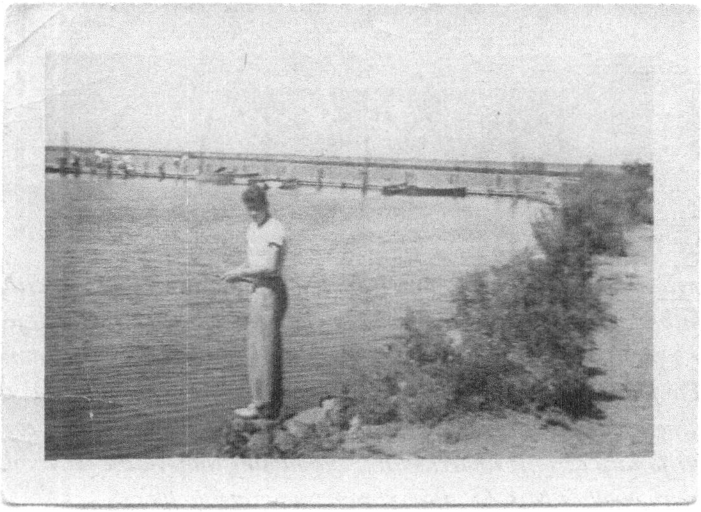

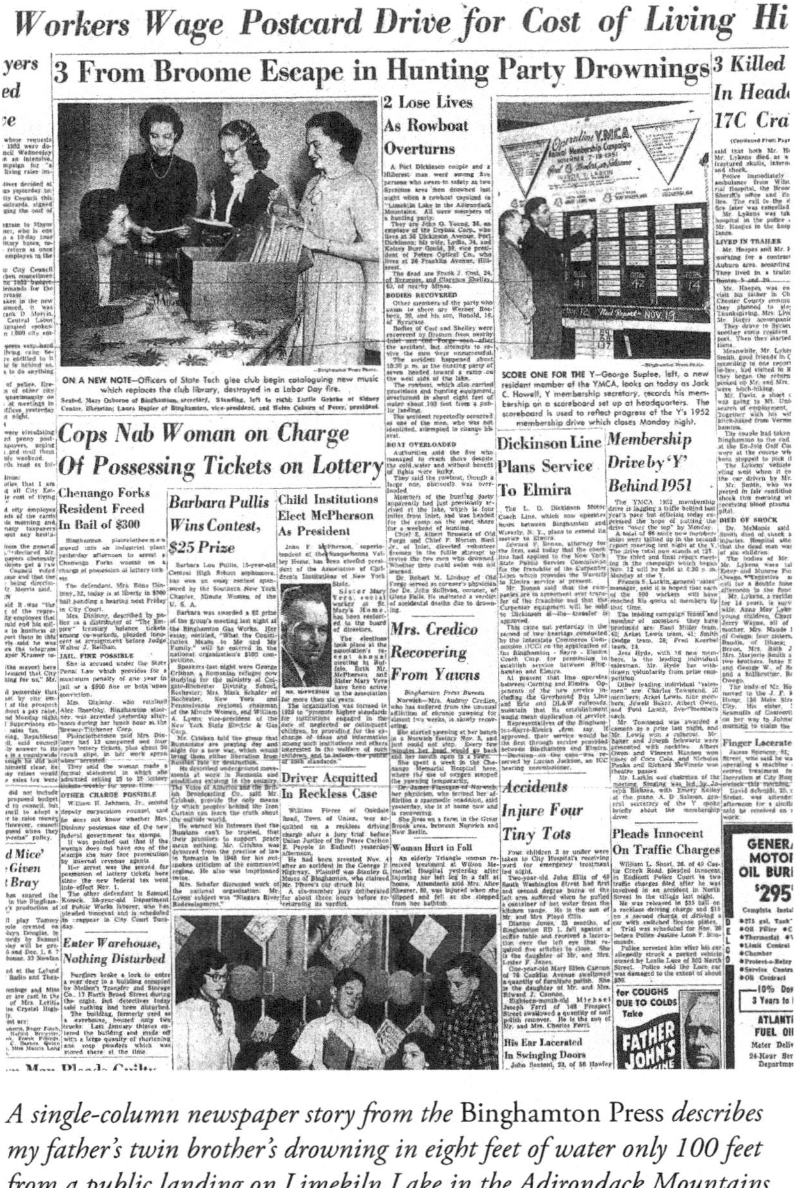

Workers Wage Postcard Drive for Cost of Living Hi

3 From Broome Escape in Hunting Party Drownings

ON A NEW NOTE—Officers of State Tech glee club begin cataloguing new music which replaces the club library, destroyed in a Labor Day fire.

2 Lose Lives As Rowboat Overturns

A Port Dickinson couple and a Hillcrest man were among five persons who swam to safety as two Syracuse area men drowned last night when a rowboat capsized in Limekiln Lake in the Adirondack Mountains. All were members of a hunting party.

They are John O. Young, 38, an employe of the Drybak Corp., who lives at 35 Dickinson Avenue, Port Dickinson; his wife, Lydia, 34, and Kelsey Burr Gould, 38, vice president of Peters Optical Co., who lives at 26 Franklin Avenue, Hillcrest.

The dead are Frank J. Cost, 24, of Syracuse, and Clarence Shelley, 40, of nearby Minoa.

BODIES RECOVERED

Other members of the party who swam to shore are Werner Rosbeck, 39, and his son, Ronald, 16, of Syracuse.

Bodies of Cost and Shelley were recovered by firemen from nearby Inlet and Old Forge soon after the accident, but attempts to revive the men were unsuccessful.

The accident happened about 10:30 p. m. as the hunting party of seven headed toward a camp on the west side of the lake.

The rowboat, which also carried provisions and hunting equipment, overturned in about eight feet of water about 100 feet from a public landing.

The accident reportedly occurred as one of the men, who was not identified, attempted to change his seat.

BOAT OVERLOADED

Authorities said the five who managed to reach shore despite the cold water and without benefit of lights were lucky.

They said the rowboat, though a large one, obviously was overloaded.

Members of the hunting party apparently had just previously arrived at the lake, which is four miles from Inlet, and was headed for the camp on the west shore for a weekend of hunting.

Chief E. Albert Brussels of Old Forge and Chief F. Norton Bird Jr., of Inlet, directed volunteer firemen in the futile attempt to revive the two men who drowned. Whether they could swim was not learned.

Dr. Robert M. Lindsay of Old Forge served as coroner's physician for Dr. John Sullivan, coroner, of Glens Falls. He indicated a verdict of accidental deaths due to drowning.

Mrs. Credico Recovering From Yawns

Binghamton Press Bureau

Norwich—Mrs. Audrey Credico, who has suffered from the unusual affliction of chronic yawning for almost two weeks, is slowly recovering.

She started yawning at her bench in a Norwich factory Nov. 5, and just could not stop. Every few minutes her head would go back and her mouth open in a yawn.

She spent a week in the Chenango Memorial Hospital here, where the use of oxygen stopped the yawning temporarily.

Dr. James Flanagan of Norwich, her physician, who termed her affliction a spasmodic condition, said yesterday, she is at home now and is recovering.

She lives on a farm in the Great Brook area, between Norwich and New Berlin.

Woman Hurt in Fall

An elderly Triangle woman received treatment at Wilson Memorial Hospital yesterday after injuring her left leg in a fall at home. Attendants said Mrs. Alice Shearer, 80, was injured when she slipped and fell as she stepped from her bathtub.

SCORE ONE FOR THE Y—George Suplee, left, a new resident member of the YMCA, looks on today as Jack C. Howell, Y membership secretary, records his membership on a scoreboard set up at headquarters. The scoreboard is used to reflect progress of the Y's 1952 membership drive which closes Monday night.

Cops Nab Woman on Charge Of Possessing Tickets on Lottery

Chenango Forks Resident Freed In Bail of $300

Barbara Pullis Wins Contest, $25 Prize

Child Institutions Elect McPherson As President

Driver Acquitted In Reckless Case

Dickinson Line Plans Service To Elmira

Membership Drive by 'Y' Behind 1951

Accidents Injure Four Tiny Tots

Pleads Innocent On Traffic Charges

His Ear Lacerated In Swinging Doors

Enter Warehouse, Nothing Disturbed

3 Killed In Head... 17C Cra...

Finger Lacerate...

A single-column newspaper story from the Binghamton Press *describes my father's twin brother's drowning in eight feet of water only 100 feet from a public landing on Limekiln Lake in the Adirondack Mountains. As if to purposely remind us of the utter indifference of the wider world to this tragic event that would so profoundly alter the lives of many people in our family, directly underneath the drowning story in the same column is a story about a Mrs. Credico's chronic yawning problem.*

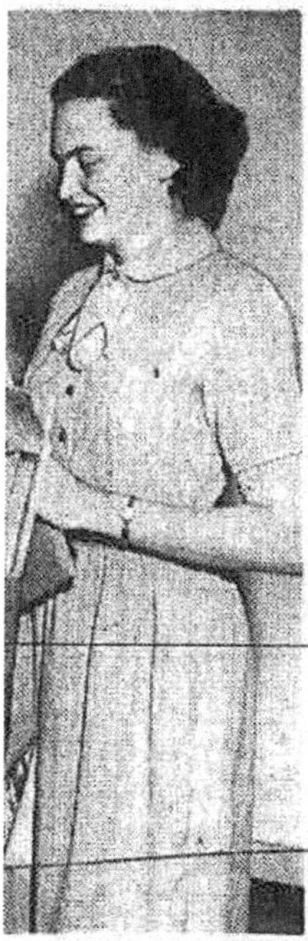

—Binghamton Press Photo.

ataloguing new music
oor Day fire.
Lucile Gehrke of Sidney
Coburn of Perry, president.

harge
n Lottery

ild Institutions
ct McPherson
President

n F. McPherson, superin-nt of the Susquehanna Val-ome, has been elected presi- of the Association of Chil- Institutions of New York State.

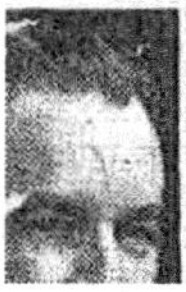

Sister Mary Vera, social worker at St. Mary's Home, has been reelected to the board of directors.

The elections

2 Lose Lives As Rowboat Overturns

A Port Dickinson couple and a Hillcrest man were among five persons who swam to safety as two Syracuse area men drowned last night when a rowboat capsized in Limekiln Lake in the Adirondack Mountains. All were members of a hunting party.

They are John O. Young, 36, an employe of the Drybak Corp., who lives at 38 Dickinson Avenue, Port Dickinson; his wife, Lydia, 34, and Kelsey Burr Gould, 38, vice president of Peters Optical Co., who lives at 26 Franklin Avenue, Hillcrest.

The dead are Frank J. Cost, 24, of Syracuse, and Clarence Shelley, 40, of nearby Minoa.

BODIES RECOVERED

Other members of the party who swam to shore are Werner Rosbeck, 38, and his son, Ronald, 16, of Syracuse.

Bodies of Cost and Shelley were recovered by firemen from nearby Inlet and Old Forge soon after the accident, but attempts to revive the men were unsuccessful.

The accident happened about 10:30 p. m. as the hunting party of seven headed toward a camp on the west side of the lake.

The rowboat, which also carried provisions and hunting equipment, overturned in about eight feet of water about 100 feet from a public landing.

The accident reportedly occurred as one of the men, who was not identified, attempted to change his seat.

BOAT OVERLOADED

Authorities said the five who managed to reach shore despite the cold water and without benefit of lights were lucky.

They said the rowboat, though a large one, obviously was overloaded.

Members of the hunting party apparently had just previously arrived at the lake, which is four miles from Inlet, and was headed for the camp on the west shore for a weekend of hunting.

Chief E. Albert Brussels of Old Forge and Chief F. Norton Bird, Jr., of Inlet, directed volunteer firemen in the futile attempt to revive the two men who drowned. Whether they could swim was not learned.

Dr. Robert M. Lindsay of Old Forge served as cornoer's physician for Dr. John Sullivan, coroner, of Glens Falls. He indicated a verdict of accidental deaths due to drowning.

Mrs. Credico

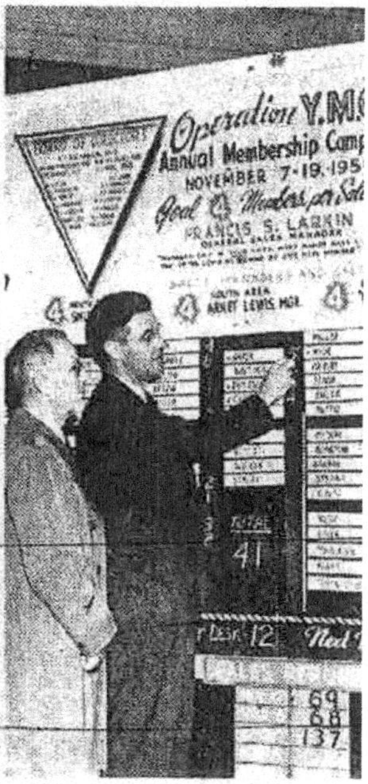

SCORE ONE FOR THE Y—Geo
resident member of the YMCA,
C. Howell, Y membership secr
bership on a scoreboard set u
scoreboard is used to reflect p
membership drive which c

Dickinson Line Plans Service To Elmira

The L. D. Dickinson Motor Coach Line, which now operates buses between Binghamton and Waverly, N. Y., plans to extend its service to Elmira.

Edward F. Ronan, attorney for the firm, said today that the coach line had applied to the New York State Public Service Commission for the franchise of the Carpenter Lines which provides the Waverly to Elmira service at present.

Mr. Ronan said that the companies are in agreement over transfer of the franchise and that the Carpenter equipment will be sold to Dickinson if the transfer is approved.

This came out yesterday in the second of two hearings conducted

M
D
B

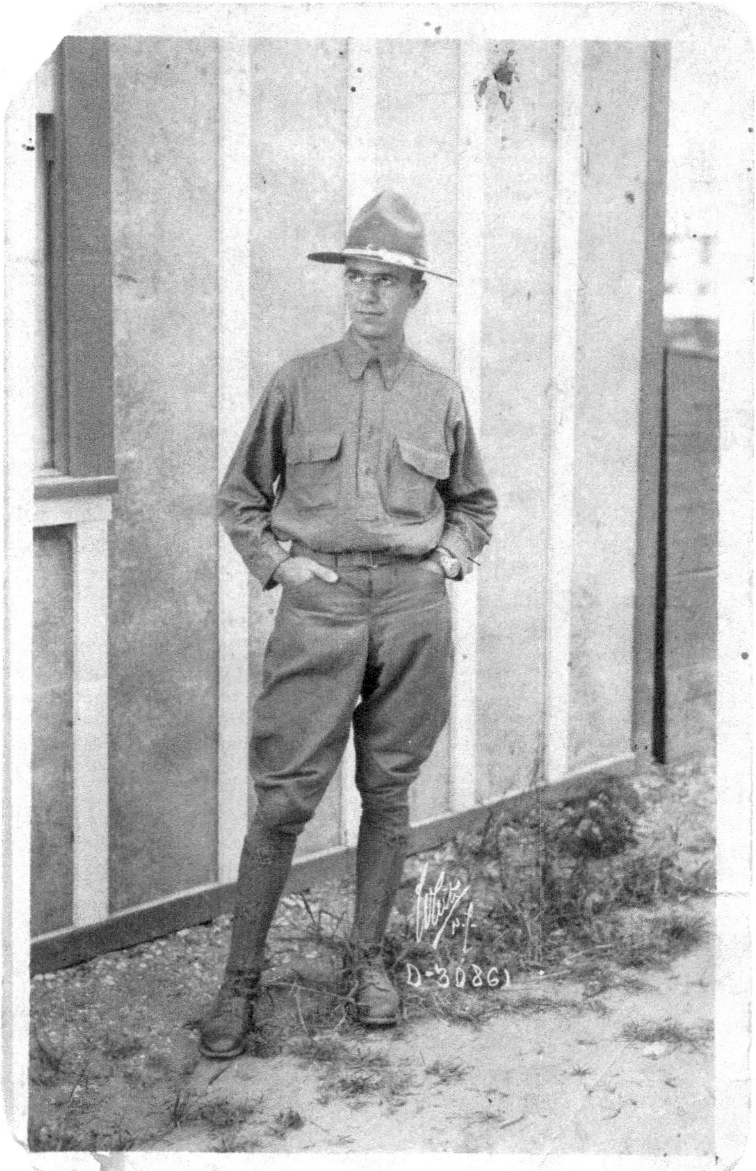

This earliest extant photograph of James Cost at Camp Dix, New Jernesy, is dated July 28, 1918. The eyes have been poked out with a pin, most likely by a child, perhaps by my father or his twin brother.

2

Like many American families, ours begins its known history with tales of flight. My father's father, born in 1894 in Bursa, near Istanbul (in what was then the Ottoman empire), was Odysseus Constantinedes, a Greek by virtue of his family heritage and a Turk by virtue of long centuries of co-existence in a place where Greeks and Turks shared a common culture until the upheavals of the twentieth century destroyed that world. He was the oldest of three sons born into a family of silk and clothing manufacturers, and was educated and fluent in both languages. He reached his eighteenth birthday in 1912, the year war began between the Greeks and the Turks as the Ottoman Empire was coming to its violent end. His father decided that Odysseus should be sent away to America to avoid being drafted into the Turkish army. Many relatives from his generation had similar reasons for coming to America.

This is all I know about my grandfather's life before he emigrated. He came through Ellis Island and his long Greek name was replaced with James O. Cost, the heroic name of the great Homeric seafaring adventurer abbreviated to a seldom-used middle initial. The earliest known photograph of Odysseus, now James, was taken at Camp Dix in New Jersey in 1918. He is standing at ease with his hands in his pockets and his body in the S-curve posture of a classic Greek statue wearing the uniform of a private in the American Army, an almost perfect snapshot of a man at the moment of transformation from Old World person to New. He was drafted into the army at the end of the First World War but was spared the experience of shipping back to a warring Europe from which he had escaped. His army service gave him American citizenship and injected him full force into a new American life with all of his dreams intact.

In July 1918, while James was stationed at Camp Dix, two Chicago-based photographers, Arthur Mole and John

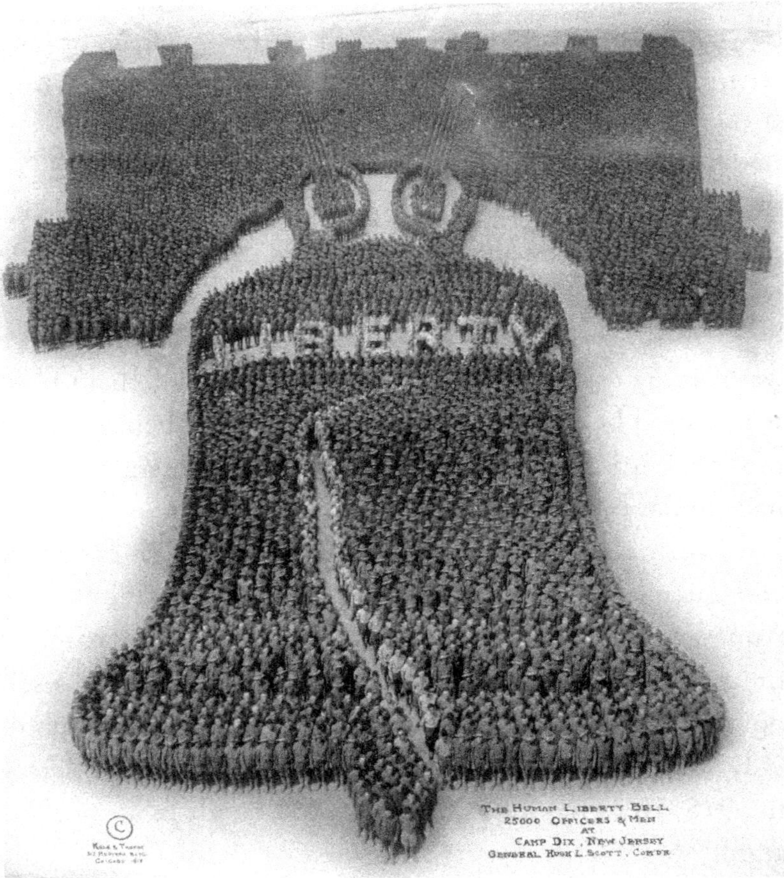

The Human Liberty Bell, 25,000 Officers and Men, Camp Dix New Jersey, 1918, Arthur Mole and John D. Thomas. (LOC)

D. Thomas, arranged 25,000 "officers and men" on the campgrounds to form the shape of the Liberty Bell. This arrangement was then photographed with an 11 by 14-inch view camera from an 80-foot-high tower constructed for the purpose. The desired shape of the Liberty Bell was transferred from an outline on the ground glass of the camera to a massive area on the campgrounds by a man shouting instructions through a megaphone to a team of men placing markers on the ground below. The soldiers were then martialed and arranged to fill the shape. From the ground it would have been impossible to imagine the appearance of the final image, or perhaps even to know the true nature of the project. The resulting photograph was intended, along with several other pictures made at other military camps and bases around the country, to be used to promote the sale of war bonds. It may never have been seen by James or the men who were in it. Although it is impossible to determine whether James participated in the making of this picture, there is some significant chance that he did. When I imagine him standing there, sweltering in his woolen uniform perhaps somewhere above the top of the crack in the bell, I'm relieved to know this may have been the most extreme moment of his forfeiture of individuality during a time when others were perishing by the millions in the trenches of Europe.

From every subsequent piece of evidence, James embraced America and nearly everything it stood for, with a few notable exceptions. For example, he did not embrace the prohibition of alcohol that became law in 1919, but instead maintained a small distillery and wine-making operation in his cellar in Syracuse, New York, throughout the dry years. Neither did he venture out into the American wilderness to find a wife, but relied on the small network of transplanted Turkish Greeks to arrange a marriage partnership with the younger sister of a fellow émigré. Dimitra Christofides had remained in Europe with her mother and younger sister throughout the war years, and was summoned to America in the early 1920s to marry James.

They lived a stable and prosperous life until the last year of the Second World War, when James suffered a cerebral hemorrhage followed by an agonizing nine months of paralyzed suffering before his death. Through all the years of the Depression and War he had maintained steady employment in the Rainbow Lounge of the Hotel Syracuse, playing the Hollywood-inspired role of sophisticated Continental waiter, displaying perfect manners and dressing in formal attire. His often-expressed ambition was for his three sons to surpass his social station, to someday be regularly waited upon themselves by such elegant help.

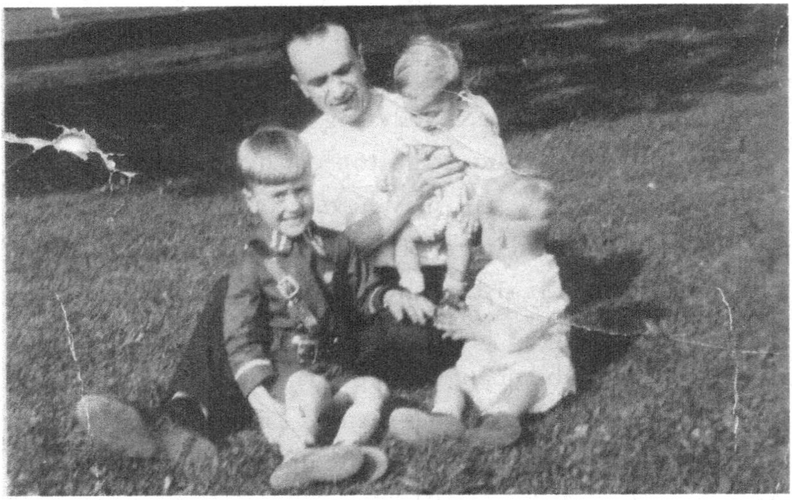

James Cost and his three sons circa 1928. The twins on the right were four years younger than their elder brother, Stephen, on the left. Steve became a physician and lived to the age of 90.

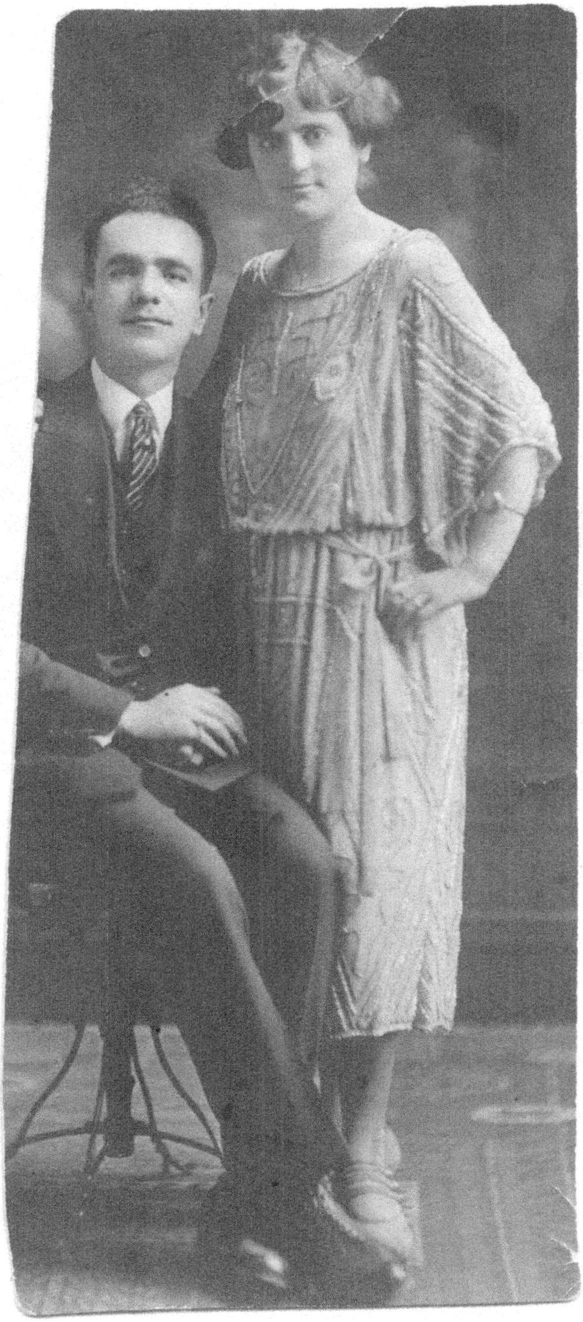

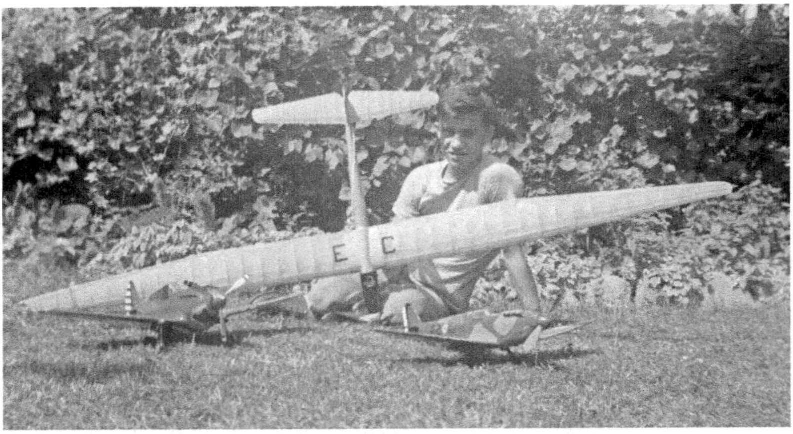

Emil J. Cost with some of his model airplanes, c. 1942.

3

The theme of aviation enters our family history in 1938, when James took his twin boys, now eleven years old, for rides in an open-cockpit seaplane on Onondaga Lake in Syracuse. My father remembers his mother protesting loudly as his father arranged for the airplane rides for himself and his two sons. He remembers that his father was the first to take a ride, but forgets who rode next. From the moment he disembarked from this brief aerial excursion, my father had a passion for flight that never diminished, a passion that became one of the dominant themes of our family life. I had always assumed that his twin brother had experienced the flight with the same enthusiasm, but recently my father told me that the only aviation-related interest his brother ever manifested was the desire to break my father's model airplanes when he was angry at him. "My brother Frank's job was to undo whatever I did, whenever he had the chance."

Just before the Second World War began, my grandfather became interested in helping the War effort with his idea of a new kind of aircraft that would employ a rotating wing with large propellers that could enable both forward motion and vertical hovering. He had his eldest son, Stephen, sketch out the concept, and my father build a model of the flying machine. On August 21, 1941, James sent a letter to the War Department describing his invention: "I have the plans and a model for a new type of bomber which can approach its objective silently and descend vertically, discharging its cargo directly above the target and escaping without being suspected." He received a response less than a month later from an organization called The National Inventors Council at the Department of Commerce. "Your suggestion for a bomber has been received and will be given prompt attention. You will be advised as soon as possible as to the disposition made of it. Thank you for your interest in national defense." As far as I know, this was the last word he received about it, but the respectful response on U.S. Government stationery was a source of great pride to him.

The three years that passed from the seaplane pleasure rides on Onondaga Lake to the proposal for a new kind of bomber in the fall of 1941 coincided with the progress

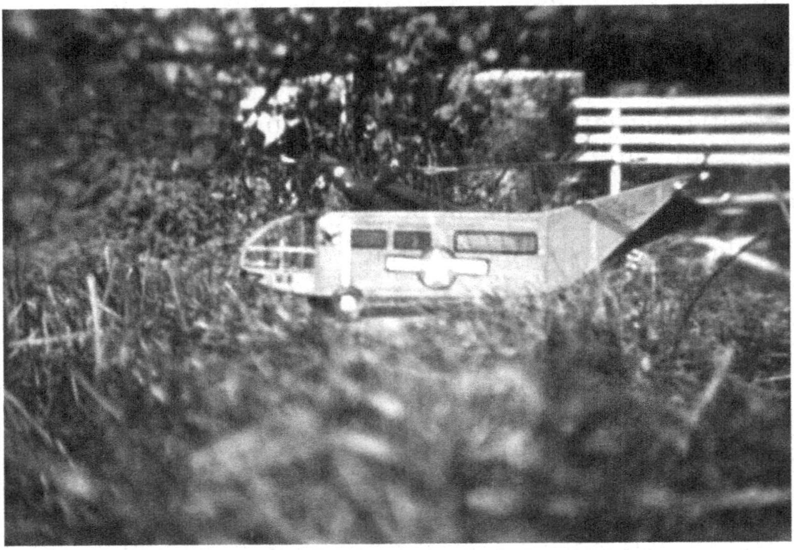

One of the thirteen recovered negatives from Emil J. Cost's darkroom bears an image of his father's invention for "a new type of bomber which can approach its objective silently and descend vertically, discharging its cargo directly above the target and escaping without being suspected."

of a world from peacetime to global war. The pleasures of looking down from the summer sky upon a resplendent and peaceful world below were displaced by fears of malevolent forces raining death from above.

The twin brothers followed separate paths during the War. Frank had always struggled in school, and when he turned sixteen in the spring of 1943, he dropped out and went to work as a laborer. When he turned seventeen, his father encouraged him to join the Navy, and wrote a letter to the War Department giving permission for his son to enlist before his 18th birthday. Frank eventually shipped to England where he overlapped briefly with his elder brother, who was serving as a medic in the army. Neither brother saw combat during the War, but photographs of each in uniform were proud indicators of their participation in the war effort. When my father, Emil, turned eighteen in March 1945, he became eligible for service, but received a deferment to take care of his dying father and suffering mother. This enabled them to keep James out of the hospital where he had been allowed to lie in a vegetative state, developing bedsores after he first fell ill. For nine months Emil and his mother nursed James at home until his death. They made it possible for him to sit in a chair in the kitchen and be in the midst of his family, even though he was unable to communicate or respond in any meaningful way.

My father found his father dead in his chair in almost exactly the same place in the kitchen where three decades later he would discover his mother's body on the floor, dead from a heart attack.

During all the years I had known my grandmother, she was rarely without a cigarette at the corner of her mouth.

She would start each morning rolling her day's supply of cigarettes with an ancient hand-rolling machine and a blue can of "Bugler" cigarette tobacco, and then stack her completed cigarettes in a triangular pile like Civil War cannon balls before a major battle. As a child I associated her with Popeye the Sailor, with his omnipresent pipe at the corner of his mouth and his infectious chuckle. During the famous "Blizzard of 1966," she was stuck at our house for days without her cigarettes and resorted to smoking one of my father's pipes, completing the cartoon picture. She had been a person of great humor and charisma. Before suffering the tragic losses that would color her later life, she had been recognized in the local Greek community as a skilled matchmaker, one who could tell the future by analyzing the patterns formed by the side-clinging grounds in empty Turkish coffee cups. During the last few years of her life, she would often express her loss of heart by declaring, "Everything baloney!" and the only prediction she would routinely make became permanently fixed in our repertoire of humorous impressions of our grandmother: "I die soon."

By the time James died in December 1945, the War had ended, and the problem of conscripting men to fight was replaced by the challenge of bringing millions home again. Although Emil had engaged in the heroic work of helping his mother tend to his invalid father during the last months of the War, his lack of military experience became a defining aspect of his adult life. When the Korean War broke out, he intended to enlist in the Army until his older brother talked him out of it. My siblings and I have speculated at times that our father's quick temper and impulsive risk-taking were his way of compensating for not having served in the

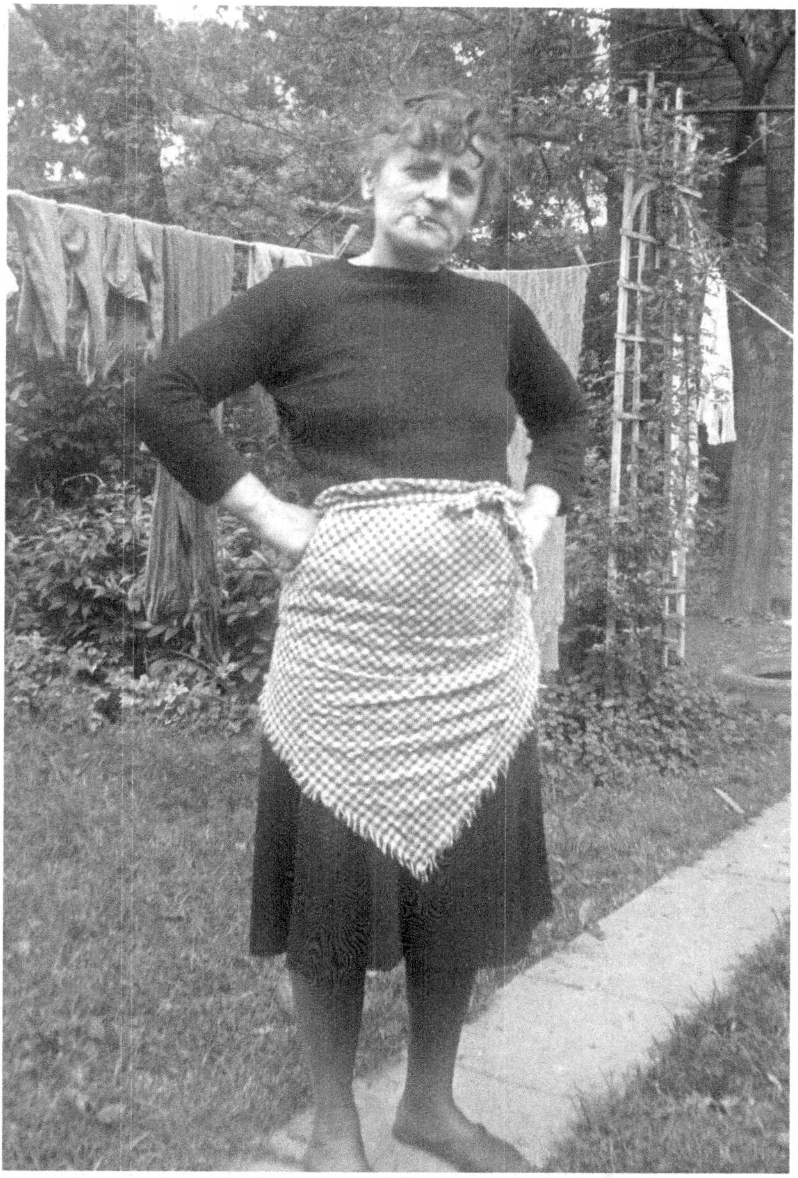

Dimitra Cost with cigarette in her back yard, circa 1950. Although she has been gone for more than 40 years, the taste of certain Greek foods, such as dolmades or Baklava, combined with the smell of cigarette smoke, will always conjure in me her powerful spirit.

military. Among our grade school friends, many of whose fathers had worn a uniform during the War, the term "4F," the classification of deferment from wartime service, was still occasionally hurled as an insult, although those who brandished it were likely unconscious of its derivation.

One of the consequences of my father's deferment from military service was a dissociation in his mind of the aesthetics of warplane design from their functionality as instruments of death. During the war years he had been a member of the Civil Air Patrol, one of many ways the government recruited the participation of civilians in the war effort. Central to service in the CAP was the ability to recognize the shapes of enemy planes. Patrol members would study the silhouettes of warplanes to train their eyes to see the subtle differences between friendly and hostile machines. Mem-

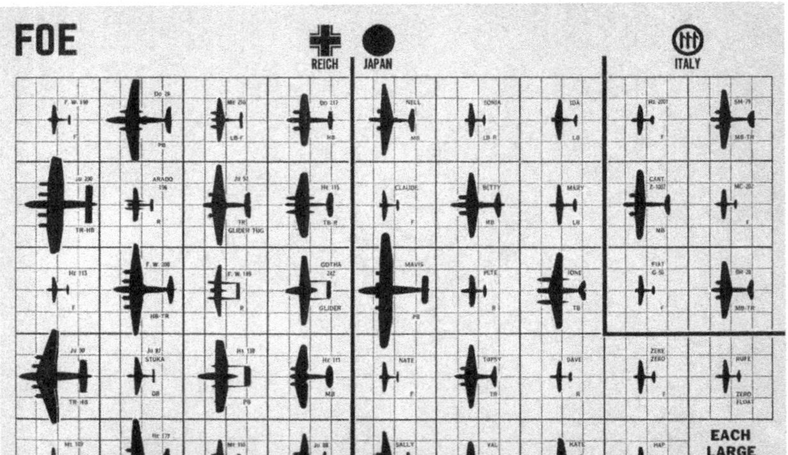

Page from the Recognition Pictorial Manual issued by the War Department to teach pilots and spotters how to identify enemy aircraft during the Second World War. (U.S. War Department)

bers would take shifts standing in key locations scanning the sky for possible threats. These memorized designs, retained from years of civilian wartime experience anticipating enemy aircraft that were never to appear, joined the shapes of other famous airplanes as icons in the household into which I was born nine years after the end of the War. Similar to the arrangement of the icons of saints and apostles around the central figure of Christ in the Greek Orthodox Church, our household aeronautical pantheon arranged these iconic airplanes around the central image of the Wright 1903 Flyer, the first airplane. To this day, whenever I see a representation of the Wright Flyer, I also feel the corporeal presence of my father, sometimes accompanied by a faint synesthetic memory of the smell of incense.

After learning the history of how the first heavier-than-

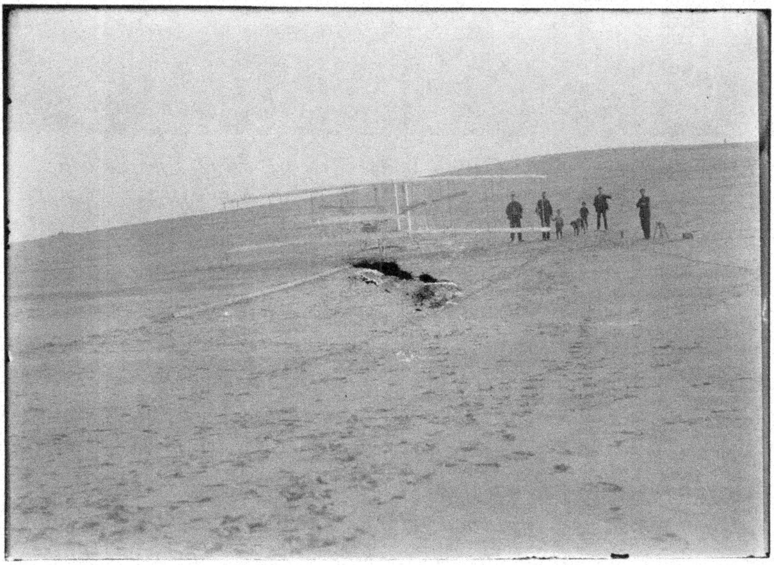

Wright 1903 Flyer on the launching track at Big Kill Devil Hill on the Atlantic coast of North Carolina. (LOC)

air airplane was designed and built by the two brothers in Dayton, I remember being unable to imagine a world before 1903, when that icon did not yet exist. I knew as a child that my father's mother had also been born in 1903, cementing that year in my mind as the official beginning of fathomable time.

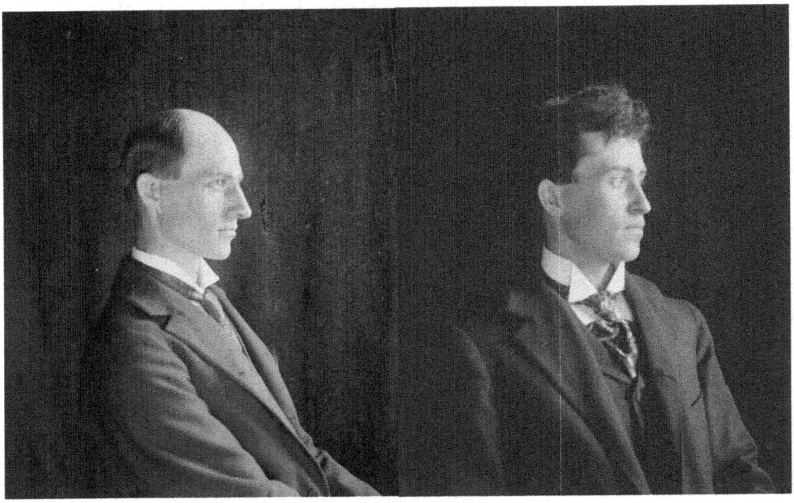

Wilbur Wright (left) and Orville Wright (right), 1897. Orville was four years younger than Wilbur and lived until 1948. Wilbur died of typhoid in 1912, two years before the beginning of the First World War. The brothers both thought their invention would make war practically impossible. Orville later explained, "We thought governments would realize the impossibility of winning by surprise attacks, and that no country would enter into war with another of equal size when it knew that it would have to win by simply wearing out the enemy." While Wilbur died before this belief would be tested, Orville lived to see the atomic bombing of cities from the air. In my childhood mind, Wilbur was paired with my father's missing twin. I thought of all the life he had missed, and this opened a window into the lives of the other members of the Wright family, rescuing them from total eclipse by the two famous brothers alone in their triumph at Kitty Hawk. (LOC)

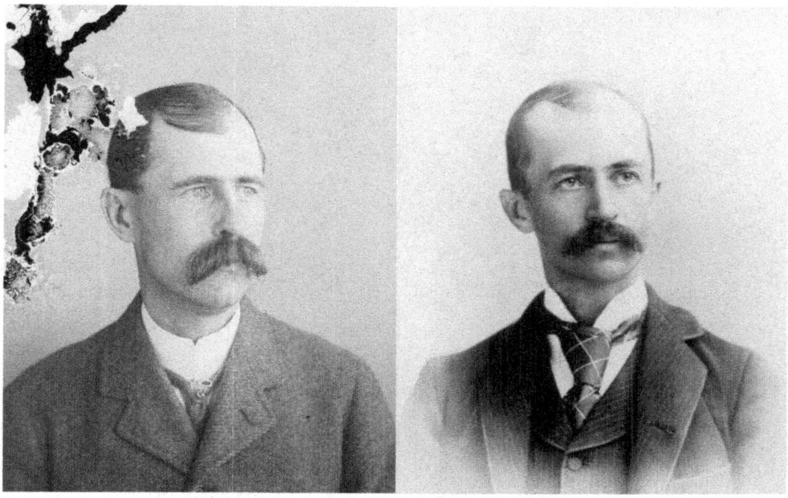

The two elder Wright brothers, Reuchlin (left) and Lorin. Reuchlin was the eldest brother, born in 1861, and Lorin in 1862. (LOC)

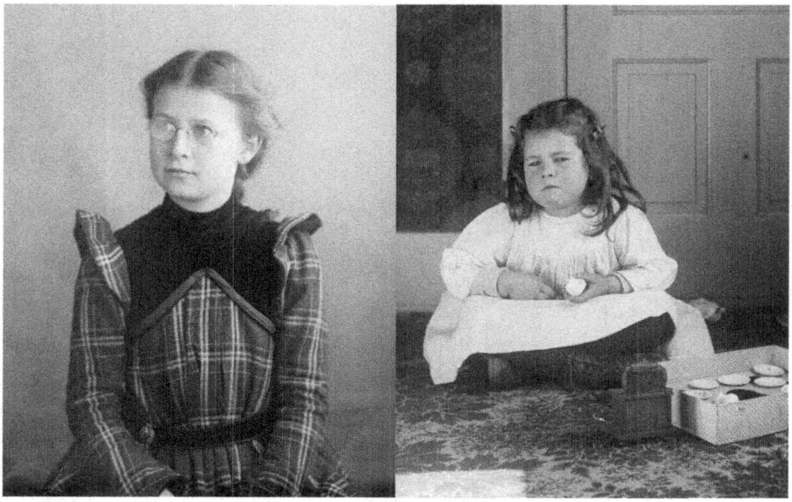

Two Wright nieces, Helen, daughter of Reuchlin (left) and Bertha, daughter of Lorin, with her tea set. Fortunately the Wrights were prolific amateur photographers, so these images were preserved along with the more famous and historically significant ones. (LOC)

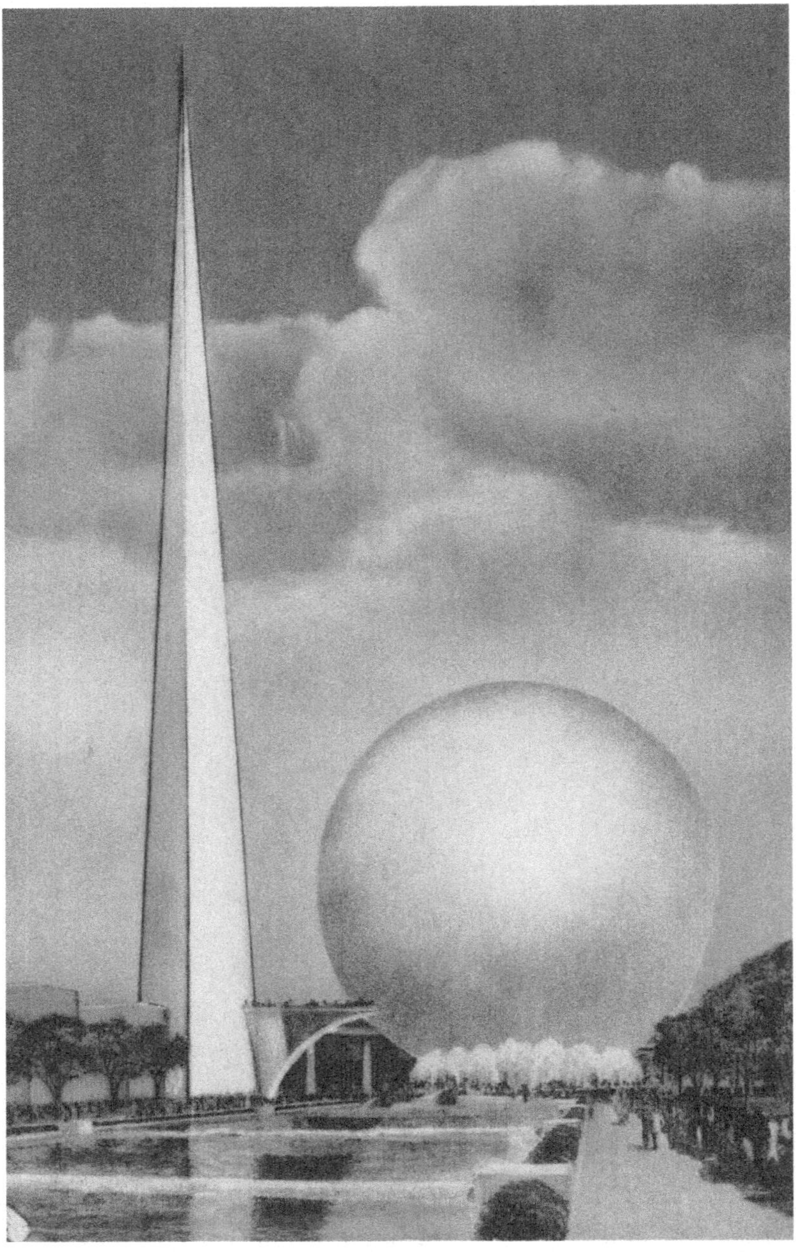

A postcard from the 1939 World's Fair in Queens depicts the 610-foot-high Trylon and Perisphere at the center of the 1200-acre fairgrounds.

4

In the summer of 1939, on the eve of the outbreak of the Second World War, James Cost decided to take his wife and three boys to New York City to visit the World's Fair, constructed on the site of an ash dump in Flushing, Queens. The fair covered more than 1,200 acres, featuring pavilions and exhibits from many countries around the world and consumer products from many of America's largest corporations. James and family drove through the Catskill Mountains in their 1937 Ford sedan. My father recalls the car breaking down and waiting to have it fixed in a small town in the mountains. Later that day they made their way to New York, where they stayed with relatives.

In my father's recollection of the trip many decades later, the next morning they drove to the Fair, parked the car, and walked to the entrance. After entering the gates, they walked directly to the Trylon and Perisphere, the massive white Euclidean structures that were the centerpiece and symbol of the Fair. They ascended a long escalator to enter the Perisphere, and once inside, my father recalls that while his father had a conversation about his car troubles with a representative of the Ford Motor Company, he obtained a small green plastic pickle lapel pin from the Heinz Ketchup company. After they exited the Perisphere, they walked back to the car and left the Fair. When I asked whether he remembered seeing a giant diorama of a futuristic city, or the first public demonstrations of television, my father said no.

He only remembered wanting and then getting the plastic pickle pin.

Even though it seems probable that James took his family to the Fair for only one day, they must have seen more than what my father remembers. They could not have missed the huge "Democracity" diorama in the center of the Perisphere, a model of a shining utopian city-of-the-future in the heart of a fair whose theme was "The World of Tomorrow."

Given my grandfather's ethnic origins and evidence of his belief system, he must have felt as Homer's Zeus, who could "view the wide world" from the summit of Mt. Olym-

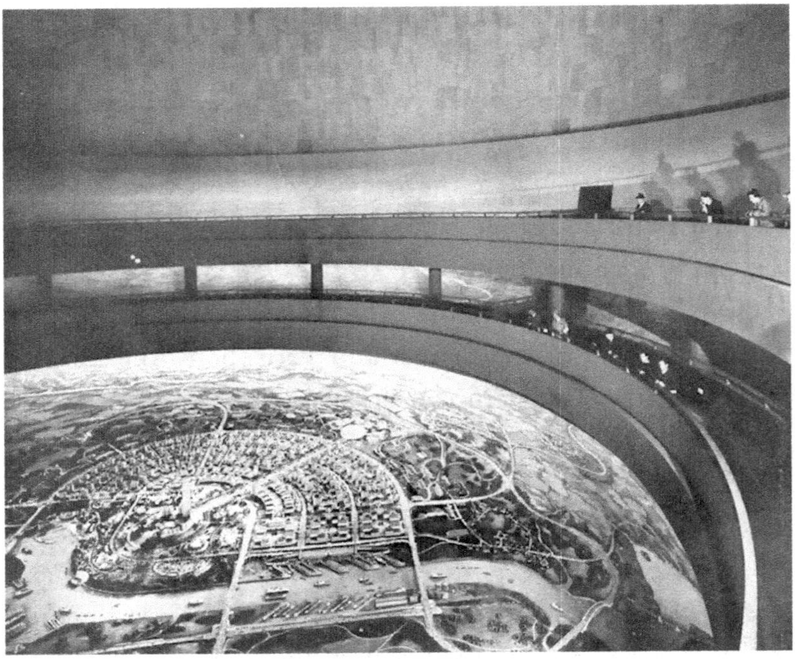

At the center of the Perisphere was a huge diorama of the utopian city of the future called "Democracity." Visitors stood on a circular moving walkway surrounding the diorama to look down on this vision of the future from an aerial perspective.

pus (Iliad, 216). By the summer of 1939 civil aviation was already promising to eventually grant Zeus's aerial perspective on the wide world to every mortal soul. Along with this perspective would come understanding, power, and dominion. While one of his twelve-year-old twin boys was obsessing about taking possession of a small green plastic pickle, it seems reasonable to assume that the son was also absorbing, through every pore of his being, the spectacular outward manifestations of the belief system of the father offered up by the Fair.

Shortly after the World's Fair closed, following a financially disastrous second season in 1940, the fast-deteriorating gypsum- and plaster-surfaced Trylon and Perisphere were torn down. The steel substructures were recycled for use in the armaments industry, their iconic power quickly draining away into the reclaimed ash dump of Flushing Meadows. Unlike the cathedrals and temples of previous centuries, those of the modern religion of scientific and technological progress do not stand for long before they cease to inspire awe, and must be recycled and replaced. The Trylon and Perisphere were not meant to inspire thought about eternal truths deeply embedded in the past, though their geometric design was rooted in purified American notions of classical Greek ideas about how aspirations toward heavenly perfection will lead to earthly utopia—the very seeds of that utopian vision contained within the testicular Perisphere. However temporary, the Trylon and Perisphere served their purpose as authoritative pointers forward for a Greek-American immigrant and his family, as well as for millions of others who were inspired by the Fair.

For many of the young men and women who passed

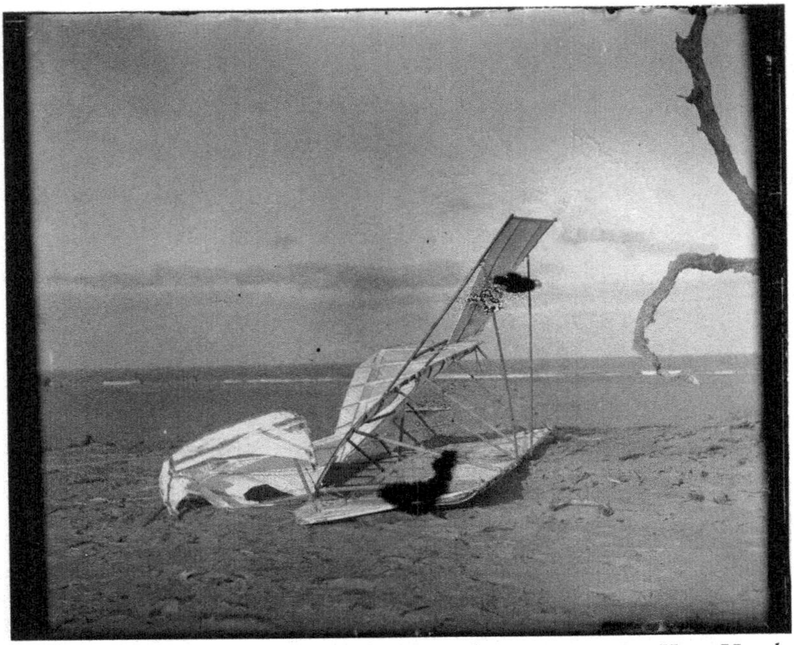

An early Wright glider destroyed during early experiments at Kitty Hawk. (LOC)

through the gates of the 1939 World's Fair, the Second World War would be a rude awakening from the utopian dream. For my father, the dream was shattered by the private tragedy of his father's illness and death. But his experience of the War was filtered through the apparatus of the news media, and he was spared the destruction of the belief system with which he had grown up. His lack of direct experience with war enabled him to retain the purely aesthetic view of flight that had been growing in his mind and body since his first airplane ride before the War. This aesthetic was alive and flourishing in the household of my childhood.

In my youthful notion of the structure of the past, December 17, 1903 marked the end of the Old and beginning of the New. On that day the first four flights of a powered airplane took place on the windy shores of the Atlantic Ocean at Kitty Hawk, bringing to an end what we believed were the many thousands of desperate years that people had desired, but had been unable, to fly. Recalling that my father's mother had been born on September 1 of that same year, I imagined that for the first three months of her life she lived in the ancient world, and then crossed over a dividing line into the modern.

The machine that drew this line had been designed by two brothers driven by a determination over many years that is still today emblematic of the American spirit. Our home was filled with Wright Brothers iconography in the form of books, photographs, and models. The photograph of the 1903 Flyer lifting off its wooden launch rail for the first time with Orville Wright lying prone on the lower wing and Wilbur standing on the sand to the right seemed to have

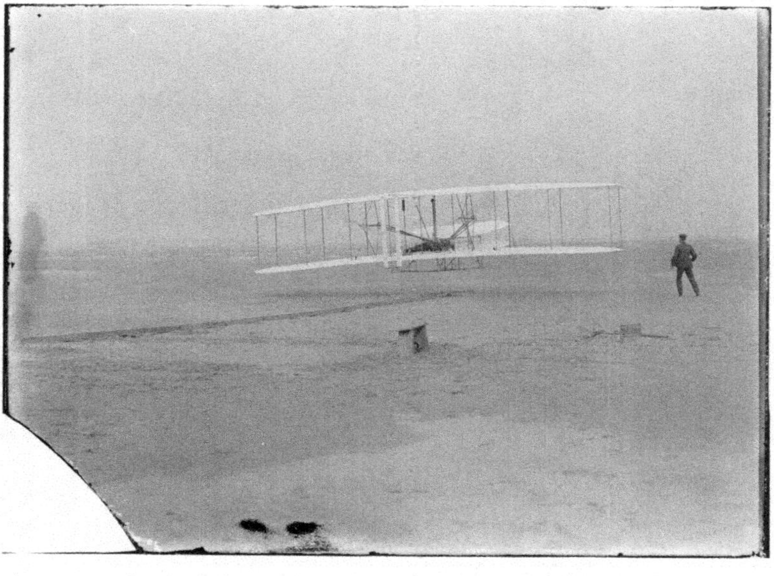

The iconic photograph of the first flight on December 17, 1903. (LOC)

always existed. It would have been as impossible to imagine a world where that moment had not happened as to have imagined a world where there was no sky.

The brothers had created the first flying machine by persisting through many years of study, experiment, design, and testing. By close observations of birds, they developed the notion of three-axis control of flight which became the foundation for every kind of flying machine to follow. The control of pitch, yaw, and roll applies to all aircraft as well as all vehicles designed for space travel. The three axes of orientation correspond to the three dimensions of Cartesian space, which can then be traversed in the fourth dimension of time. Pitch is the movement of the front of the aircraft up and down, controlled in the Wright Flyer by twin horizontal stabilizers at the front of the plane. Yaw is the movement

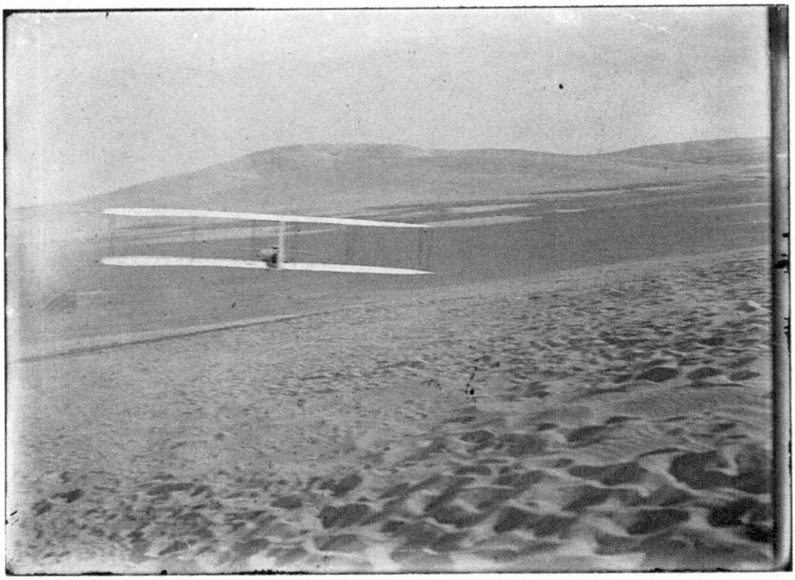

Rear view of Wilbur making a right turn in glide from No. 2 Hill. (LOC)

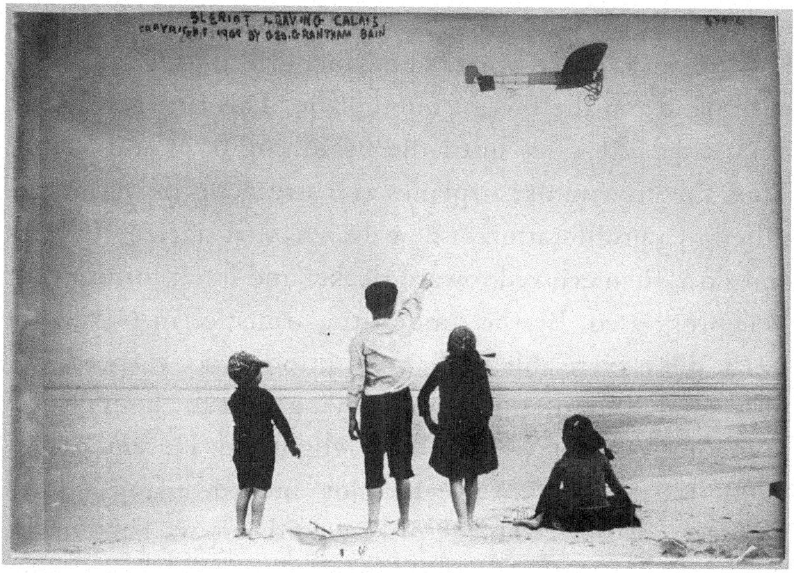

Bleriot monoplane leaving Calais for England, July 25, 1909. (LOC)

left and right, controlled by the twin vertical rudders at the rear. Roll is the rotation of the aircraft around the axis of the flight line, controlled by warping (twisting) the trailing edges of the wings up or down. The 1903 flyer enabled the control of all three movements with hand levers for pitch and yaw and a hip cradle for roll. The hip cradle controlled a series of wires that would warp the wings in a way that mimicked the movements of a bird's wingtips. The Wrights perfected their system of control in gliders flown in the strong updrafts of wind striking the dunes at Kitty Hawk. By the time of the first powered flight, they knew that the three dimensions of control were essential, and that without all three, stable flight could not be achieved.

The genealogy of the airplanes that descended from the Wright Flyer proceeded through several generations from 1903 until the time of my childhood. After the Wright Flyer came a generation of airplanes the color of unbleached muslin cloth and spruce wood. These included the Curtiss Pusher biplane and the Bleriot monoplane. This first generation dominated the skies until the beginning of World War I, when the drive to use airplanes as instruments of warfare resulted in a proliferation of new designs that started out boxy and slow, then evolved toward sleeker and faster forms as the War progressed. By the time of the armistice in November 1918, pilots were able to fly miles into the sky at speeds approaching 200 miles per hour, staying aloft for hours.

From Orville Wright's first flight on December 17, 1903, lasting only twelve seconds and traversing a mere 120 feet, the push to break prior records began. Each of the three subsequent flights on that same day broke the previous time and distance record. Wilbur broke Orville's first record with a second flight of thirteen seconds and 175 feet. Then Orville broke Wilbur's record with a third flight of fifteen seconds and 200 feet. Finally, Wilbur knocked it out of the park with the fourth flight of the day lasting fifty-nine seconds and covering a distance of 852 feet.

Thus began an era of continuous aerial record-setting that proceeded in every important dimension until limits imposed by nature were reached. These included speed, altitude, rate of climb, and distance. Each new breakthrough in materials, power systems, and aircraft design reinvigorated the competition. Wood and cloth airplanes powered by piston engines reached limits that were then shattered by aluminum monoplanes, by jets, and finally by rockets. Less than six years after the first flights at Kitty Hawk, on July 25, 1909, Louis Bleriot flew his wood and cloth monoplane across the English Channel. Eighteen years later, in

May 1927, Charles Lindbergh flew his linen-covered Ryan monoplane non-stop across the Atlantic, and twenty-one years after that Chuck Yeager flew faster than the speed of sound for the first time in his Bell X-1 rocket plane.

By the time I became interested in speed and altitude records in the early 1960s, the X-15 rocket plane was setting speed records in excess of four thousand miles per hour at altitudes of more than 60 miles, and men were orbiting the earth in metal capsules traveling four times as fast. At this rapid rate of change, it seemed that we would soon be able to fly anywhere in the universe. Television programs like *Lost in Space* (1965) and *Star Trek* (1966), and movies like *2001: A Space Odyssey* (1968) presented entirely plausible pictures of a future we believed was right around the corner.

In my childhood mind I mapped key historical airplanes onto generations of my family: The Wright Flyer to the birth of my grandmother in 1903, the Spirit of St. Louis to my parents' births in 1927, the same year Lindbergh flew, and the Bell X-1 rocket plane to a few years before my own birth. There seemed to be a kind of numerological meaning to these mappings, as though our family had been predestined to be intimately intertwined with the history of aviation. Each classic aircraft design possessed a timelessness independent of historical context. It seemed as though they were the fulfillment of designs that had existed since the beginning of time, stored away in some vault in the celestial sphere waiting to be realized in material form.

In our household, airplanes were only one part of a continuous spectrum of flying things that included the many varieties of balloons, dirigibles, zeppelins, birds, bats, flying squirrels, flying insects, flying seeds, and anything else that moves voluntarily or involuntarily through the fluid medium of the air. All were fascinating, and worthy of devotion and respect. All shared the same qualities of being, a cardinal and bluebird on the same plane of existence as the Fokker D7 and Supermarine Spitfire. Concerning each subcategory of flying creatures, there were endless ponderings and discussions about their proper place in the great chain of aerial being. There were arguments about which was the most beautiful within a given category. Was the Spitfire more beautiful than the Curtiss P-40? Would it be preferable to be a bald eagle or an Osprey, a robin or a chickadee? We would argue the relative ugliness of the homelier species. These included the Gee Bee Racer and the P-47 Thunderbolt, the turkey vulture and the pelican. (Pity

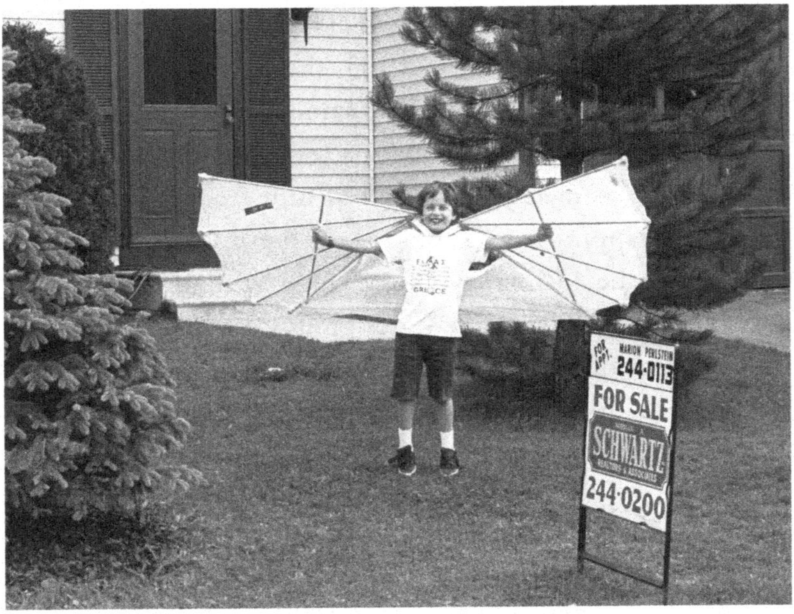

Roger Cost with a pair of wings made for him by his grandfather Emil, September 1992.

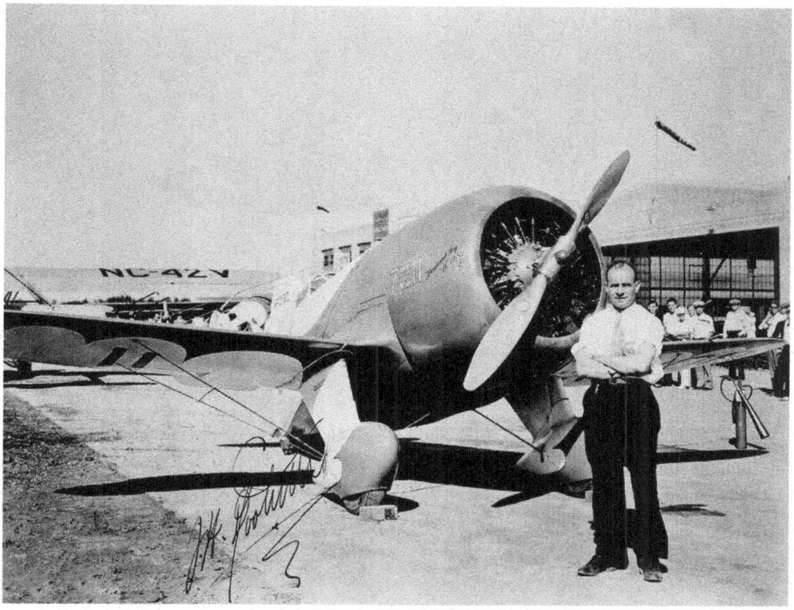

The Gee Bee racing plane is the aeronautical equivalent of the bulldog, beloved for its sublime ugliness. Flying this aircraft, Jimmy Doolittle (standing next to it in this photograph) won the 1932 National Air Race in Cleveland in what he descibed later as "the most dangerous airplane I have ever flown." Doolittle became an American hero of the Second World War when he commanded the famous 1942 bombing raid of Tokyo. (LOC)

the poor turkey vulture with his ugly naked head, and the pelican having to lug around that massive fishing apparatus on his face!)

Upon seeing any of these creatures in the flesh, or in pictures, I would attempt to conform my own inner body to their shapes. My fingers would become the feathers on the wingtip of a crow or my head would morph into the shape of the canopy on a fighter plane. I judged both airplanes and birds by how well their forms could be bodily inhabited, and how good it would feel to be one of them. Would I rather

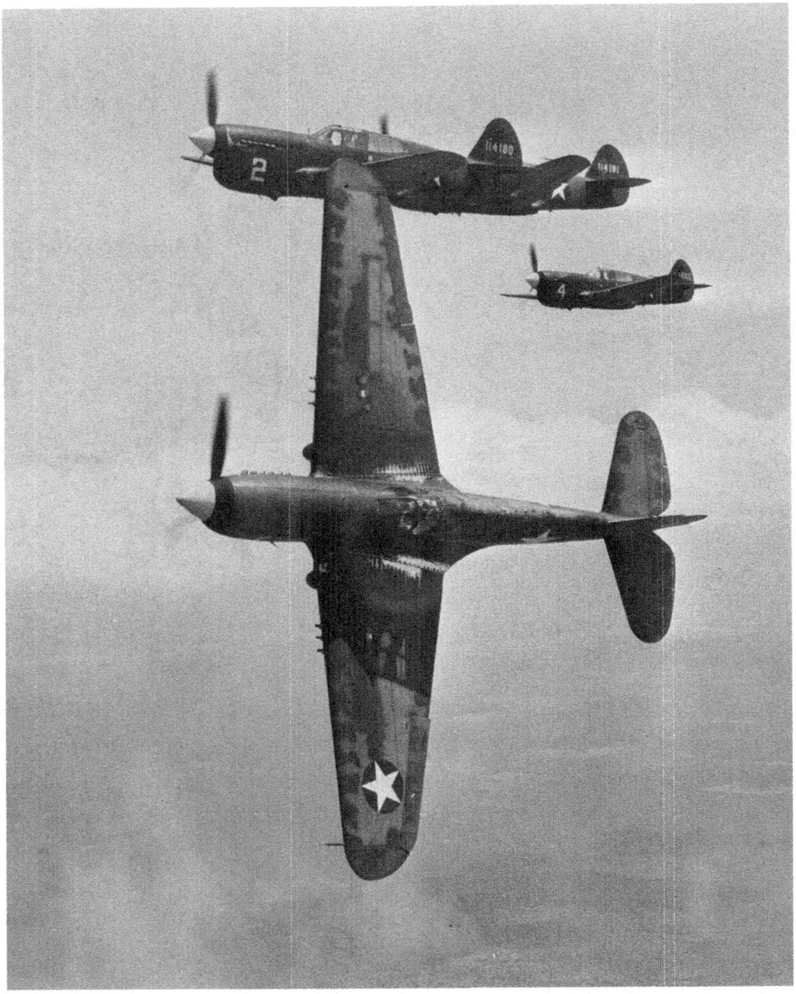

In this photograph from 1943, "the lead ship in a formation of P-40's peels off for the 'attack' in a practice flight at the Army Air Forces advanced flying school." (FSA Office of War Information)

be a Spitfire or a P-40 Warhawk? As a child I was filled with both envy and pity for the birds: envy because they could do what I could not, and pity because I suspected they did not feel any more thrill in it than I felt in walking. I would ponder the trade-off while watching them fly. Would I rather be able to fly as a bird without the possibility of knowing the thrill, or remain thrilled as a human by the impossible idea of flying as a bird? On a blustery day walking home from school, I would run into the wind holding my jacket open like wings, endeavoring to leap into the air. For brief moments it felt like the beginnings of flight. The only place where the moment extended into sustained flight was in a recurring dream that always began with a running leap, a retraction of legs, and no need for flapping. I would glide silently over the ground with head up as in a smooth walk. My flying dream was always close to the ground, never high enough to alter my view below.

This dream returns to me every so often, the latest recurrence within the past few weeks of this writing. While doing the research for this book, I learned that Neil Armstrong also reported a recurring childhood dream of flight to Dora Jane Hamblin, who profiled him and the other Apollo 11 astronauts in a July 1969 article in *Life* magazine. In Armstrong's dream, he would hold his breath and hover motionless over the ground, not realizing that someday he would similarly hover in a strange buglike landing craft over the surface of the Moon, looking for a safe place to land.

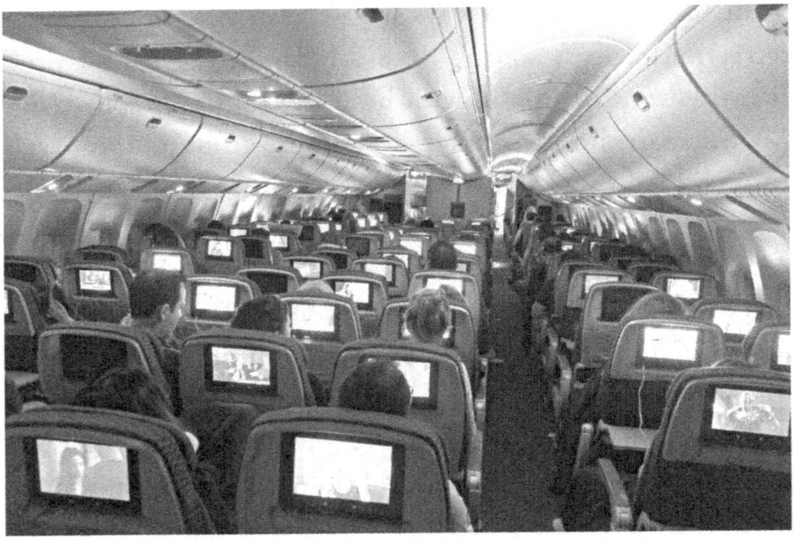

On a 2015 flight from Newark to Venice, every passenger watched a different program on a personal screen.

5

The first time I flew in a real airplane was during my senior year of high school when I traveled with a friend to Washington D.C. for a family visit. The only recollection I have of that experience was the feeling of the powerful thrust of the jet engines pushing me back against the seat during takeoff, the sensation of sitting in a stationary room full of well-behaved people suspended magically above the clouds, and then breaking through the clouds to see the Washington Monument and Capitol Building in brilliant white miniature, resembling a diorama of itself. Today, after many decades of flying as a commercial passenger, the experience has been reduced to entering a large waiting-room in one city, sitting quietly while reading, watching sanitized movies, eating snacks from tiny packages or napping, and then exiting the room to find myself in another city, with hardly any awareness of having flown there.

One of my friends is a traveling consultant who, though having served in the Air Force and achieved frequent flyer status during the first part of his professional life, became suddenly afraid of flying in middle age, and has since traveled the world by surface transportation. He sometimes claims to be Amtrak's best customer, and has crossed the oceans many times on board various Cunard ships. Another non-flying friend once told me of the moment on a long transcontinental flight when he suddenly panicked and spent the remaining hours of the flight pacing up and down the aisle in a cold sweat. After landing and disembarking, he knew he would never be able to fly again.

What makes a person afraid to fly, especially when the fear suddenly develops after many untroubled years of air travel? Occasionally, sitting comfortably in my aisle seat during a long overnight flight over some dark ocean, I have suddenly realized my physical situation, hurtling 600 miles an hour seven miles high in the stratosphere. My stirrings of anxiety could easily grow into a full-blown panic, if I allowed it. My cure is to look into the serene face of the next passing flight attendant, whereby the anxiety quickly dissipates. This has worked almost every time, except when the flight attendant's face was not serene: once when a cabin filled with smoke, once when preparing for an emergency landing with broken landing gear, and once when a gale

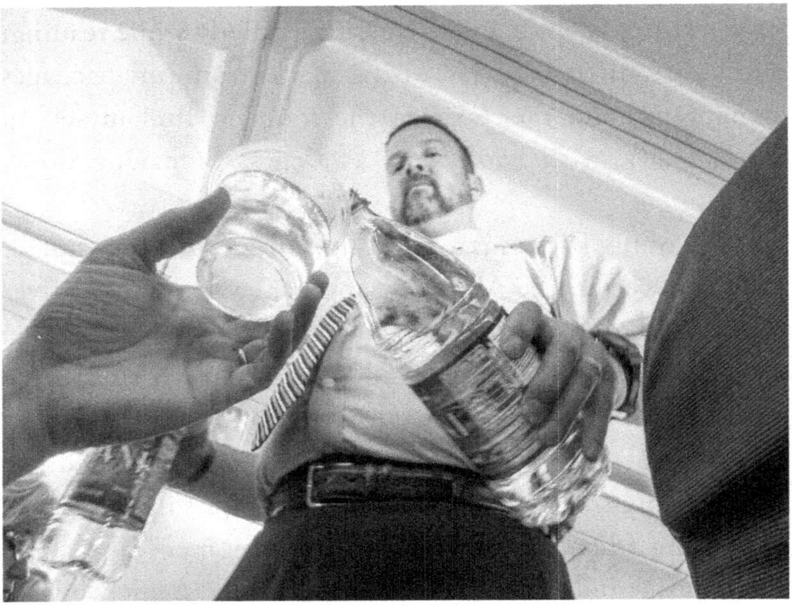

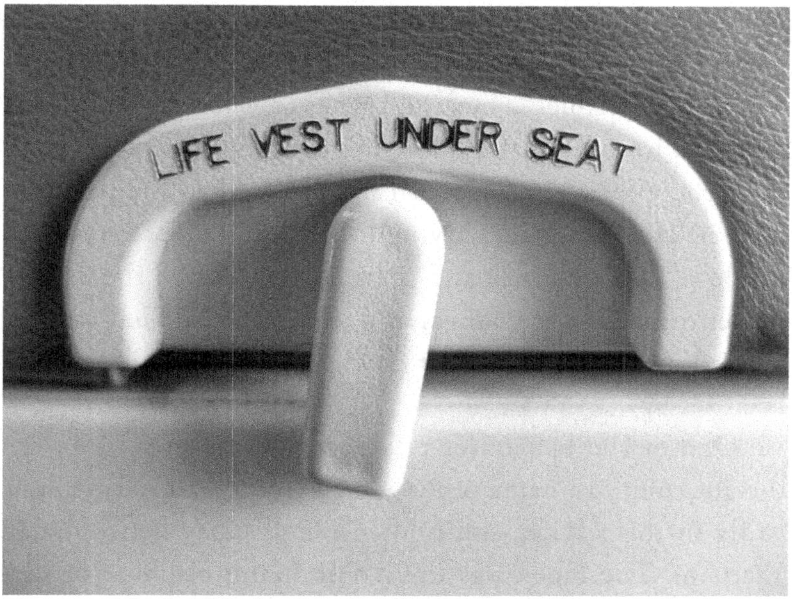

crosswind forced a pilot to abort what would have been a disastrous end to a most unpleasant flight. During these occasions I learned that the ultimate flowering of my particular strain of anxiety is not panic, but resignation. It's a good thing to know, if one is trying to overcome a fear of flying.

The summer after my first year of college I found a job at a local privately-owned airport in my hometown. The work consisted of a variety of tasks including serving as a "line boy," gassing airplanes, washing and waxing airplanes (where I discovered that an airplane has a lot more surface area than a car), mowing the grass between the runway and taxiway, painting the floor of one of the hangars (a lot bigger than a garage floor), and sometimes sitting in for the office manager, where I had the opportunity to engage in conversation with flight instructors, commercial pilots, and customers. The older mechanics called me "college boy," and one nicknamed me "Manuel Labor," with a Spanish accent on the last syllables. They sometimes gave me jobs that were strictly a form of hazing. One morning I was told to "clean the helicopter rotor," a puzzling job that had me balanced on a rickety step ladder trying to reach my objective with a bottle of spray cleaner and a rag. After a while the airport owner came into the hangar and threw a fit. "What the hell are you doing up there? Get down at once!" I realized I had been set up.

One of the helicopter pilots, a good-natured guy with the all-American name of R.C. Armstrong, had learned how to fly in the service, and piloted a Bell Huey helicopter in Vietnam. The Huey was the iconic flying machine of that War, and R.C. fit the cavalier image of a Huey pilot perfectly. He told an amazing story about flying low over a convoy of vehicles as it made its way along a jungle road in a conflicted zone, when one of the jeeps in the convoy ran over a land mine. The jeep exploded upward, one of the flying pieces knocking off his tail rotor while parts of the jeep's

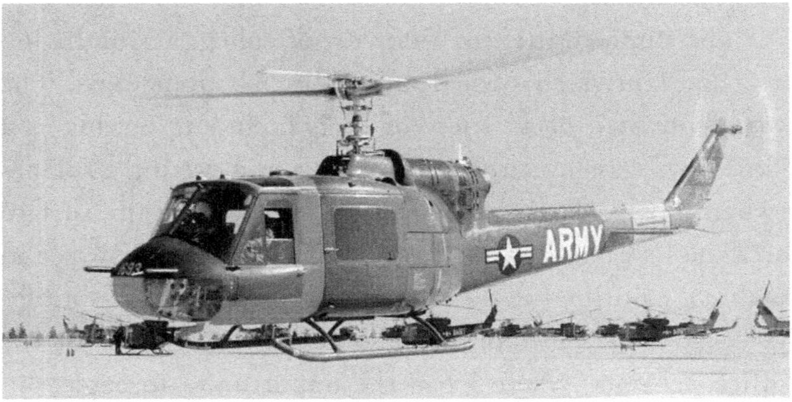

Bell Huey helicopter.

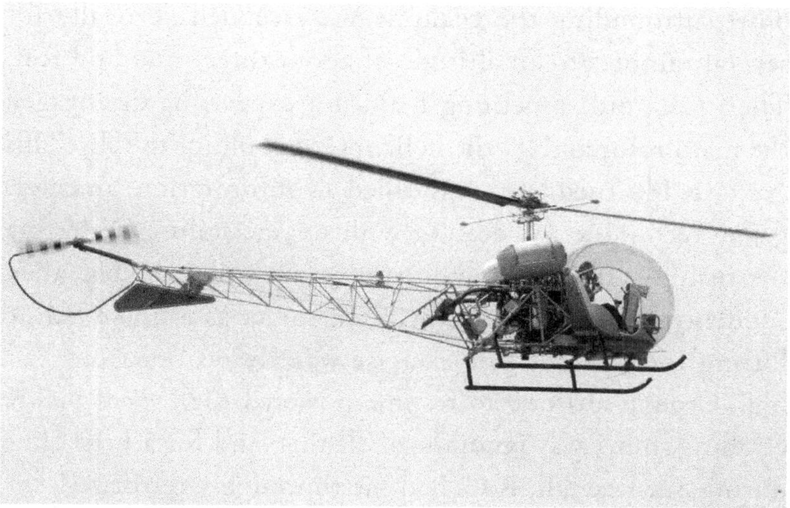

Bell 47G Helicopter.

driver splattered his windshield. This caused the helicopter to start rotating in the opposite direction to the main rotor in an uncontrolled yaw. The only possible way for him to avoid crashing was to fly forward fast enough so the large vertical fin on the tail of his helicopter would stabilize it. This gave him time to find a clearing and crash land without losing his life.

The airport was owned by a family in the construction business who employed R.C. as an airborne chauffeur, flying them around to their various construction sites in a Bell 47 helicopter, similar to the kind used in the movie M*A*S*H. Having never flown in a helicopter, I began to lobby and then daily beg R.C. for a ride. Finally, one morning he told me he had to test an adjustment in the helicopter controls, and that I could come with him. I trotted out after him like an excited puppy to the parked helicopter, and strapped myself into the passenger seat under the clear plastic fishbowl surrounding the cockpit. We ascended vertically for several minutes to an altitude of about three thousand feet. Then R.C. did something I did not expect: he disengaged the main rotor and let the helicopter fall out of the sky. This exercise, I learned later, was called an autorotation, an emergency technique for dealing with engine failure by letting the rushing air spin up the main rotor during the fall, then suddenly changing the rotor pitch to act as a brake before hitting the ground. The exercise was always practiced at a high enough altitude to resume powered flight well before crashing, but I was ignorant of all this, and for a brief time during our free fall, R.C. had me thoroughly terrorized.

Another time that summer, one of the flight instructors, a young Norwegian named Elias, offered to take me for a ride in a small two-passenger Cessna 150. We headed south into farm country. Then, flying high enough over the countryside to avoid identification, and without telling me what he was about to do, Elias proceeded to perform a series of aerobatic stunts including a loop and a barrel roll, maneuvers for which the Cessna was not properly designed. I have been thankful ever since that the wings stayed attached to the airplane and we did not lose our lives in a horrible screaming plunge to the ground. If the Federal Aviation Administration had found out about his stunts, Elias would have lost his license.

These few harrowing rides demonstrated that my pilot co-workers derived a greater thrill from my terrified reaction to their stunts than from the stunts themselves, which for them had become routine. I realized then that the only way to maintain the thrill of bodily flight would be to constantly upgrade the performance of the machinery or escalate the level of risk, or both. The end of the process would be either bankruptcy or death, or both, none of which appealed to me. This realization, combined with the dull hermetic experience of flying in a passenger jet, cured me of any small interest I might have had in becoming a pilot.

But my lack of interest in personal thrill-seeking did not prevent me from enjoying the spectacle of others risking their lives in airshow performances. This enjoyment came to an abrupt end at a show I attended with a co-worker named John who shared a family passion for aviation rooted in his grandfather's service as a German fighter pilot during the First World War. John's grandfather had flown an airplane called an Albatross D.Va. toward the end of the War. The Albatross was the first warplane with a rounded fishlike fuselage made of laminated plywood formed around a mold—a fabrication method employed later in the "Winnie Mae," a modified Lockheed Vega that the famed aviator

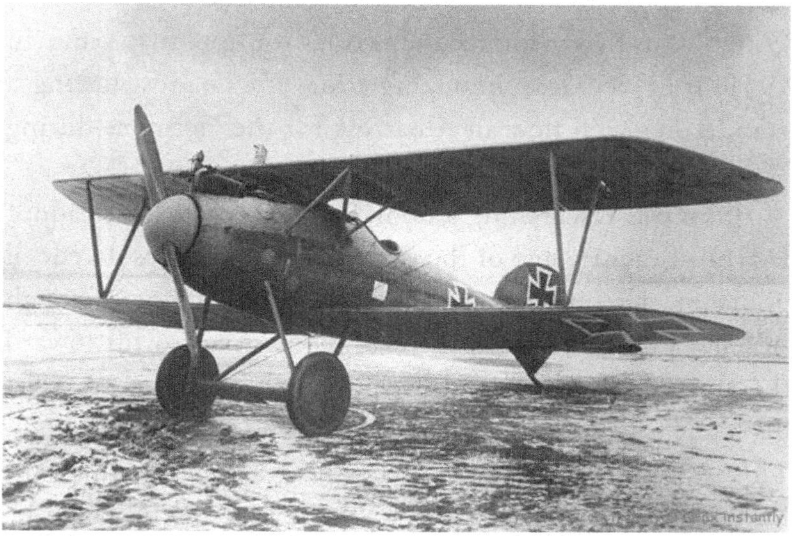

Albatross D.Va. (LOC)

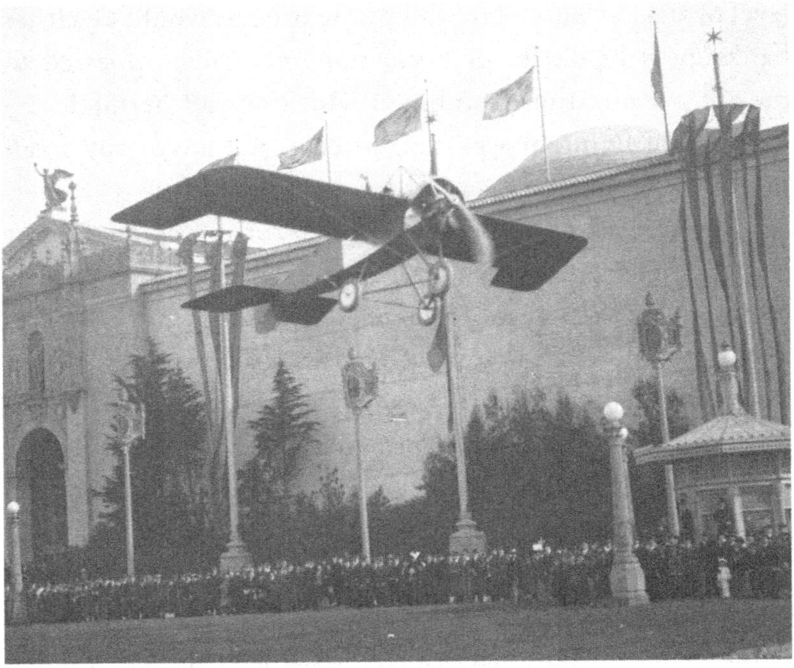

Lincoln Beachey takes off for his last flight in San Francisco on March 15, 1915. (LOC)

Wiley Post flew around the world for the first time in 1931. As a pedigree among aviation aficionados, having a grandfather who flew an Albatross for the Germans during World War I was the gold standard.

John was researching a book he intended to write about Lincoln Beachey, one of the first and most famous daredevil pilots of the opening decade of powered flight. Though Beachey's exploits were witnessed by massive crowds toward the end of his career, and celebrated throughout America, his name was never mentioned in my childhood household. This is most likely because he flew planes designed and built for him by others, including a Curtiss biplane, in which he performed the first loop, and an Eaton monoplane, which

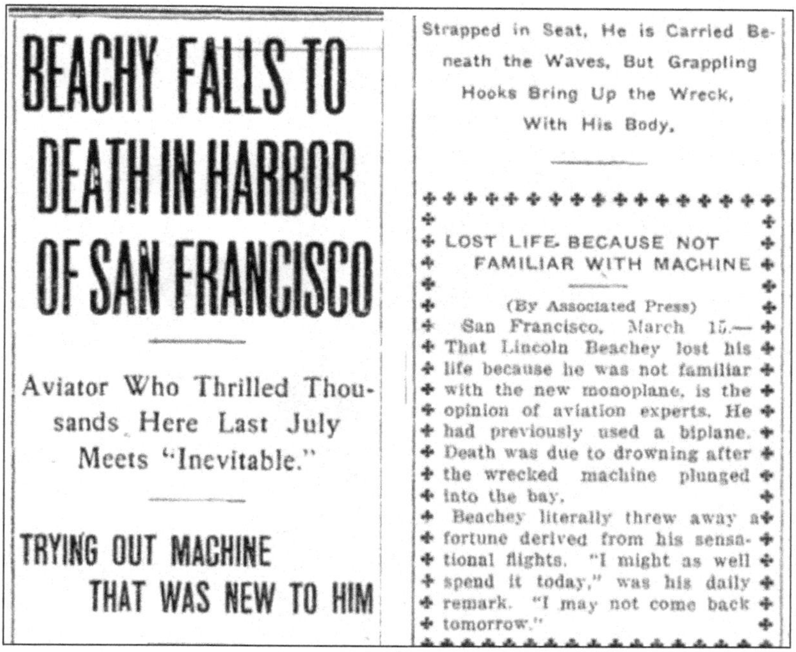

BEACHY FALLS TO DEATH IN HARBOR OF SAN FRANCISCO

Aviator Who Thrilled Thousands Here Last July Meets "Inevitable."

TRYING OUT MACHINE THAT WAS NEW TO HIM

Strapped in Seat, He is Carried Beneath the Waves, But Grappling Hooks Bring Up the Wreck, With His Body.

LOST LIFE BECAUSE NOT FAMILIAR WITH MACHINE

(By Associated Press)

San Francisco, March 15.—That Lincoln Beachey lost his life because he was not familiar with the new monoplane, is the opinion of aviation experts. He had previously used a biplane. Death was due to drowning after the wrecked machine plunged into the bay.

Beachey literally threw away a fortune derived from his sensational flights. "I might as well spend it today," was his daily remark. "I may not come back tomorrow."

he crashed fatally into San Francisco Bay in 1915 before an estimated crowd of 50,000, having overstressed the wing and broken the main spar. In my family it had always been the airplanes themselves, not the pilots, that were the stars. Even the celebrated and glamorous Amelia Earhart was upstaged in our family pantheon by her gleaming twin-engine Lockheed Electra.

John and I indulged our mutual passion for flight one Saturday afternoon in July 1985. Standing in a crowd of thousands on the hot tarmac at the Niagara Falls International Airport, we watched a performance of the U.S. Navy Blue Angels precision flying team. Two of the roaring A-4 Skyhawk jets flew at each other from opposite ends of the field in a spectacular aerial jousting match at treetop level. At the last moment before crashing into one another, both

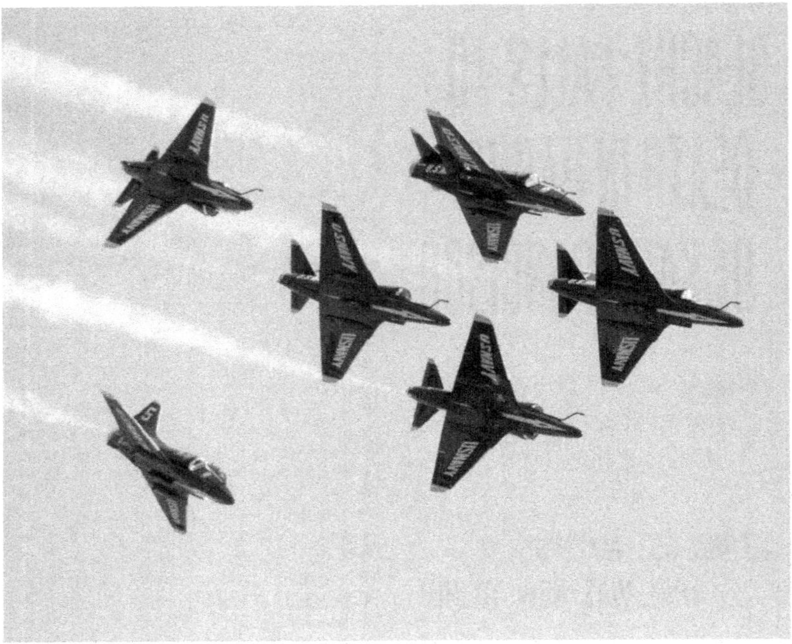

The Blue Angels A-4 jets circa 1985.

jets snap-rolled ninety degrees and passed belly to belly, leaving what appeared to be only a few feet of air between them. The experience of gasping in unison with thousands of other people is the essence of watching the Blue Angels perform.

I had attended many air shows before this one, and I was well acquainted with the physical laws that allowed supersonic fighter jets to fly perilously close to one another without mishap. So it was with a degree of excited calm born of familiarity that I watched as the two jets drew out half circles preparing for a high-altitude replay. A few moments later they came at each other once again, high above the field.

But this time, at the instant they passed, I saw what appeared to be a puff of smoke, followed a second or two later by a loud bang. Both jets began to tumble out of the sky. One of them fell directly onto the runway in front of us and exploded in a spectacular fireball. The other fell and exploded in a field to the right of the runway. Only one pilot had ejected.

We watched the fires burn furiously then gradually ebb to two piles of smoldering ash. Thousands of witnesses walked away from the field and back to the parking lot in virtual silence, all of us knowing that a person had been consumed in one of the two fires. We had never thought about aviation in such stark physical terms as we did that afternoon on our drive back home. For me, the experience put an end to any further desire to witness daredevils plying their trade. Perhaps for John it destroyed the sense of wonder about the forces that drove Lincoln Beachey to take the kinds of risks he did. No book of his about Lincoln Beachey was ever published.

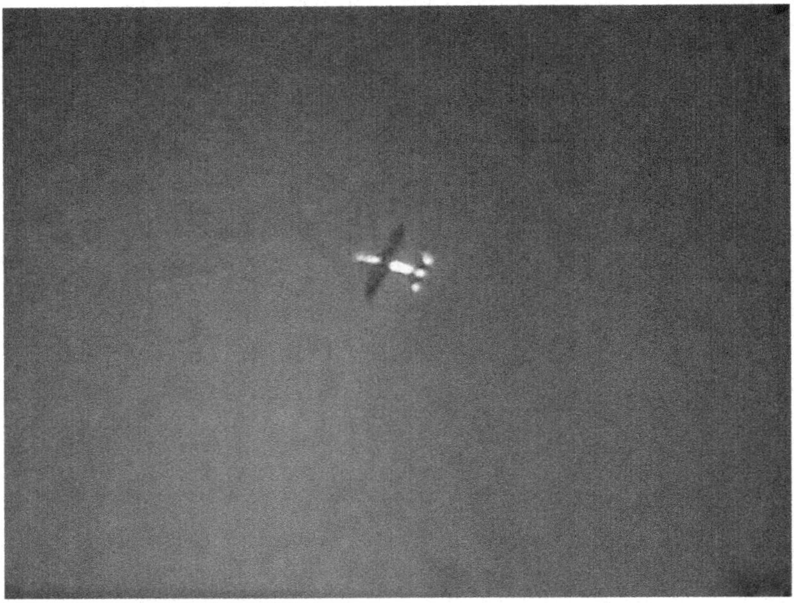

A frame from an 8mm home movie clip from around 1958 of a Lockheed Constellation airliner flying over our front yard. The Constellation was a four-engine propeller-driven aircraft used for transcontinental and transoceanic flights. Its rumbling sound still resonates deep within my bones.

6

The front yard of the suburban tract house that my parents purchased on the west side of Syracuse when I was a few years old became a platform for the observation of all variety of flying things that crossed the sky, both natural and mechanical. My earliest memories are of hearing the distinct multi-layered resonance of a propeller-driven airliner approaching from a distance while still inside the house, then running out into the yard to scan the sky for the visual confirmation. Once my eyes locked onto the airliner, I would follow it all the way to the horizon, desperately trying to imagine what it must be like to be a passenger looking down on my neighborhood, and wondering whether the passengers could see me standing there waving at them.

When smaller private planes flew over our house, it was easier to imagine a mutual visual connection. My mother, who had a way of putting her fingers in the corners of her mouth and letting loose the loudest whistle of any mother in our neighborhood, once told me she could whistle at an airplane and the pilot would respond by dipping his wing. She would demonstrate this power, and I believed that the smallest fluctuation in the wings of a passing airplane after my mother's whistle was indeed a response. I never learned to whistle like my mother, and so had to rely upon her to play this call-and-response game with airplanes for the time I remained a true believer.

During those earliest years of watching airplanes from the ground, the only person in my family I could imagine flying in an airplane was my father's mother, Dimitra, who sometimes traveled back to Europe to visit family and friends (and purchase inexpensive eyeglasses and false teeth). Once I begged her to take me on an upcoming trip. She told me she would hide me in her suitcase and smuggle me on board the airplane, a promise I took with utmost seriousness. For all the time leading up to her departure I thought about ways to survive a long overseas flight in a suitcase, devising discreet snorkel mechanisms for breathing, and systems that would make it possible to deal with bodily functions in a sanitary way. I don't remember exactly how the fantasy of stowing away in my grandmother's luggage came to an end, but a profound feeling of disappointment combined with embarrassment accompanied my realization that I had been the victim of an adult confidence game—a game all the adults in my family played with great amusement.

My father's younger cousin Tasso (Anastasio) once promised to give me his car, a lime green Plymouth of late 1950s vintage. I spent weeks and maybe months excitedly dreaming about the day I would get the car, without any practical concern that I was only six or seven years old, and would have to wait many years before obtaining a driver's license. One day I arrived home from school to find a lime green Plymouth in the driveway and assumed it had been left there for me by Tasso. I ran to the car and jumped in, proceeding to beep the horn and turn on everything that would operate without the keys. At that point my mother and a friend came running out of the house to see who was fooling around with her friend's car. So it was not Tasso's car! Oh my God! I was red-faced embarrassed for months afterwards when-

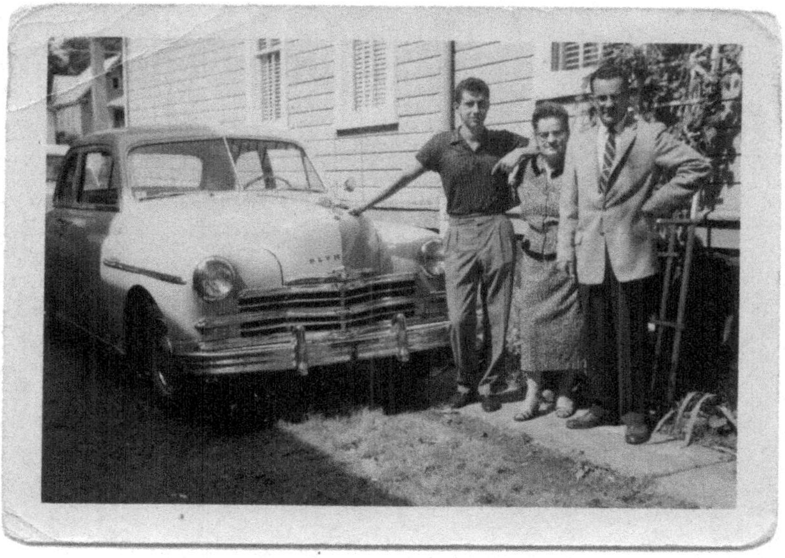

My father's younger cousin Tasso once promised to give me his car. Tasso later became an engineer working for General Dynamics on the Apollo Lunar Module, where his talents for playing confidence games would undoubtedly have had their utility.

ever I thought of my egregious mistake.

In the early 1960s our front yard became an observation platform for a new kind of flying machine. One evening as twilight was darkening to deep azure, my father took me out into the yard to watch what appeared to be a bright star crossing the sky directly overhead. I learned that this was a man-made satellite called "Echo," a giant silver balloon in orbit above the earth. Reconciling the tiny bright star with the image of the Echo my father showed me in a magazine article began to calibrate my sense of astronautical distances, which would become essential to the realistic contemplation of the possibilities for manned spaceflight.

The romance and the rapture of space travel came with

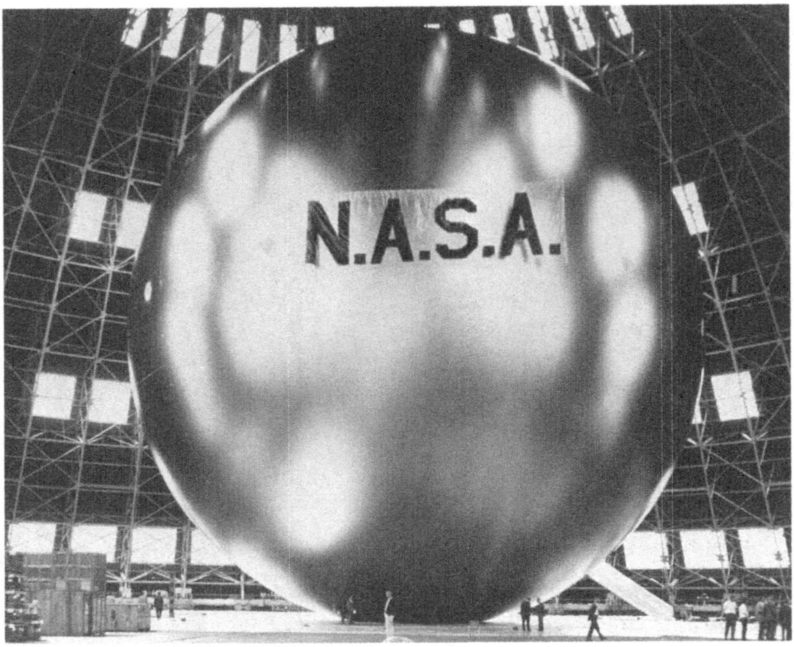

The Echo 1 satellite, an inflated mylar balloon that could be seen on clear evenings from our front yard. (NASA)

a dark underside of terror during those same years. My younger brother Emil once ran into the house from the yard screaming hysterically that the Russians had dropped an atomic bomb. We all ran outside to discover the silvery Goodyear blimp suspended silently above the horizon, looking like Herblock's "Mr. Atom" cartoon personification of the atomic bomb on the editorial page of the newspaper.

Despite the occasional reminder that Soviet rockets were always poised to attack out of a clear blue sky with only minutes of warning, the decade of the space race, beginning with our first Echo satellite sighting and ending with the Moon landing, was a time when every manner of human flight was celebrated and imitated in our family through the building and flying of models. These included models of flying machines from all the eras going back to 1903, as well as kites, mechanical flapping birds called "ornithopters," helium-filled blimps, and even large Styrofoam replicas of maple seeds we would launch into the air with rubber-band catapults, then watch helicopter down in perfect slow-motion imitation of the real thing.

The basement of our house was filled with model airplanes my father had begun to build and purchase from friends long before I existed. These included a collection of replicas of classic World War I designs that were flown by "control line," seventy-foot-long braided metal wires that allowed the operator to control the elevator and throttle on the gasoline-powered motor from the center of a circle around which the airplane would fly. I can still recall the feeling of crying hysterically in our back yard when my father started

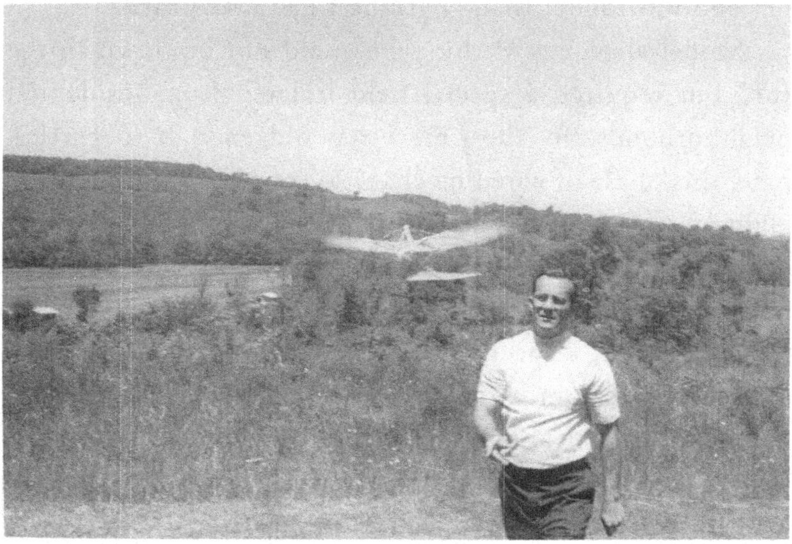

Emil J. Cost with one of his ornithopters, c. 1967.

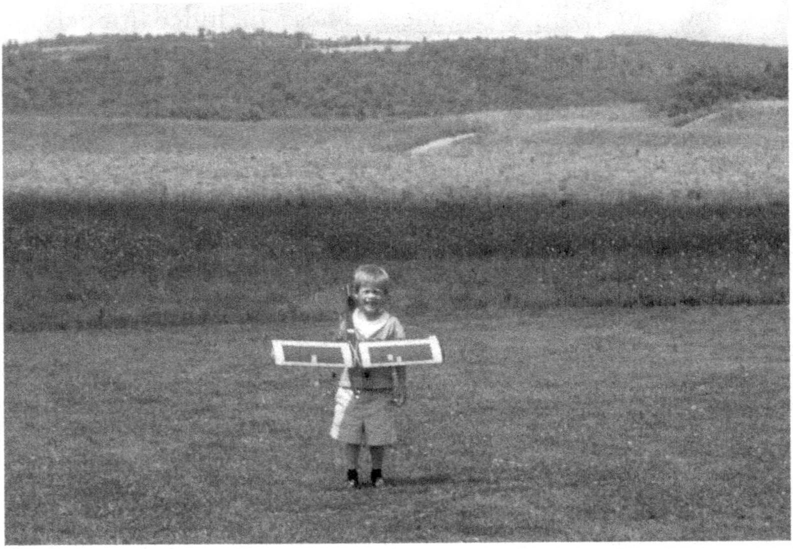

My brother Jim with one of our father's early radio-controlled models called the "Schoolboy" at the flying field on the Onondaga reservation.

the engine of a control-line model airplane that had no muffler and was louder than anything I had ever heard.

Model airplanes of this type could not be flown in the yard but required a special field isolated from residential neighborhoods. By the time I was old enough to participate, this phase of wired mechanical control technology was giving way to a new wireless era of radio-control. The first generations of the new technology relied on simple vacuum-tube-based transmitters that would generate single-tone radio signals at a specific frequency in the citizens band of the radio spectrum. A receiver on board the aircraft would detect the signal and translate it into the action of closing an electromagnetic relay. The relay was connected to a small mechanical device called an escapement which was tensioned by a wound-up rubber band. The escapement was connected to the rudder of the airplane. Controlling the rudder required only one button on the transmitter. Press and hold once for a right turn, release and press again for a left turn, then release to fly straight and level.

Model airplanes powered by gas motors and controlled by these crude radio mechanisms required large expanses of open country for flying. My father joined a club called the Aero Radio Club of Syracuse (ARCS), which leased a small plot of farmland on the southwest corner of the Onondaga Indian reservation, south of the city of Syracuse. The rectangular reservation, covering less than ten square miles, was the remnant of the expansive original territory of the Onondaga Nation that ran from the Saint Lawrence River in the north to northern Pennsylvania in the south. The Nation was part of the Iroquois Confederacy, which we studied in seventh grade New York State history class. The field was surrounded by farmland to the north and south, apple orchards to the west, and a large forest-covered glacial hill to the east.

As my father started building and flying radio-controlled models, this field became a regular destination on evenings and weekend days of good weather during the warm months of the year. My mother would pack us all off in the car, knowing we would be gone for hours and she would have the house to herself. Once at the field my father would unload his models from the car and we would stand and watch, sometimes helping, as equipment was readied. We would then await our turn to use the common citizen's band radio frequency allocated to model aviation by the Federal Communications Commission. Only one model could fly at a time, because everyone's equipment was on the same radio

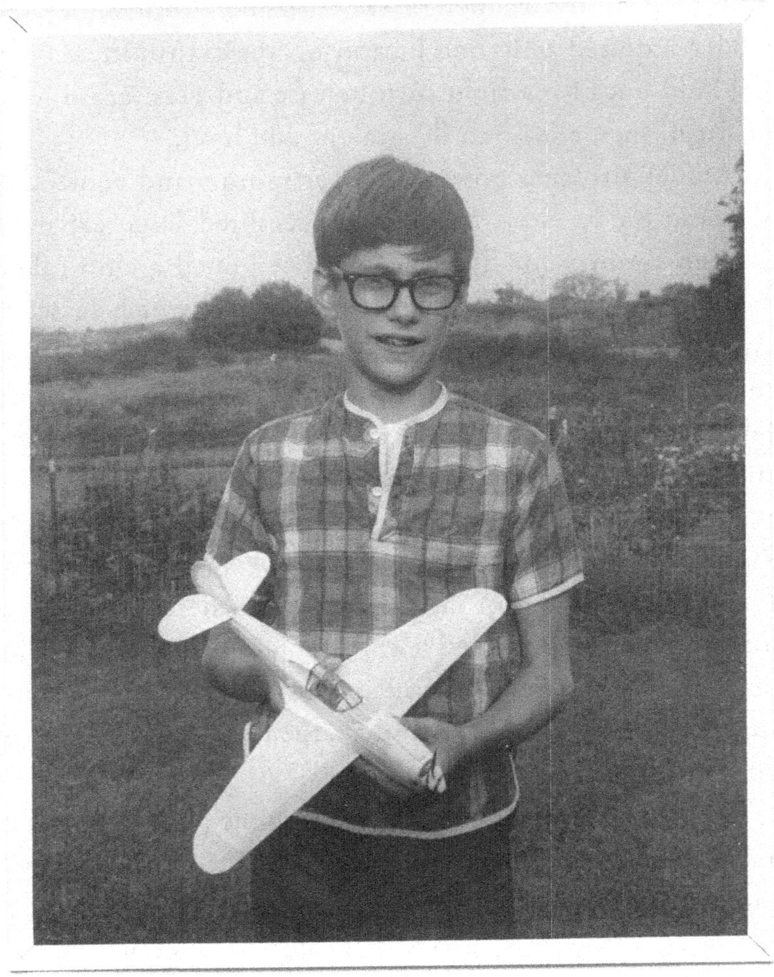

Me with a balsa wood and tissue model of a P-40 fighter, 1968.

frequency. Eventually the equipment used narrower slices of the radio spectrum, allowing multiple models to fly simultaneously. But in the early days, on a crowded warm Saturday with clear skies and calm winds, the hobby of flying radio-controlled model airplanes involved a lot of waiting until my father would frantically try to start a temperamental and finicky alcohol-burning engine, all of us hoping for a brief few moments of flight before the motor would quit, and our turn would be over.

During those years, a kind of arms race developed within the community of serious modelers, who every year would bring larger and more sophisticated models with larger gas tanks and more reliable control systems. Crowded weekend days in summer became an exercise in extreme patience for those with fewer means to constantly upgrade their equipment to stay competitive with the technology leaders. This eventually led my father to seek times and weather conditions that were not crowded with other modelers. Many of my memories of flying models on the Onondaga reservation are of barely being able to see the model in the darkening twilight, or of standing patiently on a cold autumn evening while my father desperately tried to squeeze in one last flight from a dying set of batteries. Sometimes he would lose the radio connection, and a model would start to fly away. He would yell at us to "Get in the car" and we would go driving after the escaped airplane. On a few occasions these chases led to epic adventures of climbing and bushwhacking, which my siblings and I remember variously.

My fondest memories are of the nervous anticipation of flying unreliable models with their high probability of failure, and the wonderful prospect of chasing after them into unknown, and possibly dangerous, territory. My sister Carolyn remembers enjoying the ride through the fields as a lookout on the hood of the car. Many years later my brother Emil confessed that through all the years of excursions to the flying field, he had always dreaded going there because he felt trapped and bored. Such were the stark differences between the worlds inhabited by two brothers who grew up in the same house and every night slept in the same room.

Despite our different recollections of childhood trips to the flying field, one memory my brother and I both share with our other two siblings is that our father regularly pushed against the boundaries of technology, weather conditions, and human endurance, to see his models fly, if only briefly, through the air.

The summers are short in the northern latitudes of Central New York State, and the cold snowy months of winter drag on forever. As a child, and well into my adult years, I designed and built many model airplanes during the long winter months, a time for dreaming about flight. Sometimes a model would take months to build and only moments to destroy on the first warm day of spring. The basic building materials were balsa wood, airplane glue, single-edged razor blades, pins, wax paper, sandpaper, silk or tissue paper for covering, and cellulose acetate butyrate dope (a clear lacquer-like material) for finishing. The glue and the dope were highly volatile and would make you light-headed if your space was not properly ventilated, which was almost always the case during the shut-in winter months. But in those days the only way to possess a model airplane was to make it yourself. Long hours of building were motivated by a powerful vision of the finished model, often supported by idealized paintings of the real airplane on the kit box, looking far sleeker and sexier than anything made with balsa wood and tissue paper could ever hope to be.

The general unwritten rule of model airplanes was that the more a model airplane looked like a real airplane, the worse it would fly. Of all the many balsa wood and tissue models I built of World War II-era fighters, I can only remember one small model of a Curtiss P-40 Warhawk that actually flew farther than I could throw a stone. And even if a model flew at all, it was never long before it would hit the side of a house or get tangled in the branches of a tree. The models that flew best were designed from the ground up as originals, not replicas of real airplanes. This seemed a great irony. Beautiful flight performance had to be purchased at the expense of what I thought to be the essence of beautiful design.

But gradually this idea of beauty as an imitation of something else gave way to a radically different aesthetic. The beauty of a Spitfire was not simply a consequence of its exquisite form, but also the fact that the beautiful object had flown with such superior performance and contributed greatly to Britain's success in repelling the German aerial bombing campaign during the Second World War. No balsa wood model could replicate that aspect of the Spitfire. But neither could a Spitfire hope to compete with models designed to fly gracefully above a grassy field in summer or silently within the confines of a large room in winter.

From November through most of April in Syracuse, the only way to see a model airplane fly was if it could do so indoors. So my father learned and taught us a number of building techniques for making models that were the extreme antithesis of the ferocious Spitfire. They were made of the thinnest, lightest strips of the lightest balsa wood and covered with a clear "microfilm," made by pouring dope onto the still surface of water held in a large flat pan. The dope would spread out and solidify in a microscopically thin layer that could then be lifted off the surface of the water with a wire hoop, similar to one used to make giant soap bubbles. The resulting material was like a spider web or dandelion seed—almost nonexistent. With the proper technique, it was possible to lift a perfect, unbroken membrane from the water which could then be gently draped over a balsa wood frame to complete a model's wing or tail. The microfilm would adhere to the moistened balsa frame and could then be trimmed around the edges with a needle heated over an alcohol flame.

The making of microfilm-covered indoor model airplanes required a delicacy of control of both motor skills and temper. A botched attempt to transfer a perfect diaphragm of microfilm onto the framework of a wing would challenge the most patient of the gods. At times the Spitfire-inspired part of me would force its way to the surface, and I would smash a model in anger and then run outside to play in the snow.

But when patience prevailed, the result was an airplane model that would fly so slowly and beautifully that you could walk behind it, being careful not to disturb the nearly motionless air through which it moved. The models were powered by wound rubber strands extracted from peeled golf balls. One golf ball would yield a huge pile of rubber, which it would surrender in an energetic dance across the floor once the white dimpled rind of the ball was removed.

When I was in the eighth grade, I had the opportunity to demonstrate one of these models during a science class presentation I made about aerodynamics. After explaining various aspects of flight using posters I had made for the lecture, I opened a box containing the model, which had been prepared for immediate flight with the rubber motor wound up and ready to go. The glazed-over eyes of my classmates, lulled to near stupor by my lecture, suddenly filled with excitement and fixed upon the gossamer model I held at the front of the classroom. After telling my classmates to remain motionless once the airplane started to fly, I released it to trace a slow majestic circle above their astonished faces around the perimeter of the room, returning almost precisely to the point of launch, where I was able to catch it gracefully. The class erupted in a cheer, and in my elation I moved my hand holding the airplane too abruptly, causing the wing to break away, making it impossible to perform an encore. However, the model had done its work, and I experienced a rare school triumph. For many weeks afterward, various classmates petitioned me to make models for them, which I never did, but rather basked in a brief season of celebrity during an otherwise undistinguished middle-school career.

From the beginning of his teaching career, my father always looked for opportunities to weave his passion for flight into his classes. During his first teaching assignment as a sixth grade teacher he had purchased materials for his class to build a replica of a Wright glider, and then had the students write and stage a play about the Kitty Hawk flights for the entire school. At the performance, he sat in the audience and played no role in the production, giving the students complete artistic control and credit for its success.

Watching an indoor model airplane fly slowly and silently around a room is an experience of universal appeal, especially to an audience of people who have never seen such a thing. And so the idea of calling an assembly of all the

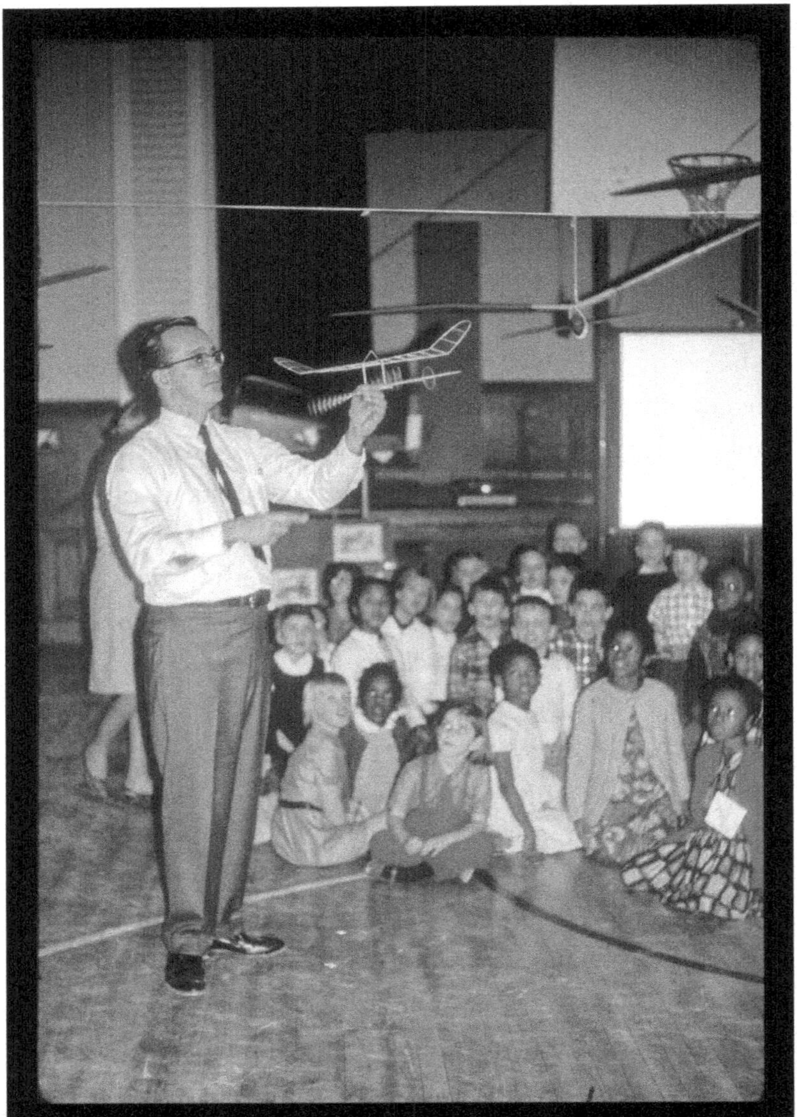

During an assembly at Percy Hughes Elementary School, on or around December 17, 1970, Emil demonstrated some of his indoor flying models to commemorate the anniversary of the Wright Brothers' first flights in 1903. These models could fly for several minutes inside a gymnasium at the pace of a slow walk.

members of his elementary school community to witness such a flight came to my father, who served as an elementary school principal during our years of experimentation with indoor flight. But how would it be possible to demonstrate the graceful, silent flight of a delicate indoor model, where the slightest movement of air would be disruptive, inside a gymnasium full of hundreds of rustling children? He decided to stage a completely silent program. The strict rule would be that students were not to speak a word from the time they left their classrooms to gather in the school gymnasium until they returned to their classrooms after the assembly. Everyone, including the teachers and my father himself, respected this rule. Instead of using words, he played an album of songs by guitarist Chet Atkins entitled *Solo Flight* through the public address system while his models flew magestically around the gymnasium. He often talked about the experience of this "Solo Flight Assembly" as one of the high points of his professional life.

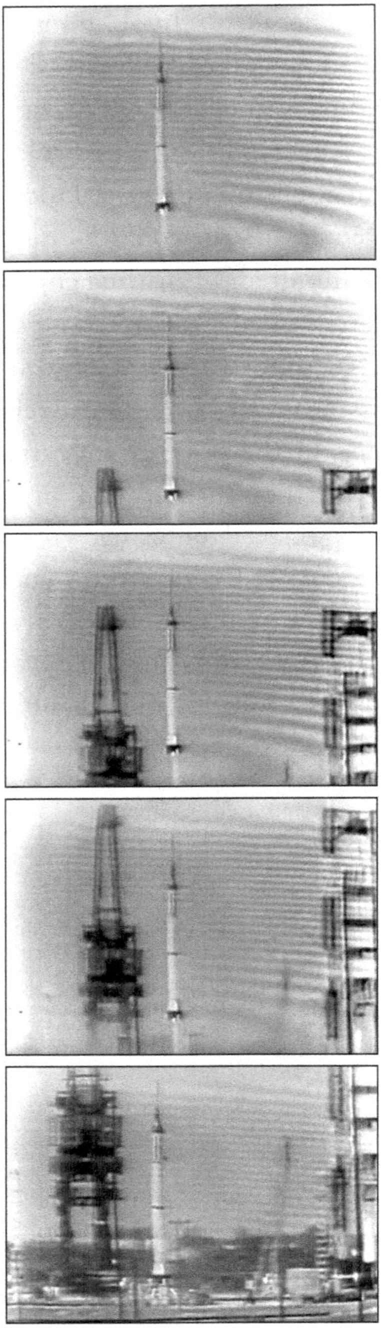

7

The decade of the 1960s seemed to promise the fulfillment of all the flying dreams of the ages, starting with the first sub-orbital space flight by Alan Shepard on May 5, 1961, and ending when Neil Armstrong and Edwin Aldrin walked on the Moon on July 21, 1969. There could not have been a more ideal person to play the role of true believer than one who witnessed Shepard's blast off at age six, and stayed tuned in for the next eight years, ultimately to see live television pictures transmitted from the surface of the Moon at age fourteen. The space program was timed perfectly to grab and hold my rapt attention. But unlike the direct experiences of flying models in the real world, flying in space was a highly mediated experience served up in flickering monochromatic images through the television screen, or in still photographs on the pages of *Life* magazine.

Each space launch reset what I imagined to be some universal clock to zero. The countdown timer on the bottom of the screen placed us in negative time—time that would count for nothing at "t-minus zero and lift-off." Time moved forward and upward, the past evaporating quickly like a trail of alcohol swabbed onto a dry glass surface. I was not yet seven years old when Shepard went up, and already believed that the time before his lift-off would soon be rendered ancient and irrelevant by the stream of fire from the end of his rocket. The television screen was a window into a constant-

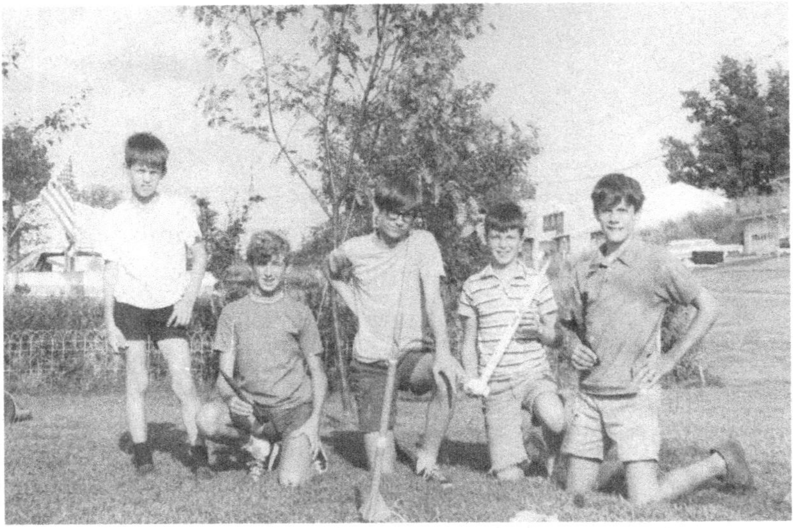

Neighborhood kids with their model rockets in 1968. I'm in the center, my brothers Jim on the far left and Emil on the far right.

ly advancing world that was quite unlike the natural world outside. Like a rocket, the television consumed the future as fuel, and expelled the past as it ascended. And as there was only one God in heaven, there was only one rocket to watch at a time on television, and no competing alternative programming on other channels.

Unlike the messy and unpredictable weather conditions through which we would try to fly our model airplanes, space was presented as a place of perfection, where the ideal forms of Plato and Euclid and the movements of Kepler and Newton reigned absolute. Space was pure and clean, where perfect men wore perfect white suits and were perfectly unencumbered by earthly concerns. Space solved the problem of flight once and for all by eliminating gravity altogether. Once space travel on television took hold of the imagination it was difficult to come back to earth. The limitations of an apelike existence, plodding about the surface of a planet held down by gravity, seemed intolerable by comparison. I felt the pull of gravity and the dreadful slowness of my own world most acutely after a morning of watching Saturday television as a child. As it must be for an astronaut returning to earth after a long period of weightlessness, the re-entry could be painful and debilitating. Fortunately, I had no choice but to come back to earth because after lunchtime on Saturday the television programming turned to dry adult subjects. One could neither live permanently in space nor in the world of television.

My mother told me a story about a time when I was a toddler, after displaying some type of unacceptable behavior she responded that I was a pretty good actor and, if I kept it up, she would "put me on television." This caused me to go into hysterics, begging her not to put me "in the television with those paper people." I have no memory of this event, but her story suggests that at one point in my early childhood I perceived what was on television to be an extension of the material world into the interior of the television set. Eventually I understood the television to be a device that synthesized images transmitted from afar. Our house was located in a hilly area, far away from the transmission towers, so reception was always a problem. The picture was often snowy, blurry, or would not hold steady on the screen, flipping vertically as though there were an endless stack of television screens popping up from below.

Sometimes the television would become so unwatchable that the TV repairman would make a house call. His name was Mr. Pigoula, and I perceived the grunting and panting sounds he made when he was on the floor in back of the television set as somehow linked poetically to the first syllable of his name. Upon reflection many years later, I realized that he had suffered some kind of breathing disorder, probably caused by smoking or possibly inhaling the blue air inside our house, where every adult smoked unfiltered cigarettes most of the time. Sometimes my father would try to fix the television set himself by extracting all the vacuum tubes and driving them over to the local drug store, where he would use a device called a "tube tester" to identify faulty tubes. The drug store had a department where dozens of different kinds of vacuum tubes could be purchased. I remember standing with him while he tested the tubes, hoping and praying he would find the culprit, and we would be able to resume our television watching that same evening.

When the television was not working it felt like we were gasping for air. Television defined universals and sought to addict us to itself. Homework was rarely assigned during my elementary school years, and the hours between arriving home after school and bedtime were relatively free and unsupervised. Until the start of the local evening news the programming was aimed squarely at us kids. The sponsors of these programs presented a garden of childhood earthly delights to send us off on missions of begging that were a constant annoyance to our parents. The greatest hope of these companies was to see a product go viral in the schools.

In some of the houses in our neighborhood, the television set was always on, whether someone was watching it or not, as though it were a full member of the family with a life of its own. In one house in particular, the always-on television, with the sound turned so low you could barely hear it, was like a resident grandmother knitting in her regular chair, quietly whispering to herself. The reign of the official culture in that household was absolute, and the family seemed to always be striving to fit the models of American perfection that television recommended. They always had a new model Chevrolet Impala in the driveway, and dinner was served at the same time every night on a fixed weekly menu cycle. Their Christmas tree was the perfect conical shape every year; their lawn had no dandelions in it; the father was always working and the mother was always cleaning.

By comparison, our house was a smoke-filled riot of improvisation. Our television set, when it was on, was merely one of the many loud voices competing to be heard above the general din. Unlike the quiet, orderly and austere Presbyterian sanctuary down the street, with simple white walls and neat wooden pews, our house was modeled on the Eastern Orthodox aesthetic—hundreds of faces peering from the walls, incense wafting in the air, and people constantly talking and jostling for attention in multiple languages.

The complex polytheistic nature of our household kept the television somewhat at bay, despite its constant aim to devour us completely, like the Cyclops making a meal of Odysseus's men when they ventured into his dwelling. This electronic Cyclops was not interested in eating our bodies, but instead in snatching them as agents for its own earthly ambitions. Its competition was the lure of the wide world of reality outside the dark confines of its cave. Thankfully, my ambition to make and fly model airplanes provided me with a means to resist falling into the clutches of the one-eyed monster completely. Despite every attempt by the monster to lure me away from reality, I never lost my ability to rise out of a television stupor at some point and turn the set off.

Sometimes, however, the television connected us to things happening in the real world which we could not have seen in any other way, such as during the weekend in late November 1963 when President Kennedy was assassinated. I first heard the news from Mrs. Huffman, my fourth grade teacher, who came into class after lunch with an ashen look on her face and said, "The President has been shot." Her words conjured the image in my mind of a firing squad, with President Kennedy wearing a blindfold. By the time school was out for the day, we had learned the terrible news that the President was dead.

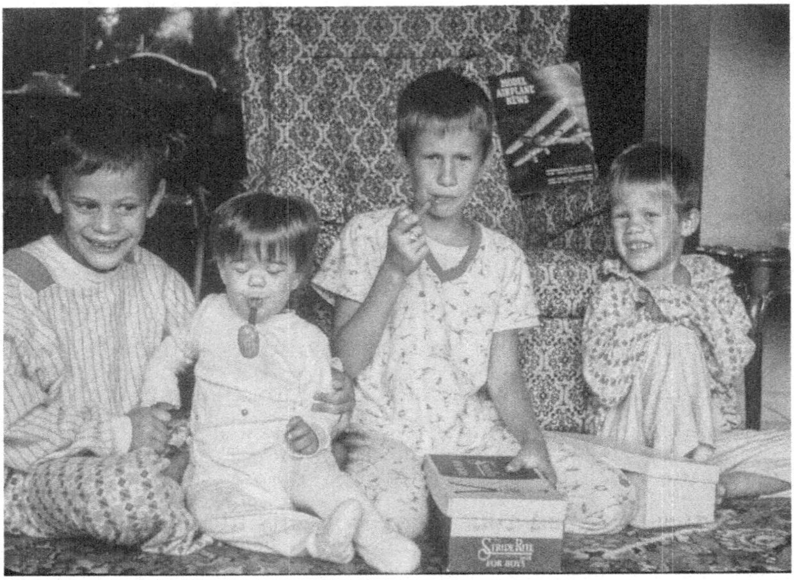

The four Cost siblings around 1963. I am third from the left. My sister Carolyn and I are pretending to smoke corn-cob pipes in emulation of all the adult smokers in our family. Emil is on the left and Jim on the right. The cover of Model Airplane News *magazine in the background is from September 1963, two months before the assassination of President Kennedy.*

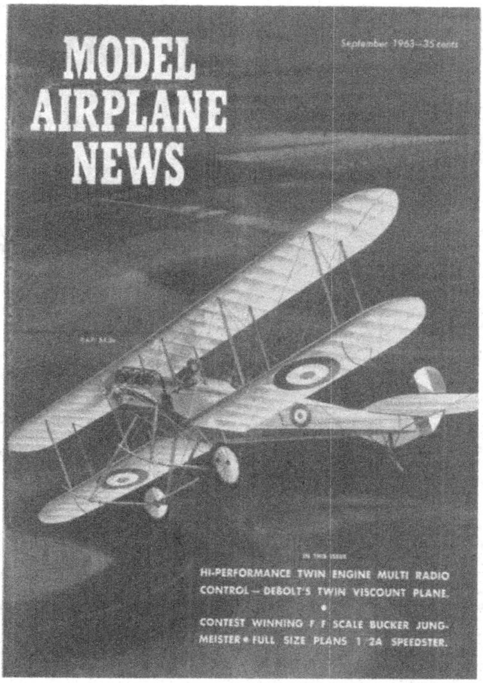

That afternoon and into the evening, all day Saturday and Sunday, and through the funeral on Monday, the television set stayed on in our house, as it must have in most others. We learned the horrifying details of the tragedy, and my storybook images of what it meant for someone to be shot were replaced by the raw realities of a sniper perched in the window of a building, an open limousine, a casket draped with a flag on a horse-drawn cart, and a burial in a place called Arlington. These were accompanied by live television images of the sniper himself being fatally shot in the stomach while being led out of a building by the police. This was my first experience of the death of anyone I knew, and marked the abrupt and brutal end of the enchanted years of my early childhood.

Chou En-lai were present at the meeting. It added that Mao also gave a banquet for the Albanian visitors.

Penn. AG, Wife 2 Others Killed In Plane Crash

SOMERSET, Pa. (AP) — The bodies of Pennsylvania Atty. Gen. Walter E. Alessandroni, his wife and two other persons were found Monday night in the wreckage of a light airplane in a snow-coated mountain gully.

Alessandroni, 51, managed Gov. William W. Scranton's unsuccessful battle to wrest the Republican presidential nomination from Barry Goldwater in 1964.

He was making the flight for a campaign speech in his bid for the GOP nomination for lieutenant governor in the May 17 state primary.

The four died Sunday when their private twin-engine plane fell in rugged Allegheny Mountain terrain — known to pilots as the "graveyard of the Alleghenies" because of the dangerous weather conditions that often prevail.

Besides Alessandroni and his wife, Ethel, the dead include James E. Staudinger of Abington Twp., who was the Republican chairman of Montgomery County and a member of the State Liquor Control Board, and the pilot, Melvin E. Ladin, 28, of Collingswood, N.J.

The plane was carrying Alessandroni from the state capital at Harrisburg to Uniontown where he was to address the Fayette County Tavern Association.

An association official said later that there wasn't much concern when he didn't arrive because it was snowing and sleeting and it was assumed that the plane had turned back.

The discovery that the plane was missing wasn't made until about 24 hours after it went down. Mrs. Staudinger phoned Harrisburg to inquire about her husband. State officials began checking.

ALBANY COUNTY DROPS ANTI-POVERTY BOARD

ALBANY, N.Y. (AP)—The Albany County Board of Supervisors, supported by Democratic Mayor Erastus Corning, has abolished the county's 20-member Economic Opportunity Commission.

The board and the mayor said private, non-profit community agencies could apply to the government for funds to combat poverty.

pointed up by the repeated reference in the nuclear test announcement of the "thought" and leadership of China's 72-year-old party Chairman Mao Tze-tung.

The statement said the complete success of the explosion was ensured by the fact that the scientists, technicians, military, workers and others involved held high Mao's banner and "gave prominence to politics," creatively studied Mao's works and followed his policies. It called the feat a "great victory for Mao Tze-tung's thought."

In exposing both "antiparty" individuals and those who have merely strayed from the correct path, the Chinese have emphasized that the culprits have either opposed or misinterpreted Mao's writings and thinking.

The use of Mao's name in the statement on the latest bomb test, a practice which was not followed in China's announcements of two previous tests, appeared to be a further effort to rally wavering elements around the Communist party leadership.

Pupils Boycott School, Protest Integration Plan

SYRACUSE, N.Y. (AP) — More than 900 children remained away from classes today to protest the city plan for the integration of Croton School.

Emil Cost, principal of the predominantly Negro elementary school, said 907 of the 1,124 pupils enrolled in the school were absent. He said the normal daily absentee average was about 70.

The school, for grades kindergarten through 6, is more than 90 per cent Negro.

The protest revolves around a plan by Dr. Franklyn S. Barry, school superintendent, that would provide for the eventual closing of Croton.

If approved, about 200 pupils would be bussed to other schools next fall in the first stage of the plan.

Civil rights organizations in varous neighborhood groups are protesting the project. They maintain that it is wrong to "integrate at the expense of a minority group."

They propose that the school board act to bring white children into the neighborhood, as well as to bus Negro children out. The board is opposed to such a plan.

The school board voted last year to close two other predominently Negro schools, Washington Irving and Madison Jr. High, and to bus pupils to other schools.

Say Car Sales Hurt by Auto Safety Issue

DETROIT (AP) — Two of the auto industry's top leaders say the auto safety issue has hurt car sales.

Arjay Miller, president of Ford Motor Co., referred to the "harassment" of the auto safety issue Monday in reporting a slowdown in Ford production.

Roy Abernethy, president of American Motors and of the Automobile Manufacturers Association, added today:

"Up to now, there have been conflicting sales reports from field offices. Some areas have reported a depressing effect on sales as a result of the Washington hearings; others report little or no effect.

"The latest survey, completed by our marketing consultants on Monday, shows that the hearings are having a negative effect on sales."

Chrysler President Lynn A. Townsend stuck by his assertion that "we will not know for some time yet what effect auto safety discussions and hearings have had on sales." He added that "we are keeping close tabs on it."

General Motors President James M. Roche said Thursday in a telephone conversation with Sen. Abraham Ribicoff, D-Conn., that he did not believe the auto safety probe had hurt sales.

from the
into New E
inches of
burgh, a re
previous hig
1.8 inches o
The snow
Placid, N.Y
dacks, was
inch fell at
day as snow
northeastern
central App
of upstate
England.
The 23 r
Mich., early
low for Ma
troit was a
10.
It was wa
Anchorage,
than at Lou
Early mor
ranged from
Marquette,
West, Fla.

WINS NOM

ALBUQU
— A State
Robert Har
has won hi
head.
Haner and
tied with 98
Tuesday's
election for
ate nomina
their right t
of deciding
toss.
The coin
by Dist.
Mcmanus a
giving the n

Gemini 9 Crew Reh For May 17 Space

CAPE KENNEDY, Fla. (AP) — America's next pair of astronauts climb into their Gemini 9 spaceship today and rehearse the complex dual countdown that will send them rocketing aloft next Tuesday to test skills needed to land on the moon.

Before next week's three-day space adventure concludes, Navy Lt. Cmdr. Eugene A. Cernan is to take a record-duration space walk and use a rocket-powered back pack.

Command pilot Thomas P. Stafford is to steer Gemini 9 on several rendezvous attempts with an Agena target satellite and jolt Gemini 9 into a new orbit by firing the 16,000-pound-thrust Agena engine while their spacecraft is hooked up with it.

The flight plan for Gemini 9 "is to date one of the most complex and sophisticated," Air Force Lt. Col. Stafford said.

Today's countdown — called a simultaneous launch demonstration — is the start of two days of

intensive re
test equipm
cians in th
cedures n
Gemini an
satellite on
apart.
Wednesda
through a
where it i
three prac
ment in th
the ground
during earl
tual flight
Preparati
noon (EST
for a scie
Atmospheri
spacecraft,
ing 465 pou
ride a Delt
shaped orbi
750 miles
study the
per atmosp
Next Tu

(Contin

8

During most of the 1960s, my father served as principal of Croton Elementary School in Syracuse. The student population of about 1,100 was mainly African American (89 percent African American in 1966, according to a U.S. Civil Rights Commission report published in June 1968). In the middle of the decade, the movement to desegregate the few predominantly "Negro" schools in the city by busing students away from their neighborhoods created social tensions among all the constituents in the community that would be impacted. The first simplistic ideas for desegregation were not acceptable to many of the families of children enrolled at Croton. Over the next few years several other ideas were proposed, ending with a complex partnership between the City School District and Syracuse University, called "Croton on Campus," which brought hundreds of Croton students in grades 4 to 6 into special classes and facilities on the Syracuse University campus every day. The complexity of this program necessitated the hiring of an administrator from the University to replace my father, who was reassigned in 1967 to Percy Hughes School.

In his last few years at Croton Elementary School, and perhaps as a way of compensating for a growing sense of frustration with his job, my father began to think about the possibility of constructing a full-size replica of the 1903 Wright Flyer. He launched into a frenzy of research, collecting every published document he could find about the

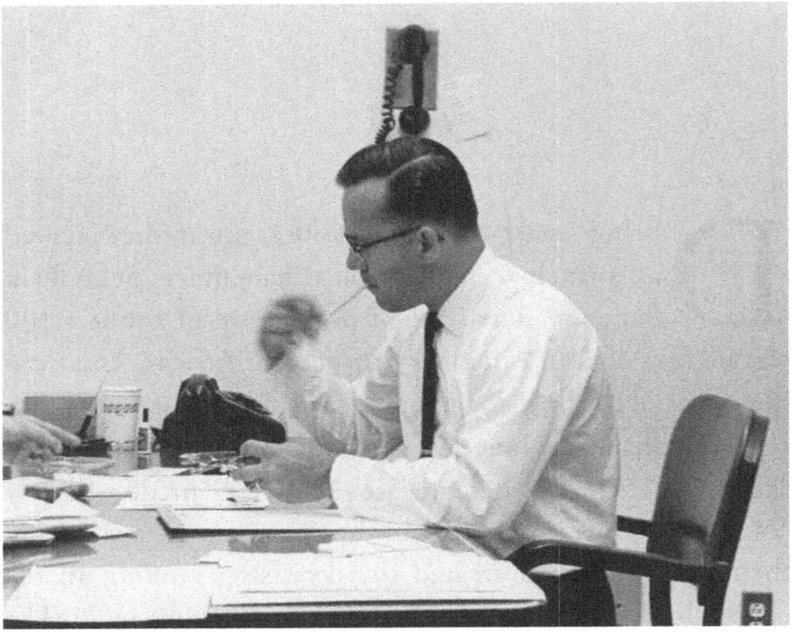

Emil Cost at his desk at Croton School in the mid 1960s. He could use the intercom on the wall to address the entire school. He could also smoke his filterless Pall Mall cigarettes while he worked.

construction of the original. The Library of Congress held all of the original Wright Brothers' papers and photographs, and had published collections of them in book form. As he accumulated these documents, he gained confidence that he would be able to learn enough about the original airplane to be able to replicate it, and the project grew into an obsession.

Our family practiced a traditional Mediterranean evening ritual that began with cocktails and hors d'oeuvres, followed by food preparation and dinner, suffused with lively conversation throughout. During these hours, the tradition held that most of the talking was done by the older people, who regaled the younger people with their stories, many of which had been heard before. I remember, as a child, begging to hear certain favorite familiar stories, whereas in later years, I would beg not to have to listen to them. My father and mother both enjoyed telling stories at the dinner table, but often disagreed about details and defended their respective interrupted versions of the narrative with an agitated, "Will you let me finish what I'm saying?!" When grandparents and older relatives joined our table, the struggle for domination of the floor would sometimes erupt into a brawl. The dinner hour could be a real workout, after which we would all withdraw to our private quarters.

During his early years at Croton School, my father's evening stories were mostly about funny things that people did and said at school that day. There were standard characters, including teachers, staff members, students, and parents, who would make regular appearances, as in a weekly sitcom. As larger policy issues began to crowd out the more personal aspects of his daily work, various bureaucrats and academics from the University became the main comic characters and villains in his stories. Their names were as familiar to us as the characters on the *Beverly Hillbillie*s or *Bonanza*. But gradually these characters yielded center stage to historical people who had played important roles in the invention of the first airplane. My father spoke often about Wilbur and Orville Wright, but also men with more exotic names like Otto Lilienthal, Octave Chanute and Samuel P. Langley.

Lilienthal was a German inventor who built and flew beautiful hang gliders resembling gigantic soaring birds. He constructed a large conical shaped hill from which he learned how to fly his gliders, and was credited with being the first person to fly successfully in one. After many hun-

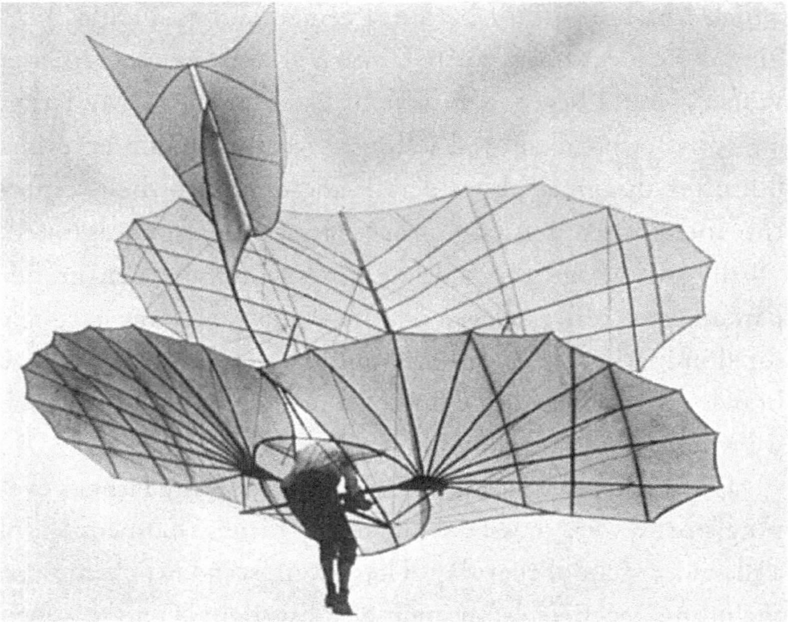

Otto Lilienthal in one of his hang gliders. (LOC)

dreds of flights over a period of several years, his luck ran out in 1896, when he stalled and fell about 50 feet, breaking his neck and dying the next day. He was celebrated and mourned on many occasions in our house.

Octave Chanute became another regular guest at our dinner table. Chanute was an American who had built and flown a boxier looking hang glider around the time of Lilienthal's death. Chanute was an engineer and a scholar of early aviation whom the Wrights credited with much of their early knowledge about the construction of airframes. Chanute's glider looked like an American model, simple and rectangular, when compared to the curvier European designs of Lilienthal. The Wright Flyer seemed to combine the straight line simplicity of the Chanute design with some subtle European curves. At one point it seemed to my childish mind that their success at Kitty Hawk was somehow magically tied to this synthesis of curves and straight lines.

Samuel P. Langley was a famous and highly educated scientist who became the secretary of the Smithsonian Institution. With generous public funding from the army, Langley designed a series of models of flying machines called "aerodromes," ungainly double-winged machines that looked like boxy dragonflies. His attempts to build a powered aerodrome capable of carrying a man came to an ignominious end as he tried to launch the machine from atop a houseboat floating in the Potomac River on December 8, 1903. Shortly after clearing the end of the launch platform, the wings folded up and the aerodrome plunged straight into the river. Nine days later the Wrights made their first successful flights at Kitty Hawk.

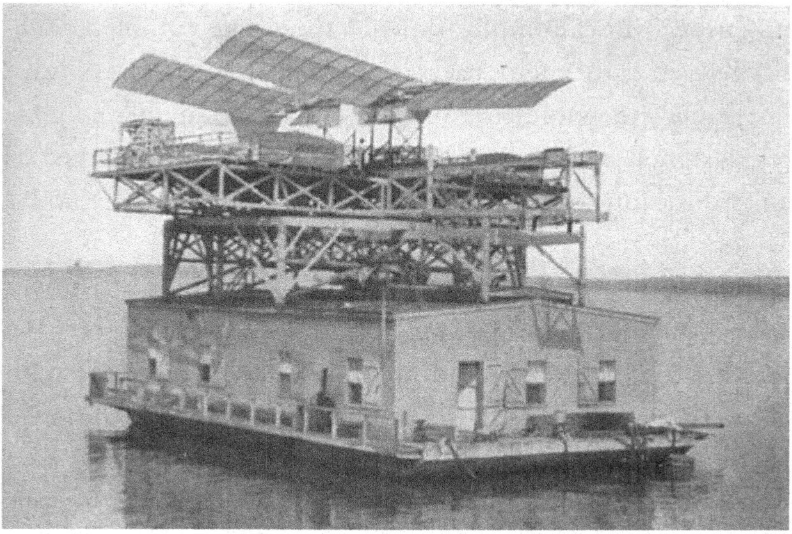

Samuel Langley's aerodrome on its houseboat in the Potomac River in 1903. (LOC)

Whereas Lilienthal and Chanute were heroic characters in the stories my father told around the dinner table, Langley was portrayed as a clown. The spectacular failure of the celebrated academic and theoretician, and the victory of two humble bicycle builders from Ohio, must have been especially enjoyable for my father to contemplate, given the ascendant authority of unpracticed university professors and social scientists in his own domain of work. The project to build a full-scale replica of the Wright Flyer would be the perfect antidote for his frustrations.

But how could he do it? Knowing how the original Flyer was constructed was one thing. Building it would require tooling that would itself need to be built. He managed to make a jig that could be used to manufacture the wing ribs of exactly the correct shape and construction, and made a sample rib. This gave him a material feel for the magnitude of the whole project, and after months of discouraged rumination over the implications of the single completed rib, he devised a different path forward that was more within his reach. He would first build a replica of one of the gliders designed by Octave Chanute in 1896, which served as an inspiration to the Wrights. This he was certain he could accomplish.

Once this decision was made our household became a chapel for the adoration of everything Octave Chanute. We learned his biography, and all about his experiments with the design and construction of gliders. We were encouraged to believe that of all the people in the world who were admirable, Octave Chanute was the most worthy of our admiration, because without him the Wrights would not have been able to do what they did. For the next few years my father fell under the influence of the god Apollo in the guise of Octave Chanute, and we were obliged to swear our allegiances.

Our devotional activities were accompanied by some real physical labor in the building of the glider replica. My father provided most of it, but there were times when he recruited us to help him do things that required four or more hands. After many months of work, sometime during the spring of 1968, we were the proud owners of a full-scale replica of an 1896 Chanute hang glider, which took up most of our basement. But what next? Could the thing possibly fly? How? Where?

Of all the contraptions in which people have tried to

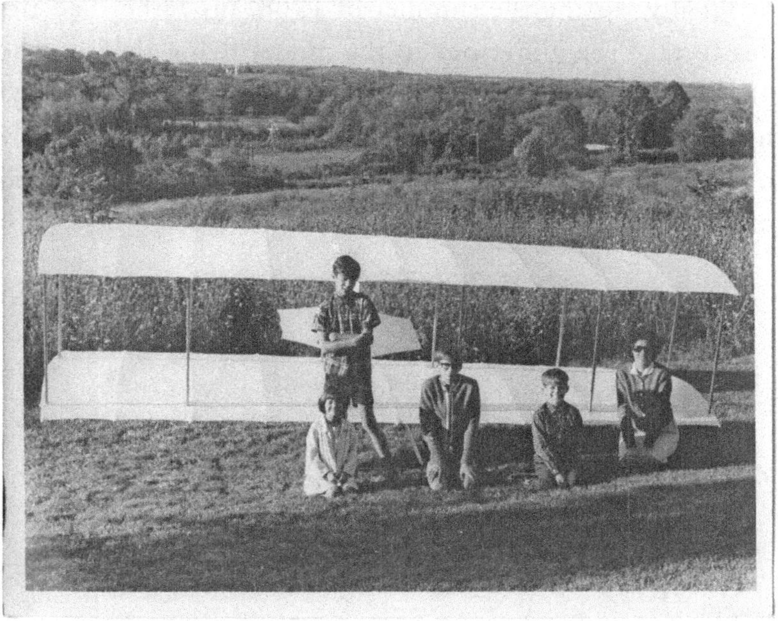

The family of Emil Cost posing with its newest member in the spring of 1968.

fly, Chanute's glider was one of the most primitive and dangerous. Unlike the later Wright gliders, it had no movable surfaces. The only way to control its flight, assuming one could find a hill or cliff from which to jump, was for the "pilot" hanging from the undercarriage to swing the lower part of his body forward and back and side to side to try to tilt the machine in the desired direction. The risk of getting hurt badly or killed seemed high. Chanute never tried to fly his own design, relying on his much younger partner and co-designer, Augustus Herring, to be the pilot. Since the most physically demanding sport among the adults in our family was vigorous argument around the dinner table, usually accompanied by smoking, the question of whether and how to try to fly the glider remained open.

Finally, during the summer of 1968, my father had the idea to take the glider out to the model flying field on the Onondaga reservation and try to fly it as a kite. We lashed the glider in parts to the tops of two cars and drove slowly to the field. Once there, we assembled the glider and tied towing lines to the wingtips and several other points. With

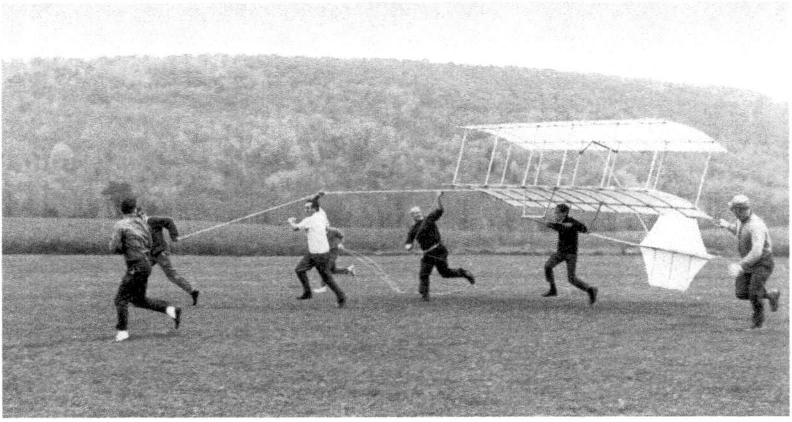

the help of several of the members of the model flying club, the Chanute glider left the ground for a few brief moments of tethered flight, first unmanned and then manned. (I was the pilot.) But my father began to realize that it would not be wise to try to fly the glider in the manner of the original. The glider only broke free of the ground once more before it was relegated to permanent storage in the garage, and eventually taken apart and recycled for materials.

My father was appointed principal of Percy Hughes School following his time at Croton. Percy Hughes was a smaller school with a racially-integrated and diverse population that was largely immune from the stresses and political complexities of desegregation. Of all the elementary schools in Syracuse, it was the furthest evolved in the direction of the ideals of the Civil Rights movement. The students included children from a broad range of ethnic, racial, and economic backgrounds reflecting the neighborhoods it served, as well as children with physical handicaps from the larger community. The experience of transferring from Croton School at the center of the turmoil of desegregation to Percy Hughes School brought with it a feeling of great optimism for my father and our family. He was again in an environment where leadership was still largely an art that could be practiced by an individual, and not a faceless bureaucratic apparatus designed by politicians and university professors.

During his years at Percy Hughes, he created some notable opportunities to share his passion for flight with the assembled community. On one occasion the students, faculty and staff were brought together for the "first manned attempt to fly the Chanute glider." My father notified the local newspapers and television stations. The faculty, staff and students assembled outdoors to watch as the glider was prepared for flight. Then my father took the microphone and described what he planned to do: gather speed running down a runway configured out of a long line of cafeteria tables arranged for the occasion, and then leap into the air. He told the students he would try to ascend to rooftop level and fly around the schoolyard. He described a flight plan as fantastic as that of Icarus. When he was satisfied that he had made believers of the children (and many of the adults), he mounted the runway with his glider and ran as fast as he could down the long line of tables, leaping off and landing

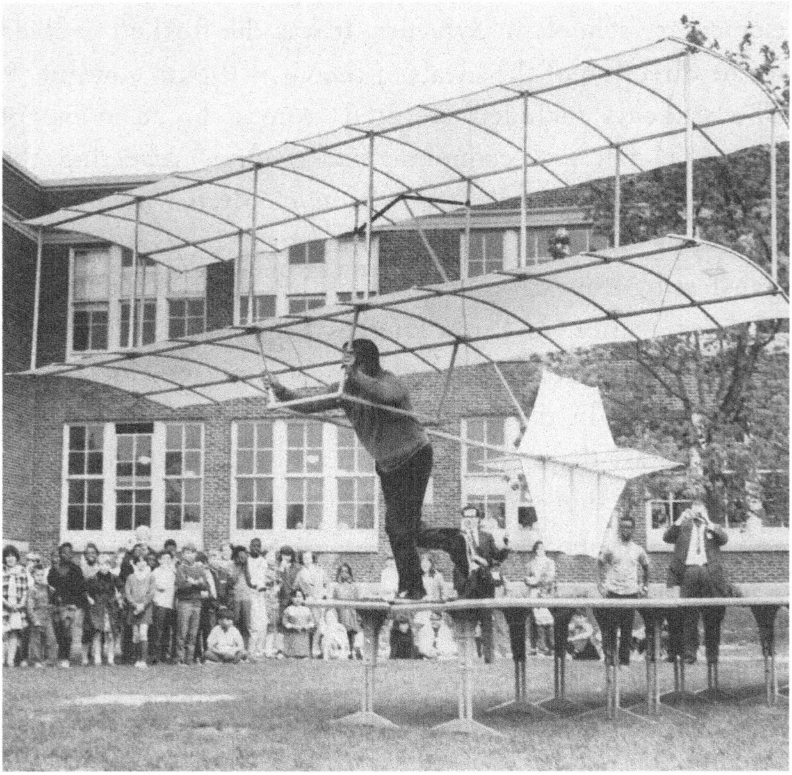

on the grass a few feet from the end of the last table. That evening we watched the event on television. I remember seeing Fred Hillegas, the anchorman for the Syracuse ABC affiliate, play the story as a serious "man attempts to fly" narrative.

My father shared two long-established family traditions with his students that day. One was an attempt to give them their own experience of the romance of manned flight as a dream yet to be realized, allowing them a sense of what it must have felt like to be Orville or Wilbur Wright before December 17, 1903. The other was the experience of being fooled by an older member of the family, as my grandmother had once fooled me into thinking she would take me on vacation to Greece as a stowaway in her suitcase. Thus he sought to share both the sublime and ridiculous aspects of our family life with his students.

The few brief flights of our Chanute glider took place during the same time period as the first lunar flights of the Apollo program, fostering in me a contemplation of the grand sweep of aeronautical history. In little more than 70 years, mankind had progressed from jumping off sand dunes with muslin-covered wooden gliders to landing impossibly complicated and miraculous machines on the Moon. People my grandmother's age had lived through the entire time.

Yet, despite all efforts by NASA and the news media to portray the Moon landing as the first giant step toward a glorious future in space, public interest in the Apollo program quickly began to wane. By the time of the third lunar landing mission of Apollo 13, the number of people planning to follow the mission closely on television had radically diminished. It was only a catastrophic failure of technology threatening to end the mission in tragedy that brought back the audience. Two days into the flight an exploding oxygen tank crippled the Command Service Module, compromising its life support systems. The crew, already on its way to the Moon, was sustained by systems on board the attached Lunar Module while it followed an improvised flight plan that swung the astronauts around the far side of the Moon and back toward Earth.

On April 17, 1970, the day the Apollo 13 astronauts were endeavoring to return to Earth, my father assembled everyone from Percy Hughes School on the playground for a group portrait taken from the rooftop of the school building. The students displayed a crude hand-painted banner that read "Welcome Back Jack Jim Fred 4/17/70."

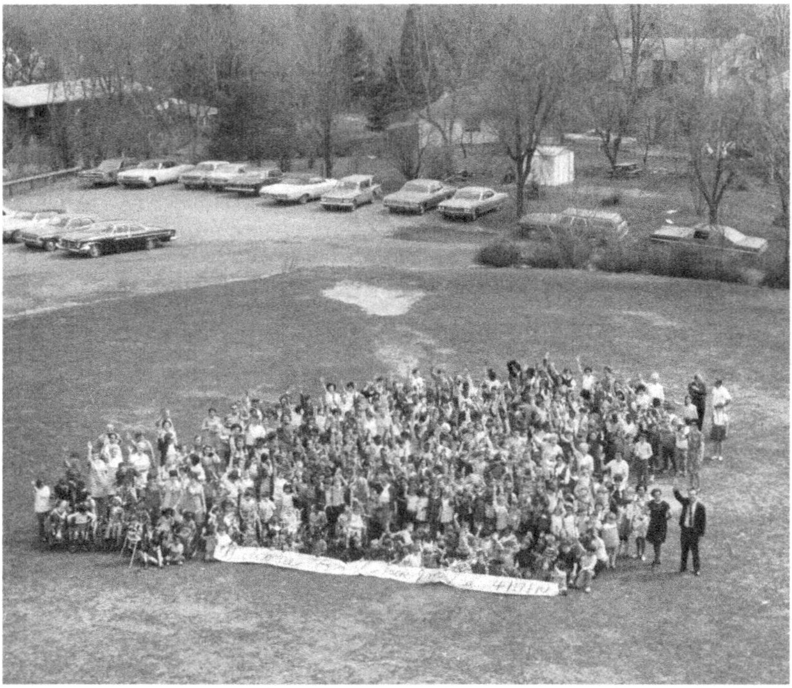

As I study the photograph now, so many decades after the last men walked on the Moon, it seems a fitting summary to the story of manned space flight—a group of diverse and imperfect people of Earth together welcoming back the would-be supermen of space into the warm embrace of home.

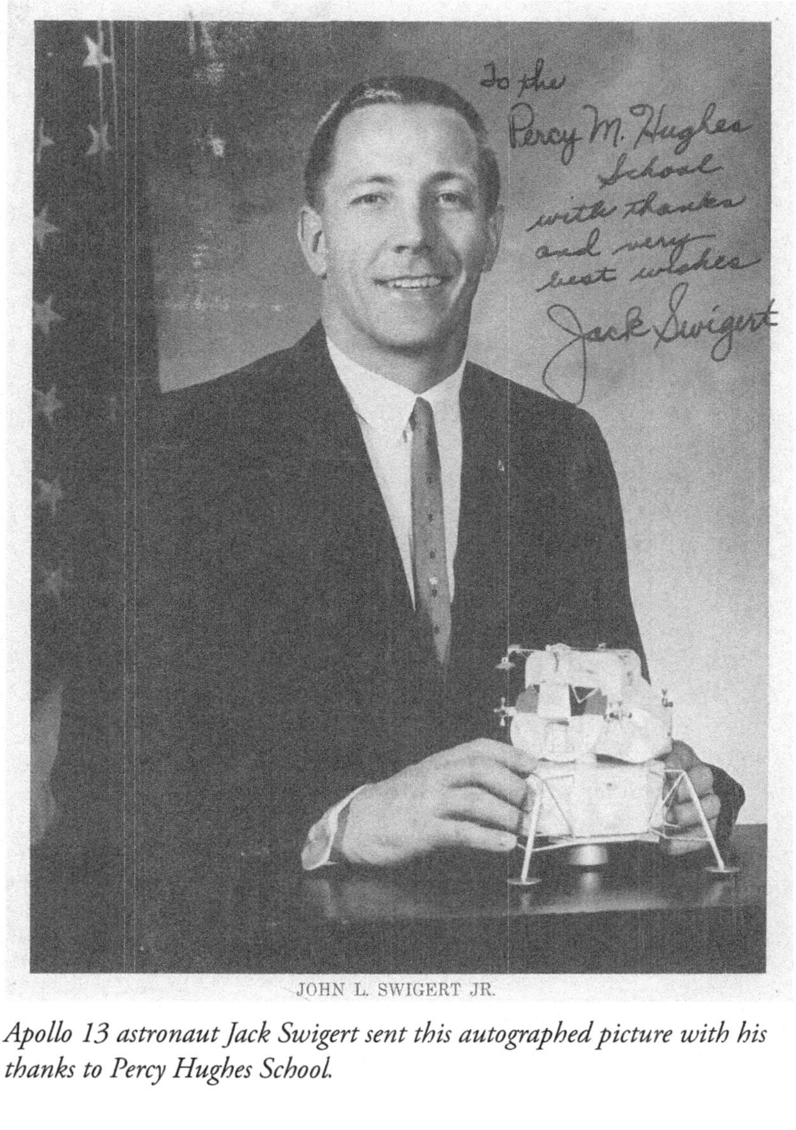

Apollo 13 astronaut Jack Swigert sent this autographed picture with his thanks to Percy Hughes School.

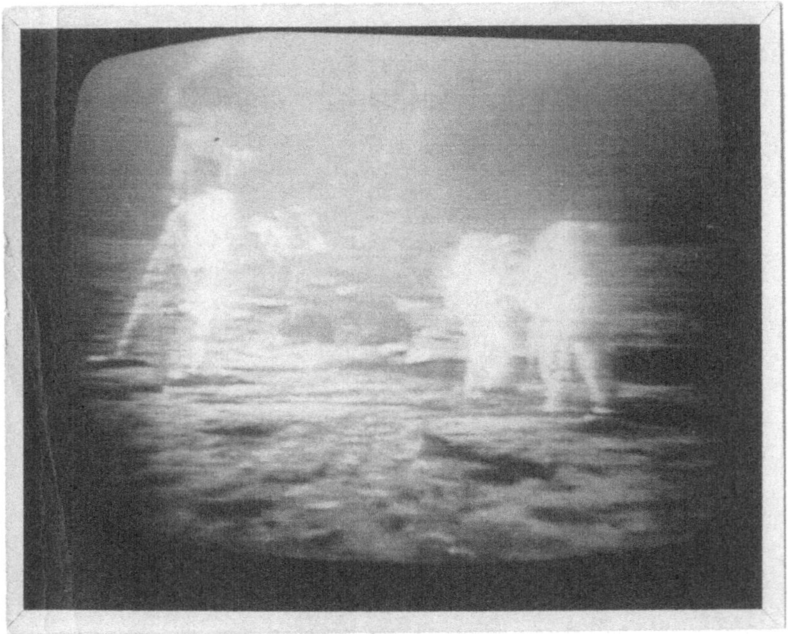

Photograph made directly from the television screen by Emil Cost during the live transmission from the first Moon walk.

9

President Kennedy had set the goal in a speech to Congress of landing men on the Moon two and a half years before his death. By the time the first boot made its famous imprint in the dark powder of the lunar surface in July 1969, there were nearly half a million people employed in the endeavor.

My cousin Tasso, who had once fooled me as a young child by promising to give me his car, was one of those half million people, employed as an engineer for General Dynamics. After the Apollo program began to recede into history, Tasso told stories about the years leading up to the Moon landing, and about how he resorted to hiding his telephone in the refrigerator so as not to be awoken at any random hour of the night by frantic calls from his colleagues working the graveyard shift.

The realities of what was happening behind the scenes of the Moon landing program were never revealed until years after it had ended. The only pictures we could see of the two-man Gemini flights and then the three-man Apollo missions were those presented on television and in *Life* magazine, which had negotiated exclusive contracts with NASA to tell the personal stories of the heroic astronauts and their perfect families to the public. When as an adult I began to read about the hidden aspects of the story, it was like peering into the guts of our broken television set dismantled by the repairman, or walking behind the altar of the Greek

Orthodox church for the first time to see the unfinished wooden substructure that buttressed the magnificent paintings of the saints visible from the pews. These moments simultaneously marked the painful end of illusion and the thrilling beginning of rational inquiry.

My years of enchantment with space travel were nonetheless real. During the Mercury flights on school days, all normal operations were suspended, and we were allowed to watch television all day long in school! We learned that when the path of an orbiting spaceship is plotted on a Mercator projection of the world map, it makes a sine wave, and that the Earth was not a perfect sphere, but a "pear-shaped oblate spheroid." I remember trying to visualize the Earth in the shape of a pear, and the delicious feeling of saying "oblate spheroid" as well as other new word pairs like "mission control," "escape velocity," and "reentry sequence."

We learned that the forward movement of an orbiting spacecraft allowed it to respond continuously to the pull of gravity while maintaining altitude. A satellite in a high enough orbit to remain clear of the atmosphere would essentially fall toward Earth forever. This fact gave space flight an aura of magical departure from Earthly limitations. In a rocket one could rise up into space and never fall back again to Earth.

Each new space mission burned hot and fast in the imagination, leaving almost nothing in its wake except anticipation for the next one. Each new feat that had never been accomplished before was quickly forgotten.

Space was presented as the "new frontier." The old frontier had been the leading edge of an expanding civilization, full of life that flourished in its wake. A normal person could

ride in a covered wagon or sail in a boat to the old frontier. But to explore the new frontier required technology that only the astronauts could possess. We could only follow the new frontiersmen into space in our imaginations. In their wake only the debris of obsolete technology littering the lifeless void of space would remain. But as long as the frontier kept moving forward, our full attention was fixed upon what lay ahead. Thus we were propelled forward by each new mission: learning how to walk in space, rendezvous with other spacecraft, escape the gravitational pull of the Earth, and ultimately land and walk on the Moon.

By the time of the first Moon landing, our family had moved to a new house and had graduated from the old black-and-white television to a new color set. When the Apollo 11 mission was launched on July 16, 1969, my childhood fascination with rockets and physics was giving way to a grow-

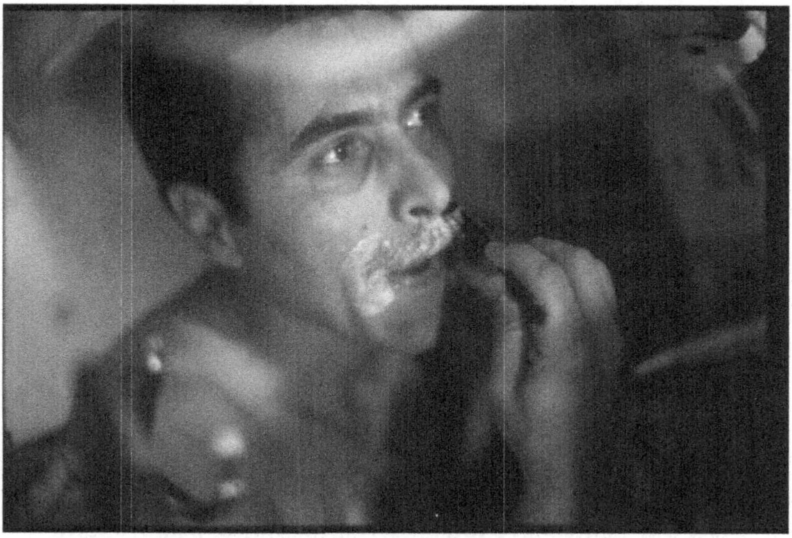

Apollo 17 astronaut Harrison Schmitt shaving after his last excursion on the Moon with Eugene Cernan. (NASA)

ing interest in the experiences of the astronauts themselves. What was it like to be in a tiny metal container as it swung around the backside of the Moon? How did it feel to finally settle on the lunar surface and hear the engines shut down? What kind of thrill was it to jump around in one sixth the gravity of Earth? How could a person possibly sleep after coming in from a walk on the Moon? None of these questions would be answered. The first men who walked on the Moon were test pilots, scientists and engineers. Some of them took decent pictures. None of them were poets.

There were a few notable attempts to enlist writers to provide the words that were not forthcoming from the astronauts themselves. On the day the Apollo 11 astronauts walked on the Moon, the *New York Times* ran a poem entitled "Voyage to the Moon" by Archibald MacLeish on its front page under the massively unpoetic headline "Men Walk on Moon." The poem was meant to express the meaning of the Moon walk as a fulfillment of an age-old dream of mankind in high ecclesiastical language. It did not reveal anything about what the experience actually felt like to the astronauts; it had been commissioned well ahead of time for the historic day's front page.

> From the first of time,
> before the first of time, before the
> first men tasted time, we thought of you.
> You were a wonder to us, unattainable,
> a longing past the reach of longing,
> a light beyond our light, our lives – perhaps
> a meaning to us ...
> Now our hands have touched you in your depth of night.
> ...

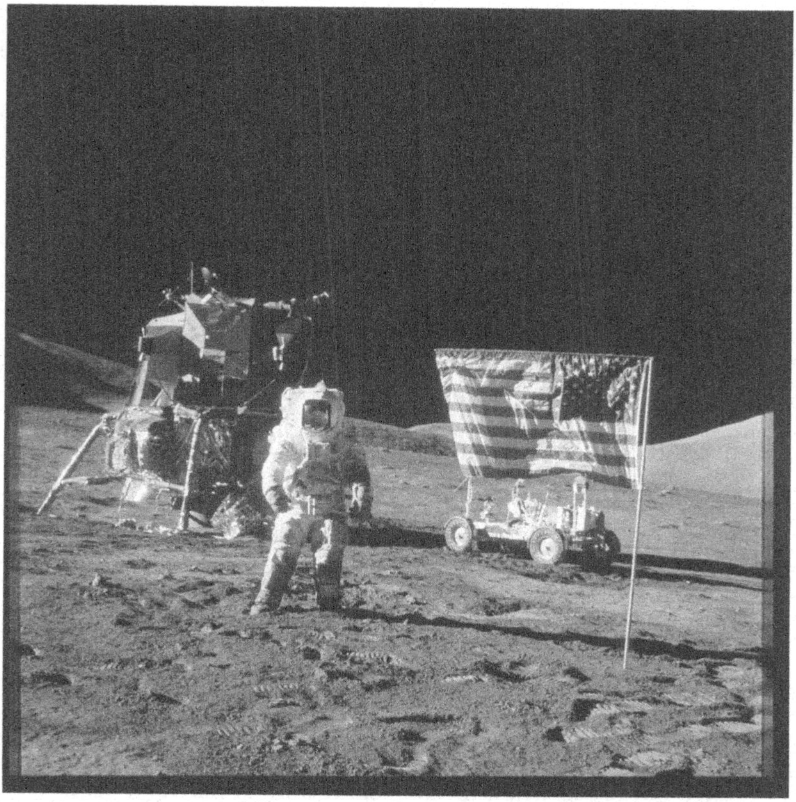

Apollo 17 astronaut Eugene Cernan poses with his Moon car and American flag on the front lawn of his Moon house. (NASA)

The Apollo program's last Moon landing took place during my first year of college in 1972, less than four years after the first Moon landing. Apollo 17 astronauts Eugene Cernan and Harrison Schmitt spent three days driving a dune buggy around a rugged area of the Moon called the Taurus–Littrow valley. The ghostly analog black-and-white television broadcast we had watched during the first Moon walk had been upgraded to clear, sharp, digitally-transmitted color.

During their final excursion on the last day of the last

Apollo mission, I went down to the main television lounge of my college dormitory and watched it out of a sense of obligation combined with nostalgia, to witness the end of something that had captivated my imagination since earliest memory. The brilliant scenes from the Moon played out on a large color television screen to an otherwise empty room. All the time I was watching, people came and went through the room without even gazing up at the screen.

Norman Mailer had written about the Apollo 11 mission in three long installments in *Life* magazine between August 1969 and January 1970. These became the basis for a book entitled *Of a Fire on the Moon*, published in 1970. In the book he described a similar scene that had unfolded at mission control during the first Moon walk.

> As the astronauts continued to walk, to hop, to flit and to skip from one vale of Moon ground to another, as the experiments were set out and the rocks picked up, so the temper of the audience shifted. It was a Twentieth Century audience when all was said, and quick in its sense of fashion. By an hour and a half of the Moon walk they were bored—some were actually slipping out. All over the room was felt the ubiquitous desire of journalists for the rescue of a drink. Boredom deepened. Now the mood was equal to the fourth quarter of a much anticipated football game whose result had proved lopsided. Now it looked as if rookies were out on the chill field running fumbles back and forth. More and more reporters departed. Even [I] left before the end. (Mailer, p. 129-30)

In the end, the space race was a race to a barren desert suspended in a black void. When the first Moon walkers returned to Earth, they were kept in strict medical quarantine

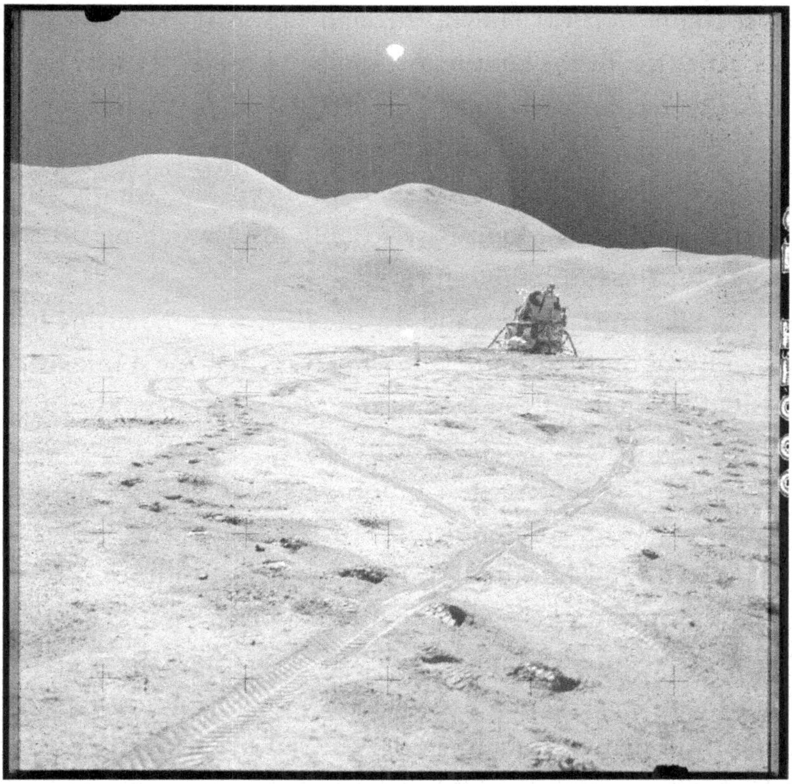

Apollo 15 lander in an area of the lunar Mare Imbrium called Palus Putredinus (Marsh of Decay), early August 1971. (NASA)

inside a sealed apartment in case some dangerous microbial life had ridden back with them from the lunar surface. Precautions had not been taken to prevent the astronauts from shedding bits of earthbound life onto the lunar surface to threaten its dead calm quiet. Even then we suspected that alien life could only spread potentially in one direction, from Moon to Earth, and not the other way.

Neil Armstrong carried with him a small piece of muslin cloth taken from the original Wright 1903 flyer during his walk on the Moon. Despite attempts to draw a line from the first flight at Kitty Hawk, through Lindbergh's crossing of the Atlantic, to the landing of Apollo 11 on the Moon, there actually was no such line. The first two flights had opened new frontiers for millions of people to follow, whereas the final Apollo astronauts blasted off from the Moon after abandoning their Moon base to oblivion, switching off the lights for the foreseeable future.

We began to understand, by the time the quarantine had been lifted on the Apollo 11 astronauts, that the outer space visited throughout the race to the Moon was devoid of life, unable to sustain our own form of life without first enveloping it in complex life-support technologies, engineered back on Earth. We understood that without continuing to spend tens and hundreds and thousands of billions of dollars, the spread of sustainable life to a place even as close as the Moon would be impossible. And we knew that participation in space exploration would remain for the foreseeable future an entirely imaginary adventure for all of us not chosen to be astronauts.

During the space race years, many young boys like me, wearing thick glasses and corrective shoes, who knew they would never fly to outer space, nevertheless searched for ways to connect themselves to the great adventure. They built replicas of spaceships and launched model rockets made of cardboard and balsa wood that would ascend hundreds of feet toward the general direction of space, and then parachute slowly down onto the treetops and rooftops of neighboring houses. They watched television programs like *Lost in Space* and *Star Trek* transform paper mâché and spandex into the settings and costumes of other worlds.

Of all the models I built during the years of the Moon

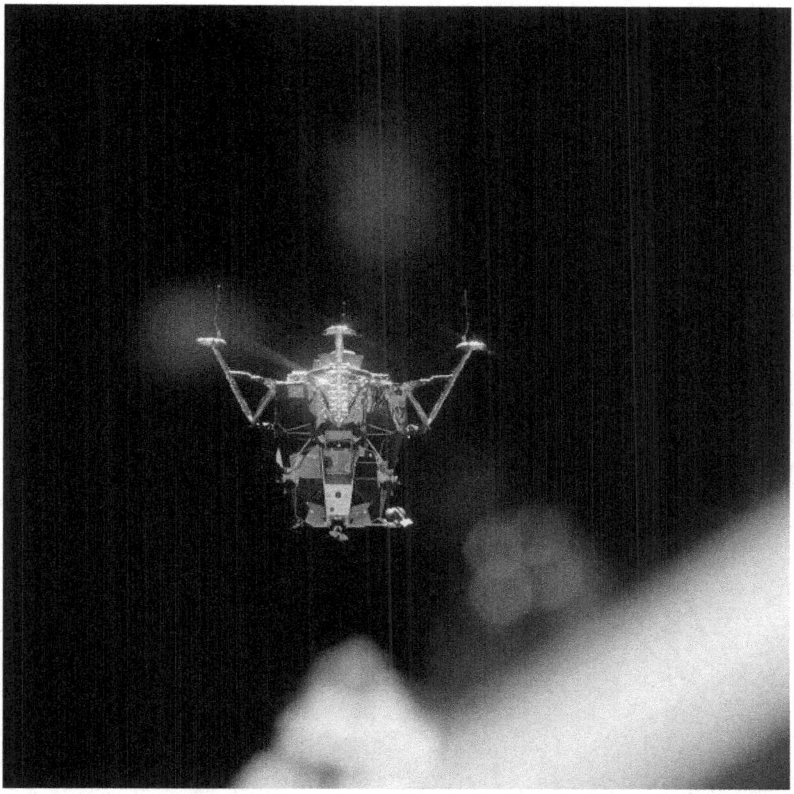

The Apollo 11 Lunar Module photographed by Michael Collins prior to its historic descent to the lunar surface in July 1969. (NASA)

race, one stood out as exceptional. It was the lunar landing machine used in the later Apollo missions, called the "Lunar Module," the only flying machine in our family pantheon designed to fly only in the vacuum of space, never to feel the rush of air flowing over its surface. The word "module" seemed to perfectly befit the bug-like machine that was folded up and stored in the streamlined thorax of the Saturn 5 rocket during its ascent into orbit. Once there, the sleek Command Module, which contained the astronauts as they blasted into space at the top of the giant rocket, would separate from the thorax, turn around, attach itself nose-first to the Lunar Module and pull it out of its protective sheathe. The two modules would then travel together to the Moon, attached head to head, like an awkward pair of fraternal Siamese twins. At one point on the trip, the spacecraft passed from the dominant gravitational pull of Earth and entered that of the Moon, enjoying a brief instant when it was compelled to fall neither toward one nor the other. When the twins reached lunar orbit, they would separate to pursue radically different, but fraternally-bound destinies.

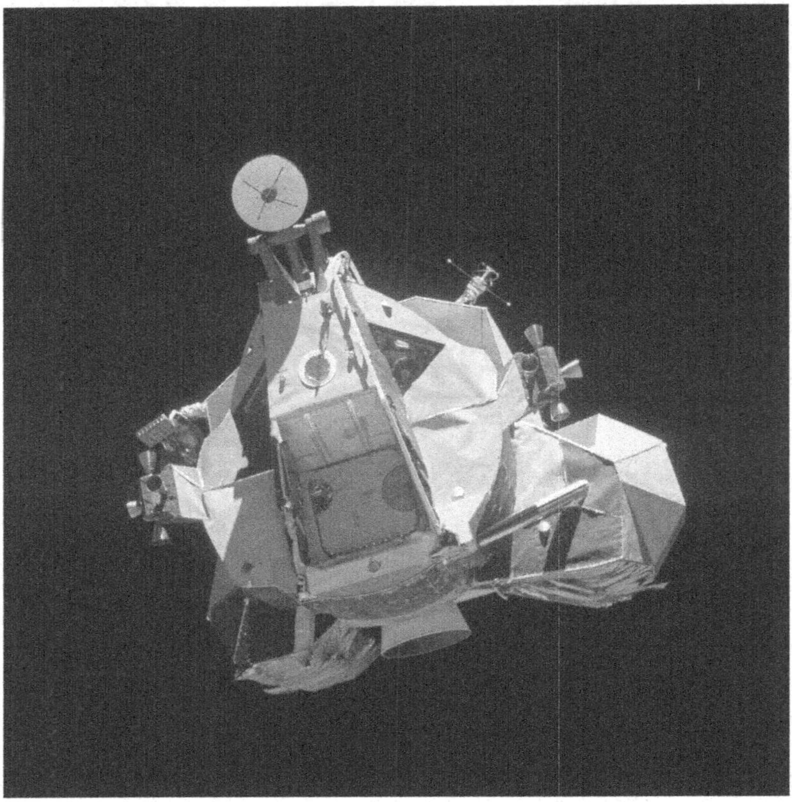

Apollo 17 ascent stage of the Lunar Module after returning to rendezvous with the Command Module, December 1972. (NASA)

The Lunar Module was the uglier twin, but the one that did the important job of transporting two of the three astronauts down to the lunar surface and then itself dividing into two parts, one to be left permanently on the Moon and the other to take the Moon walkers back to rejoin the Command Module, reuniting all three astronauts for the return ride back to Earth. The design of the Lunar Module was entirely determined by its function as a flying machine that would never touch air, and thus had no need for any kind of aerodynamic shape. None of the aesthetic considerations that had guided aircraft designers from the Wright brothers onward were relevant to its design, and nothing observed in the flight of creatures or machines through the atmosphere of Earth would apply to its flight down to the lunar surface and back up again. Its inner beauty lay entirely in its functionality as a machine without Earthly reference. Nothing bespoke as conclusively the impossibility of ever following the new frontiersmen into the cosmos as did the bizarre shape of the lunar landing machine.

Long after my fascination with the machines of the Apollo program had been abandoned, as though left behind on the lunar surface, my fascination with the men who went there remained strong. The politicians, corporate leaders, and NASA officials who had decided early on to make the space program a human adventure story had instinctively understood that unmanned space exploration would never inspire enough interest to convince citizens to spend the kind of money required to pursue it. Opposing voices, arguing rationally that unmanned space exploration would be far more cost-effective in advancing our knowledge of the cosmos, were overwhelmed by the soaring rhetoric of President Kennedy, and defeated by the public's willingness to believe in the romance of the New Frontier.

Only after the last three Apollo astronauts had returned home did we begin to learn about the physical realities of space travel. First there was the complex problem of sustaining human bodies when they are completely removed from their natural environment and sealed up in tiny airtight containers for more than a few hours. The first American astronaut, Alan Shepard, had waited for hours in the sealed capsule atop his ballistic missile through delay after

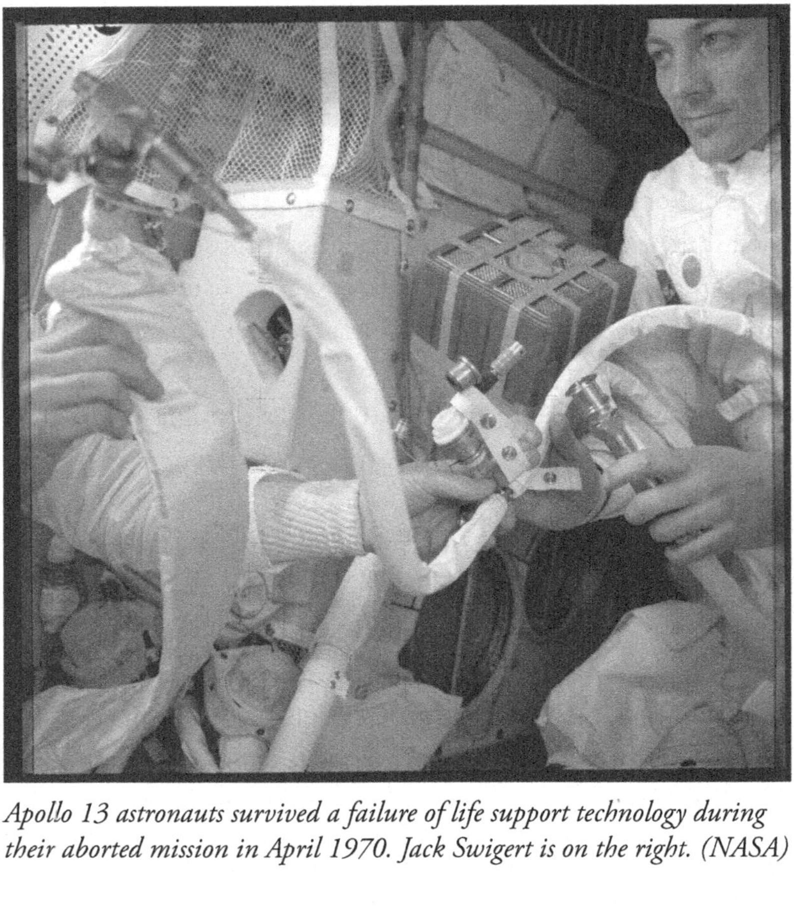

Apollo 13 astronauts survived a failure of life support technology during their aborted mission in April 1970. Jack Swigert is on the right. (NASA)

delay until he had no choice but to urinate in his spacesuit. Frank Borman and James Lovell orbited the Earth 206 times in 14 days in their sardine-packed two-man Gemini capsule, struggling with extreme cramped boredom and leaking waste materials. After the capsule splashed down in the ocean, one of the frogmen who opened the hatch to extract the astronauts threw up because the smell was so bad. On Apollo 8, the first mission to leave the Earth's gravitational field and orbit the Moon, Frank Borman became ill on the first day, filling the cabin with small floating globules of vomit and diarrhea. When we watched a television transmission of the Apollo 8 astronauts reading passages from the Book of Genesis on Christmas Eve 1968, we had no idea they were enduring such difficulties.

A few years after the first Moon landing flight of Apollo 11, Edwin Aldrin published a book entitled *Return to Earth* in which he described in great detail both the physiological hardships of the flight to the Moon and the difficulties of returning. He had to make the transition from a hard, technological, and purely Apollonian state of mind that had enabled him to be the second person to set foot on the Moon, to one that could cope with the demands of a wet, sloppy, and emotionally conflicted life back on Earth.

The raw physical realities of spaceflight, once revealed, inverted our pre-conceived ideas about the relationship between the earthly and heavenly spheres. As children we had looked up toward heaven and imagined ascending from the muck and mire of our grounded lives to the perfect, weightless cleanliness of space. As adults we came to understand the true value of a long hot shower back on Earth after living in a rapidly fouling orbital prison cell for days on end.

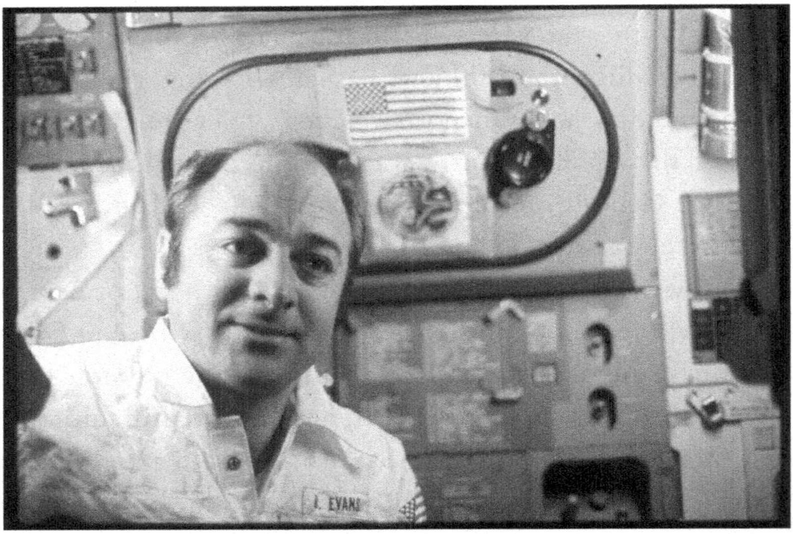

Apollo 17 astronaut Ronald Evans stayed behind in the Command Module while fellow anstronauts Gene Cernan and Harrison Schmitt walked on the lunar surface for the last time. (NASA)

10

The remaining Apollo flights after Apollo 13 played to dwindling television audiences and waning political support, while the Vietnam War continued to absorb American lives in its last throes. In the draft lottery for the year I was eligible to serve (1974), my birthday drew the high number of 304, making it almost certain that I would not be drafted. Like my grandfather and father before me, the timing of my birth placed me just beyond the reach of Ares, and I was privileged (and perhaps disadvantaged in some ways) to remain innocent of war.

The last years of the War, and the social unravelling that accompanied them, provided a dispiriting backdrop for my coming of age and that of my three younger siblings, and the cause of much disappointment for our parents. The entire sweep of human progress, from the first flights of the Wright Flyer through the landing on the Moon, was called into question. Had all of this progress led us only to the napalming of villages and mass slaughter in a pointless war on the other side of the world? What was to follow?

As the War was grinding down to its bitter end, my parents were emerging from the bunker of child-rearing to a changed world. The idea of building a replica of the Wright Flyer had been conceived in the past world, and now the gods who had commandeered my father's imagination during the Chanute glider years released him from their grip. Instead, they came to him in new guises and he decided he wanted to learn how to pilot a real airplane.

My father's father, like his Homeric namesake Odysseus, had set sail from his native land to cross the sea to a distant shore to find his adventure. However, unlike his namesake, our Odysseus found his home and hearth in the new place, and never returned to his place of origin. He never saw his parents again after the age of eighteen. The domestic life he constructed with my grandmother Dimitra—buying a house, raising three sons, and working as a waiter—must have felt like a great adventure.

The possibility of a life of seafaring adventure while remaining at the same time nestled in the comforts of home must have made an impression on my father. To live the life of a latter-day Odysseus, while simultaneously enjoying the benefits of domestic life, became his quest. He knew that one without the other would be problematic: the adventurer would long for home, and the domesticated man long for adventure. The soldier who patiently awaits the end of a tour of duty, only to re-enlist shortly after returning home, must know this dilemma well.

My father's quest was to figure out how to have it both ways. Fortunately, my mother, who shared her name with Helen of Troy, also possessed her own duality of desire. She was herself a restless person who wanted both domestic happiness and adventure. Her father, Charles, had left his childhood home in a city on the Sea of Marmara near Istanbul, called Kios by the Greeks and Gemlik by the Turks, around the same time as my father's father had left Bursa. Charles had been sent on a ship to America at the age of 15 by his parents, who wanted to save him from being drafted into the Turkish army. When his ship reached its first port of call on the Greek mainland, he disembarked and found another ship to take him back home. But he was again sent away, this time to make his way to Ellis Island and the kitchen of a Greek restaurant in Carthage, New York, near Watertown, to find work as a dishwasher.

My mother's mother, Eriketa, had come as an infant with her family from Tripolis, an inland city on the Peloponnesian peninsula near Sparta. She grew up in Bennington, Vermont, and was fluent in both Greek and American English, which she spoke with the Yankee refinement of a screen actress of the golden age of Hollywood. Among my other three grandparents, who spoke with heavy Greek/Turkish accents and chain-smoked unfiltered cigarettes, Eriketa was polished and modern. She married Charles when she was nineteen and they raised five children, three daughters and two sons. She insisted that her daughters go away to college, a decidedly modern idea among many of the members of the Greek American diaspora at the time.

My mother was the youngest of the three daughters and was granted the greatest amount of freedom. She attended Syracuse University, where she was more interested in the social life than in academics, and after failing to achieve the required grades to remain matriculated, was sent to a two-year finishing school in Connecticut called Larson College, now Quinnipiac University. After graduation she moved to Washington, D.C., where she worked at *Time* magazine for three years. This was her great adventure on the high seas. After her years in Washington, she transferred to New York to work for the *March of Time* television news program, before deciding to return home in order to find her way into marriage and family life. From her stories and photographs

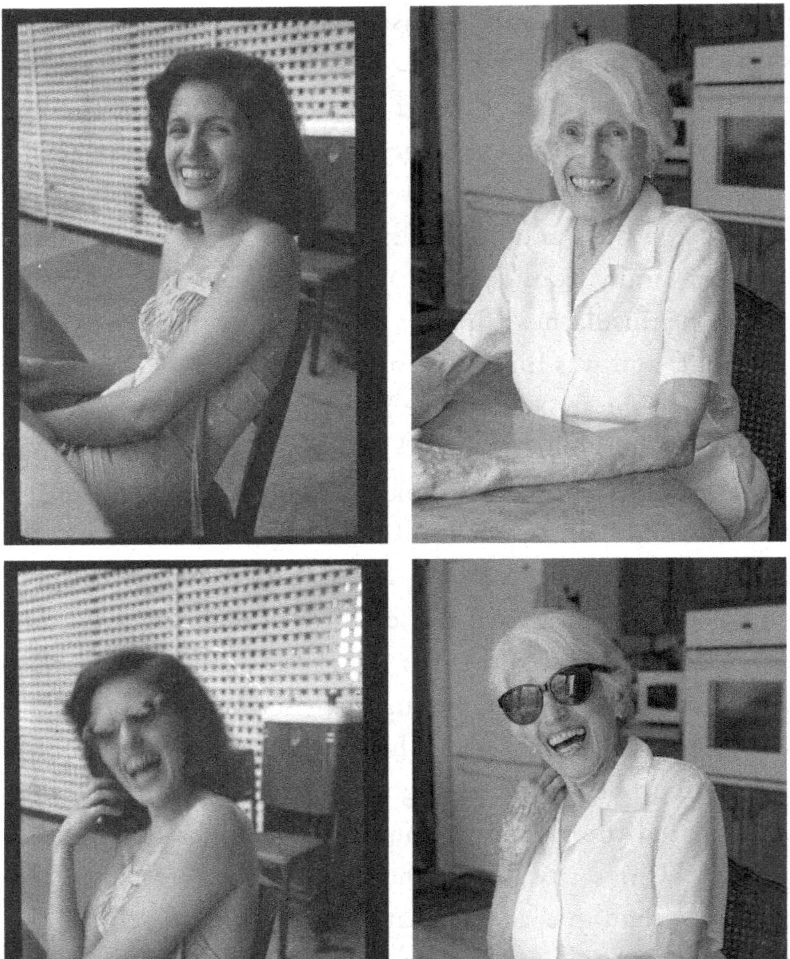

On the left, Elaine Cost circa 1950 during her years at Time *magazine in Washington, D.C. On the right, Elaine attempts to strike the same poses 66 years later. The original photographs were taken by a friend and Time/Life co-worker, John G. Zimmerman, who later became a famous sports and celebrity photographer. The photographic moment is fleeting, but the essence of the subject is indelible.*

of her time in Washington and New York, I have always equated my mother during this period of her life to a young Katherine Hepburn or Lauren Bacall. Although when they first met, my father could easily have played the part of Cary Grant or Humphrey Bogart, by the time our family life was in full swing, my siblings and I often associated our parents

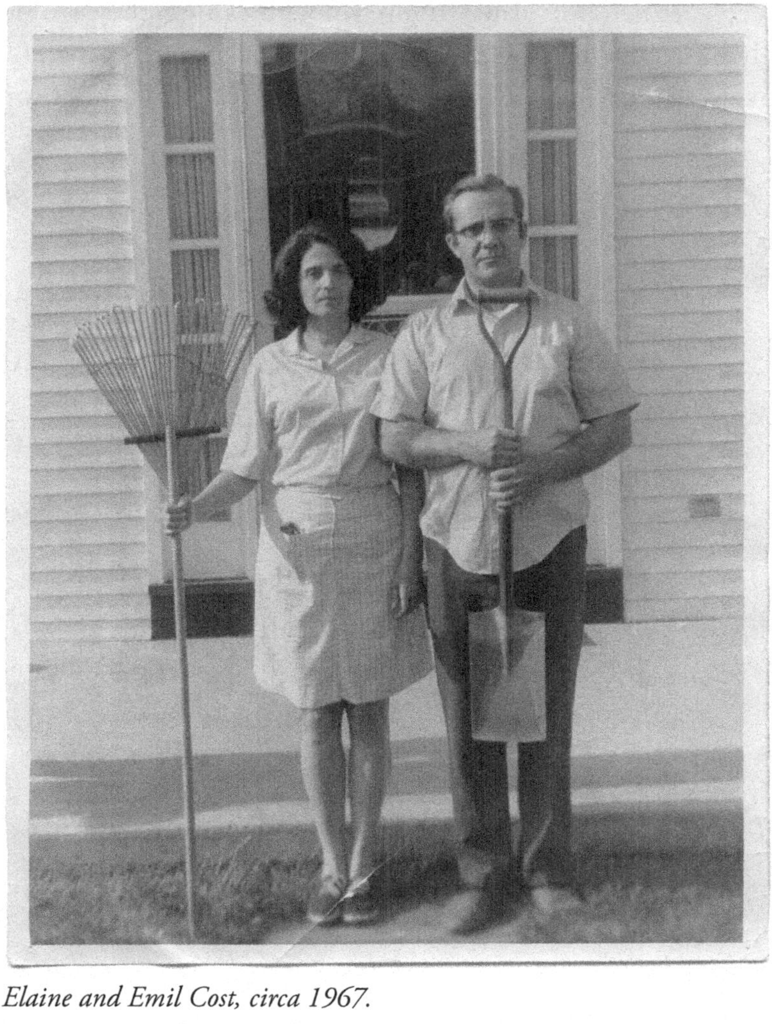

Elaine and Emil Cost, circa 1967.

with the comic characters of Alice and Ralph Kramden on *The HoneyMooners* television show.

When my father decided he wanted to learn how to fly, he instinctively knew that the best way to secure my mother's support would be to invite her to join him in the pursuit of her own pilot's license. So they took flying lessons together, and eventually both became licensed pilots. They were certified for visual flight rules, meaning they would rely on navigating by "dead (deduced) reckoning," progressing from one identifiable landmark to another. This form

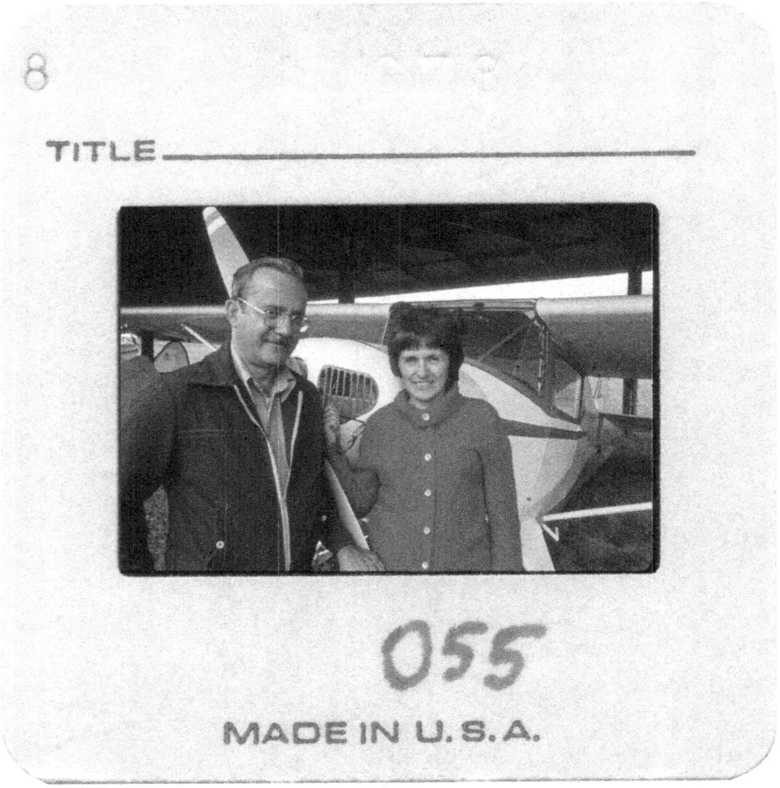

Emil and Elaine Cost with their two-passenger Taylorcraft monoplane, August 1978.

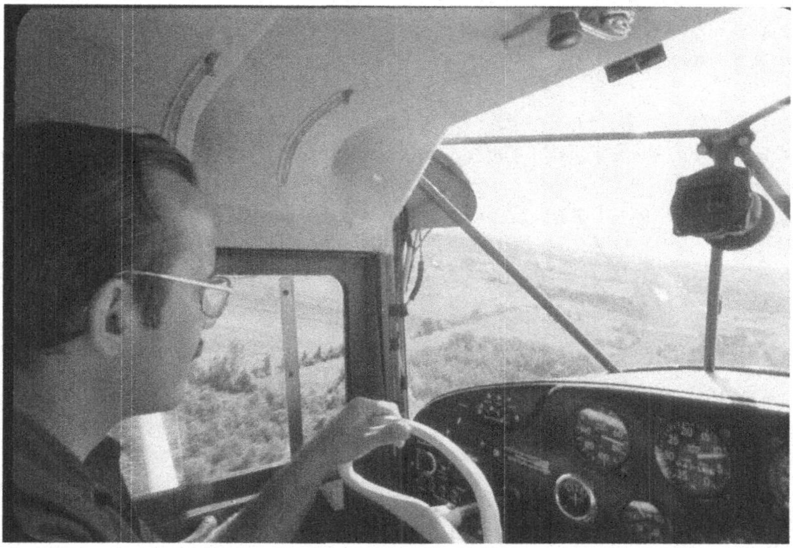

Emil Cost makes a final approach for landing the Taylorcraft at a small private airport near Syracuse in 1978.

of navigation requires that the pilot maintain sight of the ground and knowledge of his or her position on the map at all times. It is the same method Lindbergh used when he crossed the Atlantic in 1927.

They purchased an antique 1946 Taylorcraft airplane, similar to the classic Piper Cub but with seating for two people side by side rather than "tandem" seating (one person sitting behind the other). The Taylorcraft was covered with Irish linen and weighed less than a thousand pounds. It had an ancient 65 horsepower 4-cylinder engine, and could cruise up to about 100 miles per hour. If it had been an automobile, it would have been a Model T. They rented a hangar at a small airport close to our home, with a grass field for taking off and landing. There they found others who shared their passion for flying. For the next quarter century, until

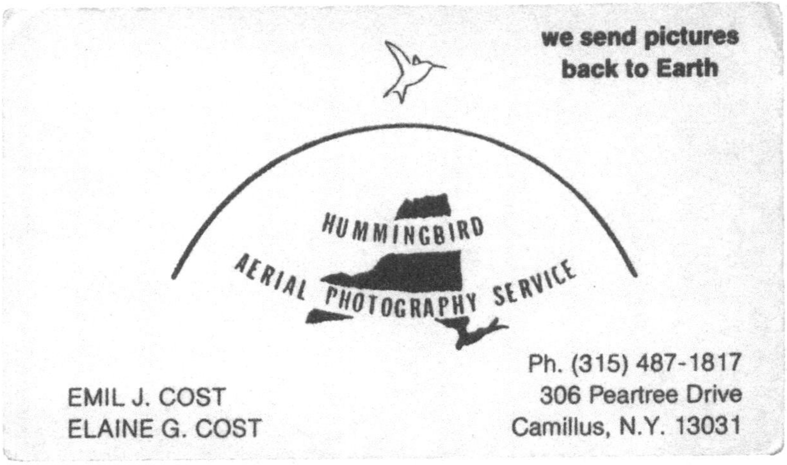

age and medical conditions prevented them from renewing their licenses, they flew together. Most of their flying was within a 100-mile radius of central New York, with a few longer trips to neighboring states. I had many opportunities to fly as a passenger with one or the other of them.

Once they gained confidence as experienced pilots, they decided to help defray the costs of airplane ownership by establishing an aerial photography business called "Hummingbird Aerial Photography." Over the next two decades they produced a collection of aerial images for private and commercial customers. My introduction to aerial photography was as a passenger/photographer in the right seat of the airplane. They developed a technique of using the ailerons and rudder to "slip" the airplane sideways once the photographic target was in sight, to give a clearer view out the side window for the camera. The act of taking pictures from an antique, cloth-covered airplane slipping sideways through the air brought a certain physical thrill that still lingers in my muscle memory. Because the fixed-wing airplane always had to be moving forward, and wind direction is always at least somewhat unpredictable, getting the camera to the perfect position for the desired composition was a great challenge.

None of their children became interested in obtaining pilot's licenses, but my interest in aviation as a source of aesthetic enjoyment remained strong. (It had been hard enough for us to learn how to drive a car with our temperamental parents as instructors, spoiling any appetite we might have had for flying lessons.) I was quite happy to ride as a passenger, except on the occasions when flying through an afternoon sky full of cumulus clouds was like driving fast down a road full of deep potholes that could not be avoided, with no opportunity to pull over and rest. During one long ride through such turbulent conditions from Saratoga to Syracuse, the last vestiges of desire I may have had to become a pilot were shaken vigorously out of me.

I once had a similarly choppy ride on a business flight in a small turboprop with a colleague named Tony who was deathly afraid of flying. Aware of his rising alarm in the seat next to me, I forced myself to remain completely relaxed and calm, reading my *Sky Mall* catalog and keeping a big smile pasted on my face, which I believe helped keep Tony from descending into a full screaming panic. Tony was clutching my shoulder by the end of the flight, and I realized that a lot of practice with that kind of flying as a passenger in my parents' airplane had helped prepare me for whatever unpleasant flying experiences lay ahead in my future.

Once one begins to participate in the world of private aviation, the dangers associated with the sport become more visible. Rarely do these dangers come from the failure of equipment. But occasionally an engine will stall, and a pilot will be forced to land in a cornfield. The worst kinds of engine stalls are on take-off, when the pilot does not have time to find a clear field for landing, and sometimes pilots and their passengers "buy the farm," a euphemistic way of saying, "get killed."

More often, accidents are caused by pilot error and the results can be embarrassing—a bent propeller or collapsed landing gear. Any incident within a certain radius of a private airfield, where a plane fails to perform in the way it was intended, becomes a story that spreads like wildfire in the flying community. The accidents I heard about during my parents' years of aviation involved male pilots, and while research shows that accident rates among male and female airline pilots are statistically equal, based on my small sampling of flying mishaps, I came to prefer flying with my mother. She was naturally more cautious and unwilling to take even small risks that were routine for my father. While risk-taking may be exciting for the person flying the plane, it is decidedly not so for the passenger.

My mother's first solo cross-country trip as a student pilot came on July 1, 1974, when she flew from a small airport west of Syracuse to Watertown, New York. On her return flight, she did not factor in the strong westerly winds correctly, and ended up drifting off course to the east of where she thought she should be. As soon as she knew she was lost, she radioed the control tower at the Watertown airport and told them she was a student pilot and didn't know where she was. The air traffic controller asked, "How much gas do you have left?" She answered, "Half a tank." The controller started laughing, and said, "That's good!

If you were a man, you would have waited until you were down to your last drop of gasoline before calling us." He located her on radar and directed her back to her correct route. After getting her pilot's license, she flew safely for more than twenty-five years without another incident.

One flying accident during those years involved my mother's cousin, Ted Limpert, an instrument-rated aviator with thousands of flying hours. We were shocked to receive the news that he had fatally crashed his private plane into the top of a mountain in the Catskill Mountains in a rainstorm on Monday, June 29, 1987. His two passengers, a friend and the friend's son, also lost their lives. The consensus within our family, and within the aviation community, was that Ted had taken too big a risk. (My mother and Ted had been very close because they were nearly the same age and their mothers were sisters. Ted had come to live with my mother's family for two years after his father, who suffered from manic depression, took his own life. Ted had become a successful lawyer and judge, and had remained close to our family. After his tragic death, his son Ted Jr. went on to become a decorated Air Force combat pilot, deployed many times overseas, starting with the first Gulf War in 1991.)

My father combined an almost cavalier willingness to take risks himself with zero tolerance for any of his children to do the same. Even as a child I thought this was because he projected onto us the potential for tragedy that had befallen his twin brother, and not himself. I reasoned that knowing his brother had drowned so close to shore caused him to worry about our taking the smallest risks. The thought of exposing my father to further tragedy stifled any attraction to physical risk that may have been inside me.

After he and my mother had been flying for several years, my father decided to build an ultralight airplane from plans he found in *Popular Mechanics* magazine. The airplane, called the "Woodhopper," was similar to the first generation of airplanes built during the decade after the Wright brothers' first flight. The only significant difference was that this airplane had no ailerons, hence no control over the roll

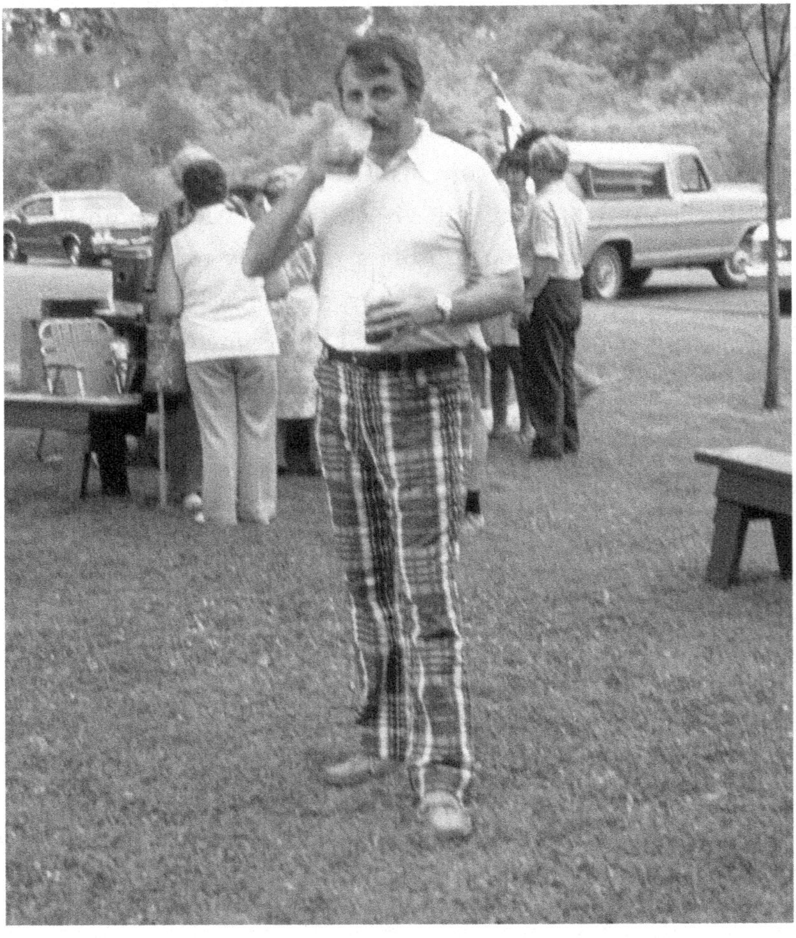

My mother's cousin, Ted Limpert, here dressed in a period costume of the 1970s, crashed into a mountain top in the Catskills on June 29, 1987.

axis. Even though he knew better than anyone that control of this axis was a critical aspect of the Wright design, in his enchanted mind, the Woodhopper was just a big version of a model airplane, and ailerons were not entirely necessary. He began to fly the Woodhopper in perfect windless conditions, and slowly gained enough confidence to take cross-country flights away from the airport. He would disappear over the horizon, then return twenty minutes later, much to our collective relief.

Eventually he tried to take off in a crosswind strong enough to compromise the stability of an airplane with no ailerons, and he crashed. Fortunately, he was able to walk away with minor injuries. This was one of two crashes in his aviation career; the other was a stall and crash in the Taylorcraft when he was trying to land on a grass field in Weedsport, New York. Again, he was able to walk away. However, this time the FAA came to investigate. My brother Jim once

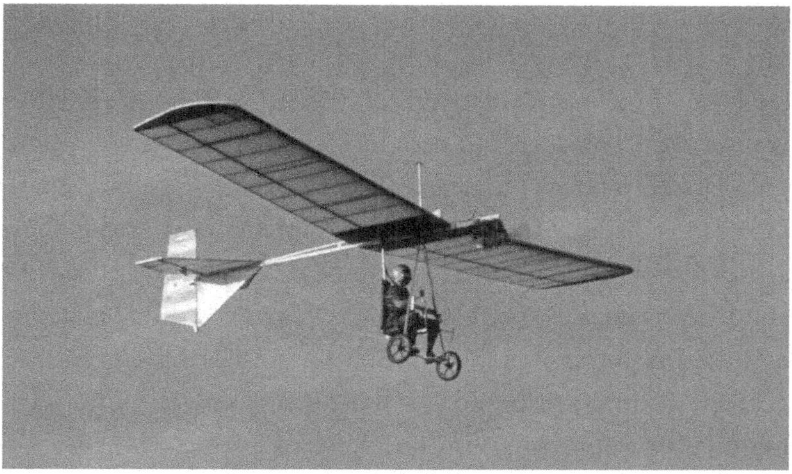

Emil Cost in his home-built Woodhopper, an airplane with no ailerons, thus no control over the critical roll axis.

remarked that our family was like the one in the Icarus story, except in our version, it was the father who was driven by the desire to fly too close to the Sun.

Those years were yet another port of call in my father's personal odyssey. Researching, building, testing, and flying the Woodhopper held my father in a state of enchantment as powerful as the original Odysseus had been held by the goddess Kalypso on her island paradise. It was only after the crash that my mother finally played the role of Penelope and called him back to the family hearth, which, fortunately for him, was still the cockpit of an airplane. Nonetheless, my father never stopped wanting to fly an ultralight, and well into his eighties, when my mother was out of earshot, he would disclose his secret plans to get back into the air.

The thrilling pursuit of the elusive is something my father understands well. It explains why he would remain committed for so long to primitive radio-control technologies that were prone to failure long after newer, more reliable technologies became available. It explains why almost every airplane model he designed was slightly underpowered, barely able to keep itself aloft. And it explains why he would even consider building and then flying an airplane that lacked ailerons. In each case, he designed elusiveness into his creations, inviting risk to come to him rather than aggressively going out and looking for it. He also knew that an unrestrained pursuit of raw adventure would suck up endless amounts of money, which he did not have. Thus he perfected the art of being a seafaring adventurer while staying close to home on a limited budget.

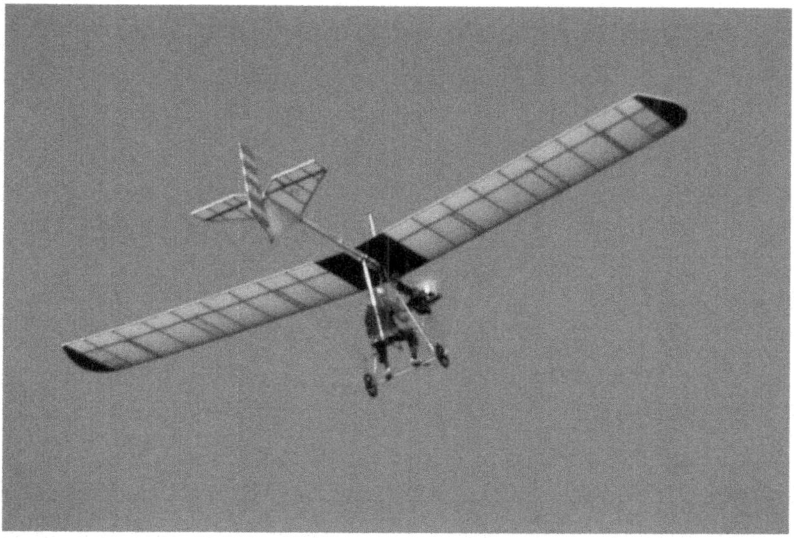

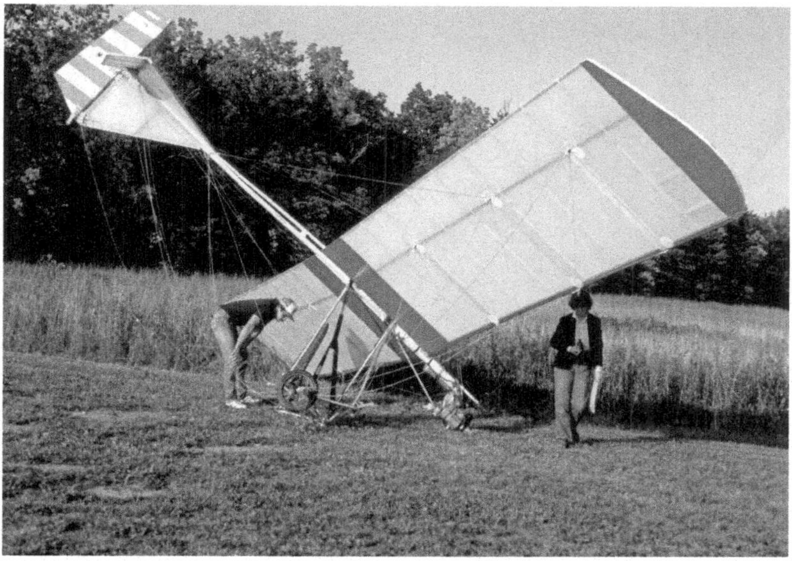

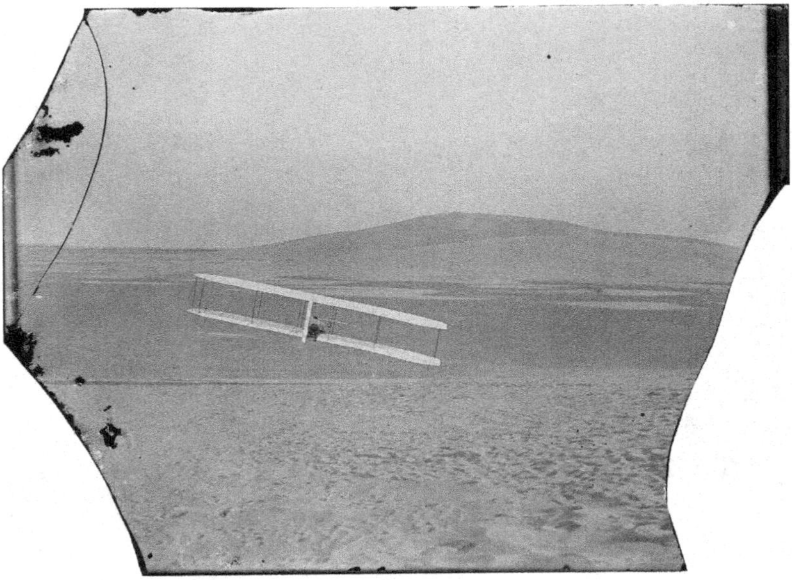

11

By the time the last Apollo astronauts had returned from the Moon my childhood aspirations to transform my body into the shape of a Spitfire or P-40 Warhawk had also ended. The domain of powered flight had become the too-familiar place where my parents made their home, from which I was compelled to flee. Throughout the years my parents spent as aviators, my interest in flight remained a vicarious aesthetic experience to be enjoyed with both feet on the ground. Remote-control technology had evolved to a point where one could control the flight of a model from the ground with all the nuance and reliability of its full-scale counterpart.

I found my new aerial inspiration in the soaring flight of the beautiful sailplanes that flew along the ridges of the Alleghany Mountains in places like Harris Hill, near Elmira, New York. I had always tried to imagine what it had been like for the Wright brothers on the dunes at Kitty Hawk when the silence of their initial years of gliding was broken by the terrible noise of their first crude internal combustion engine, and the elegant slipping of their glider down the slope of Kill Devil Hill was replaced by the chugging awkwardness of their complicated flying machine. We had always been taught that the gliders gave birth to the powered machines, and there the branch of aviation most relevant to our family lineage was established. Yet gliding had its own progeny, as my uncles and aunts had theirs, and my discovery of soaring was like meeting a long-lost cousin.

The challenge with unpowered sailplanes has always been how to get them into the air. One is to tow them like kites, and the other is to launch them from elevated ground such as a hilltop or a cliff. With manned sailplanes, the towing operation is sometimes accomplished with a cable attached to a powered airplane, or winch. But with models, a simpler towing method employing a long stretch of rubber surgical tubing attached to an even longer length of strong fishing line will silently launch a glider to an altitude of several hundred feet, where once released it can sail through the air searching for rising air currents called thermals.

Thermals begin to form during the morning hours when the Sun heats up the ground, which then radiates heat into the air just above the ground. This heated air expands and begins to rise. The rising air breaks away from the earth in

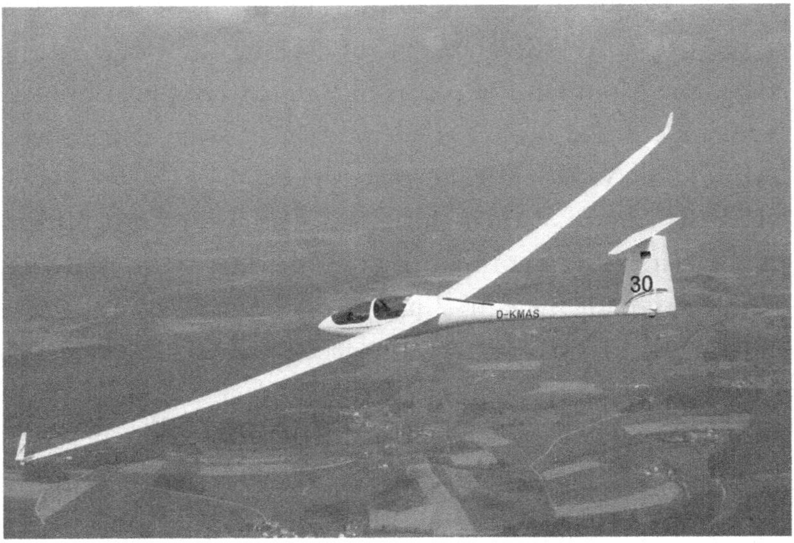

Schleicher ASH30 sailplane.

the form of an invisible bubble. If you fly either a manned or model sailplane into one of these rising bubbles of air, it will begin to ascend relative to the ground.

Sailplanes are designed to fly extremely efficiently, losing very little altitude as they move forward in the air. The most efficient modern manned sailplanes will only lose one measure of altitude for every 60 measures they move forward in calm air. This performance characteristic is expressed as a glide ratio of 60 to 1. This means that a modern sailplane starting its glide one mile above the ground will travel 60 miles before landing. A typical airliner has a glide ratio closer to 10 to 1, meaning that from an altitude of one mile, a gliding airliner would travel about 10 miles before reaching the ground.

Modern hang gliders, descendants of the primitive wood and cloth models of Chanute and Lilienthal, take many forms, and are usually lightweight enough to be "worn" almost in the same way Daedalus and Icarus wore their feathers. A typical hang glider has a glide ratio of about 15 to 1, so it will not glide as far as a sailplane from the same altitude. But because they fly much slower than sailplanes, their rate of descent over time in calm air is about the same, and they can find sustained lift in more confined volumes of rising air.

Each type of aircraft, depending on its size and weight, the size and shape of the wings, and the overall efficiency of the design, also has a minimum flying speed before there is not enough air moving over the wings to keep it aloft. Once this happens, the aircraft will stall: abruptly stop flying and start to fall. Pilots must learn certain things about any airplane they intend to fly, whether powered or glider. These include its stall characteristics and how best to recover flying speed after a stall. Many airplane crashes are the result of stalls from which the pilot cannot recover before hitting the ground, so periodically practicing stall recovery is an important exercise.

My father perfected his own stall recovery practice as a form of recreation. In the middle of an otherwise routine flight, he would say, "Let me demonstrate a stall." He would slow the engine and pull back on the controls to pitch the nose of the airplane higher and higher, until finally it would stop flying and the nose would drop suddenly. He would then push the controls forward and accelerate the engine to recover enough airspeed to resume flying. The moment just before the stall seemed to place him in an ecstatic trance while only giving me a feeling of rising nervous anticipation. The resumption of normal flight brought satisfaction to him and relief to me.

As large thermals rise up into the atmosphere, moisture in the warm air eventually begins to condense into fine water droplets. The cumulus clouds (that cause the bumpy air which can make flying in a powered airplane so unpleasant) are actually "crowns" atop giant masses of rising warm air. Sailplane pilots learn how to visualize these rising columns of air beneath cumulus clouds and navigate through them to gain altitude. The warmer and wetter the rising air, and the greater the temperature differential at higher altitudes, the more powerful the thermal. This is how thunderheads or cumulonimbus clouds form.

In some cases, rising air can ascend so rapidly that a sailplane or hang glider will be unable to escape being drawn up into a thunderhead. This phenomenon is called "cloud suck." The challenge for sailplane pilots is to fly into air that is rising fast enough to keep them aloft, but not so fast that they end up in the middle of a thunderhead. The consequences of failing to do so can be frightening and sometimes fatal. As a sailplane is drawn up into a cloud, visibility of the ground disappears in a white-out, the temperature drops, and the air gets thinner. Pilots can black out from lack of oxygen or suffer from hypothermia. All modern sailplanes are equipped with devices called "spoilers" that can be deployed to break the flow of air over the wing surfaces and kill the lift, allowing the sailplane to escape most situations where the lift becomes too strong. Cloud suck can be especially dangerous for hang glider pilots, who have less protection from the elements. Pilots have been sucked up into storm clouds where they have lost consciousness and frozen to death or gotten struck by lightning before being disgorged and deposited in a tangled heap far from where they entered the clouds. It is far more likely that Icarus was sucked up into a cloud and frozen to death than that the Sun melted the wax on his wings.

While the experience of getting swept up by a strong thermal is not physically dangerous for a person flying a model glider remotely from the ground, it can nevertheless be dramatic and alarming. A glider with a ten-foot wingspan can quickly disappear out of sight, and even a small hand-launched glider can be swept up into a thermal and be lost to the heavens. Before the advent of radio-controlled flight, free-flying models were often equipped with "de-thermalizers" that would pop up a horizontal stabilizer after a calculated amount of time had passed, to stun the glider out of a thermal and send it fluttering back to earth. On a warm

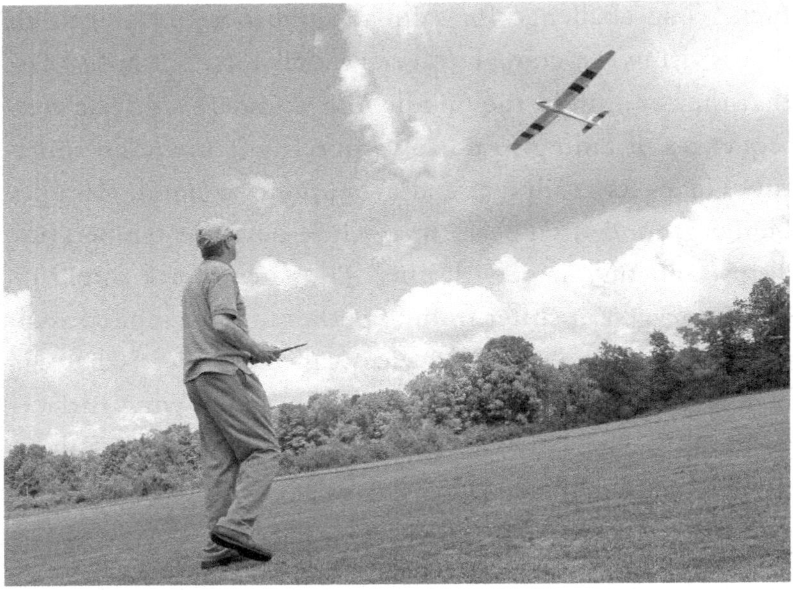

My father took this photograph of me flying a model sailplane searching for thermals on a warm summer day.

summer afternoon when large cumulus clouds are forming in the sky, it is often the case that what goes up, continues to go up.

As one gains experience flying model sailplanes in thermals, the air becomes a visible ocean of moving currents. Living in the ocean are other creatures that now become colleagues or potential adversaries. If you find some rising air and start circling in it, often a hawk or turkey vulture will see you from far off and fly over to share the same thermal. Others may join. Some soaring raptors like vultures do not mind sharing, but more solitary predators may try to do battle. If a red-tailed hawk attacks your glider, you will probably lose the contest, so it is best to run away from such a confrontation.

A model glider looks like a large predatory raptor to smaller nesting birds. When flying low and slow over the countryside, you will sometimes be greeted by angry birds flying up from their nests to attack, like German Messerschmitt fighter planes attacking an American B-17 bomber during the Second World War. The feeling of having an aggressive songbird pecking at my tail feathers is an experience I share with crows and hawks, whom I have come to regard as respected colleagues. I've never lost a model sailplane to such an attack, but neither have I ever seen a crow downed by a perturbed red-winged blackbird. The experience of flying a large model glider chased and harassed by a small bird is akin to that of taunting a cat with a laser pointer, but the pleasure is more elusive.

The West coast of California meets the Pacific Ocean abruptly in many places, mountains and cliffs rising high above narrow beaches and the great outstretched ocean beyond. Prevailing winds from the west flow across the vast flatness of the water until they encounter the rising coastline, moving up and over the land as they continue inland. All along the cliffs are zones of constantly rising air whenever the winds are blowing from the West. If you launch a glider out toward the ocean and fly parallel to the edge of the cliff, the glider will stay aloft for as long as the wind blows. Unlike a thermal, which drifts and rises in the direction of the wind, the wave of rising air along the coastline is stationary.

There are places along the California coast where the rising air is so strong and consistent that people are willing to step nonchalantly off the edge of the cliff in a hang glider, knowing they can stay aloft for as long as they desire. For an Easterner visiting a place like Torrey Pines State Natural Reserve near San Diego, the abundance of lift seems almost decadent, like many aspects of life in coastal California. If the Wright Brothers had tested their gliders at Torrey Pines instead of Kitty Hawk, they may have scrapped the idea of powered flight. Why bother putting a motor on something that will stay in the air all day long without one?

Flying a glider in rising air along the edge of a cliff is called "slope soaring." Back East it's a lot harder to accomplish than at Torrey Pines. But there are a few places along the shores of the Great Lakes where the prevailing winds blow against cliffs and create similar conditions on a smaller scale. One is in Sterling, New York, along the southern edge of Lake Ontario. Another is west of Cleveland on the edge of Lake Erie. The main weakness of these sites is that they are situated on the "North Coast," and so the ideal wind direction for slope soaring is from the north. The wind doesn't cooperate often, and when it finally does, it often comes as a frigid blast from Canada rather than a warm breeze from the South Pacific.

Once you move inland, the challenge of finding good sites for slope soaring is greater. When the ice sheet began to recede around 10,000 years ago from the Northeastern part of our continent, it left behind a terrain of elongated hills called drumlins running primarily in the direction of the receding ice, south to north. Prevailing westerly winds blowing across surrounding expanses of flat land will sometimes move up and over a drumlin to form a standing wave of rising air similar to the rising air at the cliffs of Torrey Pines, but on a much smaller scale. When the wind is

blowing at the perfect velocity in the perfect direction, it is possible to slope soar from the top of one of these drumlins.

The search for suitable drumlins for slope soaring was a quest that absorbed much of my leisure time during the 1980s. My brother Jim and I discovered a few sites that provided a setting for several memorable experiences. One hill in the town of Farmington, east of Rochester, would produce small zones of rising air if the wind was blowing from the northwest. The whimsical nature of the winds in Western New York often meant that the long drive and then hike up to the top of the hill would be met with the disappointment of sinking, rather than rising, air. But on some occasions, the wind would be right, and our gliders would rise up into the sky along with our elated spirits. My children

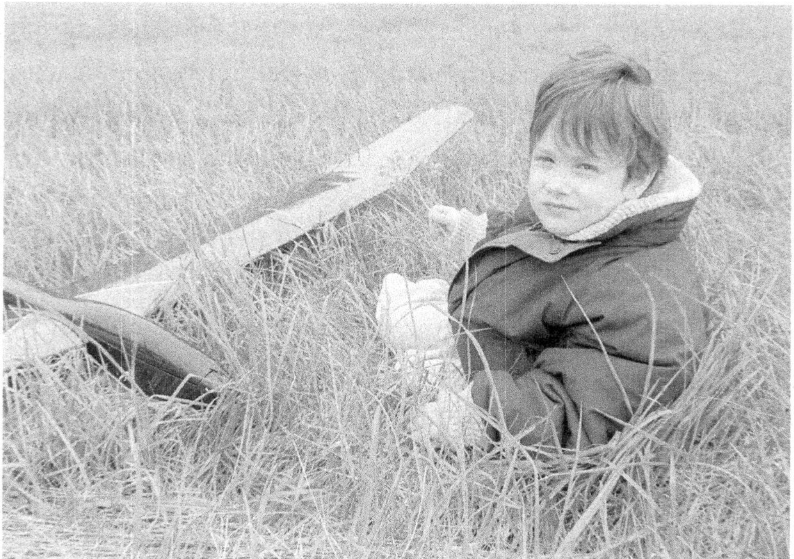

My son Roger sits with one of our sailplanes in the grass on top of the hill in Farmington. A handful of grass thrown into the air would indicate the direction of the wind.

each have their own memories of the hill in Farmington, as we did of our childhood flying field on the Onondaga reservation.

During my first years teaching at the Rochester Institute of Technology (RIT), I was fortunate to have a senior colleague who shared a passion for slope soaring. He was Bekir Arpag, a Turkish immigrant who had been born near Istanbul and grown up in Vienna, the son of the Turkish ambassador to Austria. Bekir was fluent in six languages, with a sweetness of disposition and gentleness of soul that was captivating. When he talked about soaring, he nearly sang the words with a rapturous cadence that I can still hear today. Bekir told stories about building model airplanes as a young boy and flying them down the long corridors and in meeting rooms inside the embassy. He remembered seeing Hitler at various parties and embassy events.

Bekir knew of a hill in a town south of Rochester that was ideal for slope soaring, and we drove there together with our gliders on a few occasions. He had built a huge white fiberglass scale model of a full-sized sailplane with a wingspan of ten feet. The first time we took it to the hill the wind was coming from the west but the lift it generated was not enough to keep the glider aloft. On another evening there was a rare easterly wind and we were both able to fly along the eastern edge of the hill for a brief time against the backdrop of a dramatic sky, painted brilliant by the setting Sun. This would be the only time Bekir and I would successfully fly together, but for many years afterwards whenever I saw him, he would rhapsodize about the experience, like Homer retelling a favorite story we both knew by heart. What Bekir and I both realized was that our families had come from the same place in Asia Minor, had been at war, had followed radically different paths to America, and had ultimately come back together through our friendship and our common love of soaring flight.

The elusiveness of the experience of trying to find rising air on the side of a hill in our part of the country is unknown to the overindulged Californian standing 300 feet above the Pacific Ocean on a cliff from which it is almost impossible not to fly. As with all pleasurable things, scarcity amplifies the pleasure, and abundance eventually anesthetizes. Bekir and I often talked about wanting to go to Torrey Pines one day with our gliders, but neither of us ever did. If we had met as faculty members at the University of California at San Diego, and not at RIT, we could have enjoyed much greater success at flying our gliders together, but perhaps neither of us would have retained an interest in such a sure thing for long, and the memories we shared about our one moment of triumph together would not have been possible.

A recurring contemporary graffiti attempts to put a frame around the device that presumes to frame all of reality, thereby liberating the artist and viewer from the device's undue influence upon the imagination.

12

The oldest cave paintings have been estimated to date as far back as 40,000 years. Their incredible anatomical sophistication and graceful beauty give evidence of a long-established craft.

What were the cave painters trying to do? Many theories have been put forth since their discovery: Maybe the caves were places of religious worship and the paintings were meant to call upon supernatural forces for help in the hunt. Maybe the paintings are externalized expressions of desire. Or perhaps the painters were working out their fears through art therapy.

These paintings are the first evidence we have of the constant human impulse to step away from our current reality to better understand our predicament. As we step away, we place a frame around reality to better see it. The process is recursive—once we put a frame around one level of reality, we're tempted to put another frame around the frame. The evolution of language has allowed us to step away from ourselves in the realm of thought; the evolution of visual art allows us to step away from ourselves in the realm of physical existence.

Our visual ascent into the sky has been gradual. William L. Fox, in his 2009 book *Aereality*, claims that the earliest known aerial painting was made more than 8,000 years ago in a Neolithic agricultural and trading town called Çatalhöyük, in Anatolia (present-day Turkey). The painting depicts the settlement from directly above, as in a map, but extends to the horizon where the profile of a then-active but now extinct volcano 60 miles distant can be seen. Fox asks,

> How did someone make this image, which accurately represents the scale and relationship of houses to one another, two thousand years before the invention of writing and four thousand years before the invention of any known alphabet? How did they assume an aerial view, as if they were standing above a roughly gridded street map? There were no hills nearby Çatalhöyük, and although the residents apparently climbed up the volcano to obtain obsidian, the town was effectively invisible from that distance. Perhaps standing on the roofs, on the mound [of the settlement] itself, helped inculcate an aerial view of the town—but it wouldn't have been a vertical view like this. And why make this composite image in plan and profile? (Fox, p. 6)

Fox explores the evolution of aerial image-making, from earliest history onward, from the perspective of an art critic. He is concerned about the relationship between visual art and language, attempting to develop a philosophical synthesis, and I recommend the book to anyone who is interested in philosophy. Personally, I'm content to keep the visual aspects of aerial seeing separate from spoken and written language, and concentrate on aerial seeing as an experiential pursuit, not a philosophical one.

Other early maps dating back almost 4,000 years have been found in ancient Babylon, suggesting that the techniques of deriving an aerial perspective from the results of land surveying have been practiced for thousands of years. The uses of maps in the ancient world are not difficult to imagine. Just as today, they must have helped people plan for construction and navigation. Some maps were drawn proportional to the actual dimensions of the land, and others, especially those used for navigation, distorted the actual geometry of the land for purposes of graphic efficiency. A modern-day equivalent of such a distorted map is the famous Vignelli subway map of New York, which sacrifices the actual proportions of the subway system to create a graphically efficient and compact representation for navi-

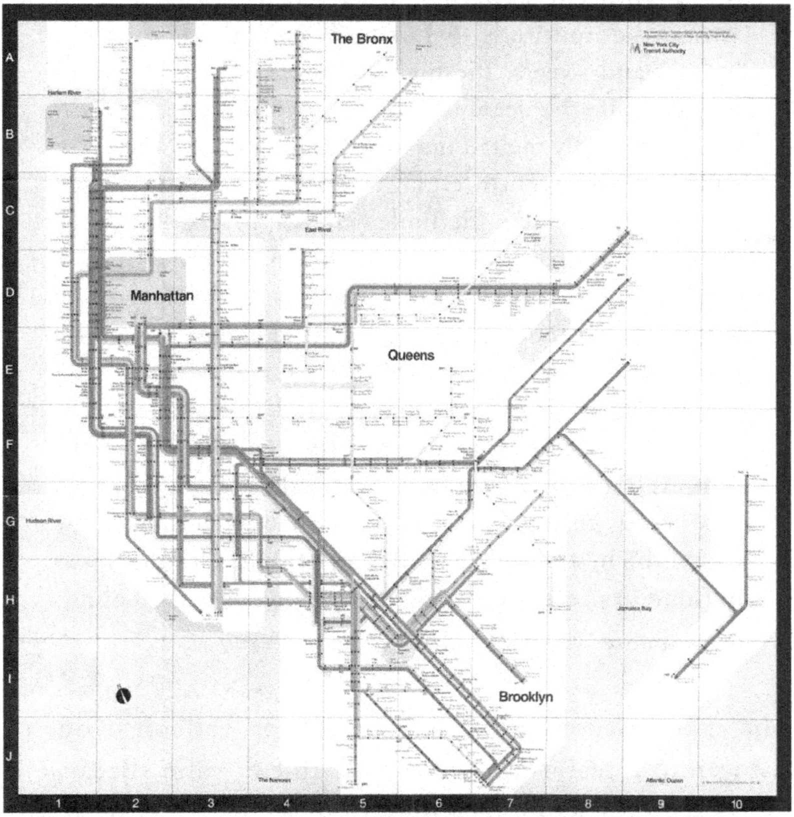

The Vignelli map of the New York City subway system dispenses with spatial accuracy to achieve navigational clarity.

gating one's way through the underground labyrinth.

When humans began to ascend in hot air balloons in the late eighteenth century, they were for the first time able to see with their own eyes what others had only been imagining for thousands of years before. One of the earliest descriptions of what a landscape looked like from above was written by Prince Pückler-Muskau after ascending in a balloon over the city of Berlin in 1817.

> No imagination can paint anything more beautiful than the magnificent scene now disclosed to our enraptured senses: the multitude of human beings, the houses, the squares and streets, the highest towers gradually diminishing, while the deafening tumult became a gentle murmur, and finally melted into a deathlike silence. The earth which we had recently left lay extended in miniature relief beneath us, the majestic linden trees appeared like green furrows, the river Spree a silver thread, and the gigantic poplars of the Potsdam Alee, which is several leagues in length, threw their shadow over the immense plain. We had probably ascended by this time some thousand feet, and lay softly floating in the air. ... I never before witnessed anything comparable to this scene even from the summit of the highest mountains; besides, from them the continuing chain is generally a great obstruction to the view, which, after all, is only partial; but here there was nothing to prevent the eye from ranging over the boundless expanse. (Newhall, p. 11)

The experience of riding in a free-flying balloon is one of rising into a realm of quieter and quieter calm. Because it moves with the wind, regardless of its velocity relative to the ground, it always seems to be sitting in calm air. Our modern hot air balloons come equipped with their own large propane burners, which rudely interrupt the silence when fired up occasionally to keep the air heated inside the balloon. But earlier hot air and hydrogen balloons never broke the silence.

During the same historical period, while some men were creating new balloon technologies for ascending into the air, others were obsessing about the possibility of permanently capturing and fixing camera images on surfaces using chemistry. The race to create the first photograph was won by a Frenchman named Joseph Niépce, but his process never became a practical commercial reality because it required hours of exposure in bright sunlight to form an image.

Not long after, faster photographic processes requiring only several minutes for an exposure were invented almost simultaneously by Daguerre in France and Fox-Talbot in England. These were ideal for making photographs of subjects that did not move, but they were almost immediately put to use to make portraits of uncomfortable people who had to have their bodies and heads clamped to ensure that they would remain motionless during long minutes facing the camera. Even blinking was discouraged. Not until the 1850s, with the invention of the wet plate collodion process, requiring only seconds for an exposure, did photography begin to look possible from a camera lofted by a balloon.

The first person to successfully make a photograph from a balloon in 1858 was an eccentric French inventor named Gaspard Félix Tournachon, who called himself Nadar. Nadar became the Annie Leibovitz of his era, known throughout Europe for his celebrity photographs. He was prepared to take action when, finally, balloon technology and the collodion photographic process were ready to be assembled into a new system.

After flying in a balloon for the first time, Nadar described the thrilling experience of stepping away from his normal reality and gaining a new, higher perspective.

> Free, calm, levitating into the silent immensity of welcoming and beneficent space, where no human power, no force of evil, can reach him, man seems to himself really living for the first time, enjoying, in a plenitude until then unknown to him, the wholeness of his health in his soul and body. Finally he breathes, free from all the ties with this humanity which ends up disappearing in front of his eyes, so small even in its greatest achievements—the works of giants, the labors of ants—, and in the struggles and the murderous strife of its stupid antagonism. Like the lapse of times past, the altitude that takes him away reduces all things to their relative proportions, to Truth. In this superhuman serenity, the spasm of ineffable transport liberates the soul from matter, which forgets itself, as if it no longer existed, vaporizes itself into the purest essence. Everything is far away: cares, remorse, disgust. How easily indifference, contempt, forgetfulness drop away from on high—and forgiveness descends … (Nadar pp. 57–58)

It makes perfect sense that an artist whose tool was a camera would want to try to frame and capture this new view of reality. Nadar was also a businessman, constantly searching for commercial opportunities that could be protected by patents. He saw an immediate opportunity to revolutionize the practices of land surveying with the use of a balloon and a camera.

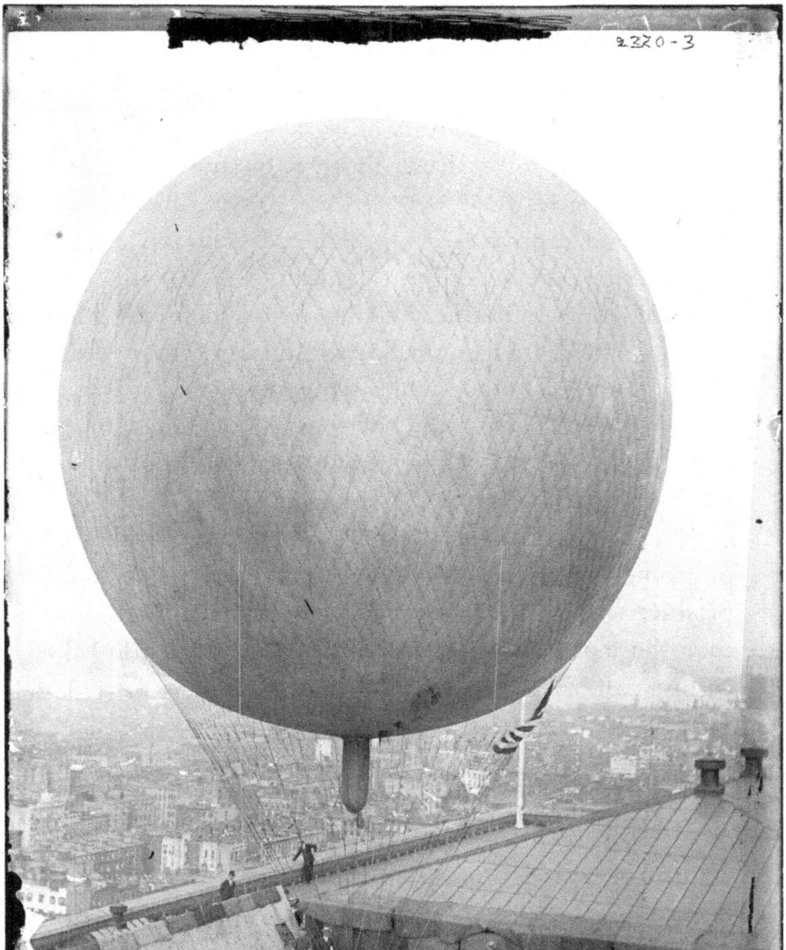

A hydrogen balloon launched from the top of Wanamaker's Department Store in Manhattan in the early 1900s. (LOC)

"This gigantic work of registering the land," I said to myself, "with its army of engineers, surveyors, chainmen, draftsmen, accountants, had required more than a billion and more than half a century of work—to be done poorly.

"This year, today, I can finish it by myself in thirty days—and perfectly.

"A good captive aerostat [tethered balloon], a good camera, these are my only weapons.

"No more preliminary triangulation, painfully built up on a stack of trigonometric formulas; no more dubious instruments, plane tables, compasses, alidades, graphometers; no more chains of convicts to drag through the valleys, hills, plowed fields, vineyards, swamps: we do not have to bother people at home anymore.

"... Miracle! I who all my life have professed a hatred of geometry that is equal only to my horror of algebra, I produce with the rapidity of thought plans more faithful than those of Cassini, more perfect than the maps of the Ministry of War! ..." (Nadar, p. 60)

Driven by his enchantment with the aerial perspective and the possibility of great fortune, Nadar set his goal of making a photograph from a balloon. The story of his many expensive and failed attempts to produce the first collodion image from a balloon is entertaining to read in full. In short, Nadar was foiled many times by the fact that hydrogen sulfide gas escaping from the vent of the balloon as it ascended reacted adversely with his photographic chemistry.

Now, during each of my ascents, this valve, gushing, would spew out sulfured hydrogen in torrents onto my developing baths: silver iodide with hydrogen sulfur, a wicked couple irrevocably condemned to never produce

> children. By not having imposed here an immediate divorce, and from the very first encounter, I undoubtedly had deserved to pay even more dearly for my lack of observation and deduction. (Nadar, 68)

With great focus comes great peripheral blindness. The irony in this particular case is that while Nadar was striving to create the first framed picture of the world from the highest perspective then imaginable, he was not paying attention to something happening much closer at hand.

Most of Nadar's predictions about the value of aerial photography to replace land surveying would eventually be fulfilled. Today we live in a world where Google cars are navigating down every drivable road on the planet creating street views, and Google backpackers are hiking walkable trails to do the same for the wilderness. (One of the great losses I have lamented on behalf of my current and future students is the experience of getting lost, something that has been rendered almost impossible by the advance of modern mapmaking.)

Nadar predicted another use for aerial photography:

> From a strategic point of view, we are aware of what good fortune it is for a general in a war campaign to encounter the bell tower of a village from where a Master Sergeant can make his observations.
>
> I was carrying my bell tower with me and my lens was able, successively and indefinitely, to shoot positives on glass which I would send directly from my basket to the headquarters, by means of a very simple form of delivery: a small box which would slide down to the ground through the length of a rope that would bring instruc-

> tions back up to me, if necessary.
>
> These images, immediately enlarged by projections under the eyes of the commander in chief, would represent to him the entirety of his chessboard, as they would register progressively the minutest details of action and ensure for him incomparable superiority in conducting his part in the game. (Nadar, p. 59)

From the very beginning of human existence, when we first felt the need to step away from ourselves to try to better understand our situation, we have also felt the fear of unknown danger lying beyond the horizon. As far back as our ancestry can be traced there were always birds flying overhead, and it is impossible that a person fearful of an invisible approaching danger would not have wished he were a bird, or at least had a bird as an ally. Think of doomed MacBeth standing on the ramparts of Dunsinane, struggling to see whether Birnam Wood was truly advancing on him—how at that moment he would have wished he were able to fly up and confirm what he thought he saw.

The use of balloons for aerial observation during war began in France shortly after the Montgolfier brothers pioneered manned balloon flight in the late eighteenth century. From that time through the American Civil War, balloons were used for reconnaissance of battlefields, mostly behind the front lines. They served as the portable bell towers Nadar had envisioned, but there is no evidence that any photographs were ever taken from balloons during the Civil War.

The first successful aerial photograph in America was made of the city of Boston in 1860 by James Wallace Black, using wet plate collodion photography. But the long exposures and the need to prepare wet plates in a flying

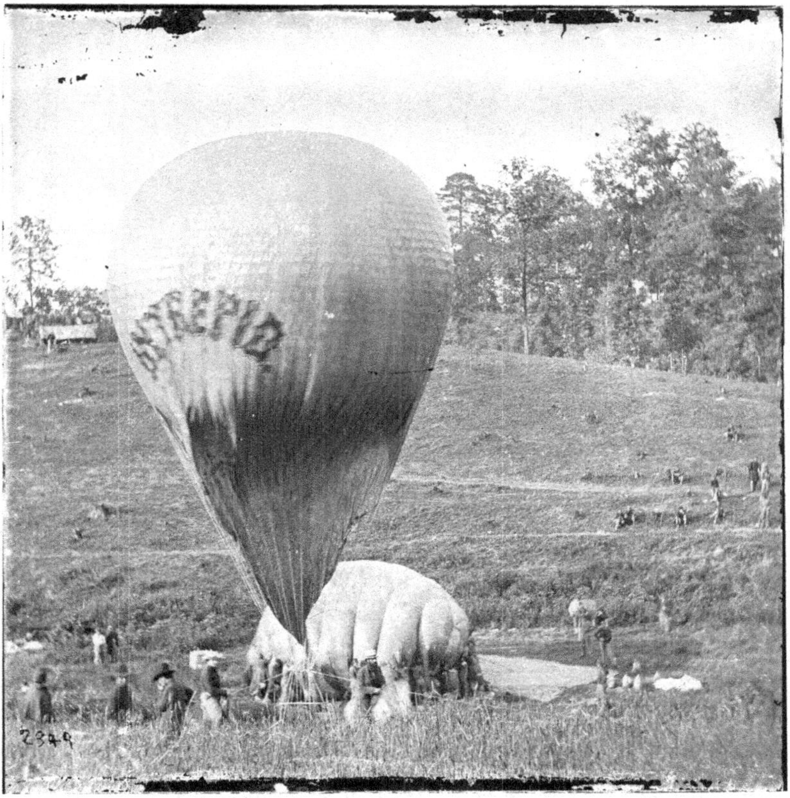

During the Civil War Thaddeus S. Lowe built a small fleet of hydrogen balloons used for aerial reconnaissance of Confederate troop movements. This photograph depicts the replenishment of hydrogen in the balloon Intrepid *from another balloon in Fair Oaks, Virginia, in May 1862. Lowe's balloons were used for visual reconnaissance, since the wet plate collodion photographic process (used to make this image) was not yet fast enough to be usable for aerial photography. (LOC)*

balloon made aerial photography barely possible on a perfect calm sunny day in peacetime, let alone during the heat of battle.

The inventions of dry silver-gelatin glass plates and, later, roll film, made practical, reliable aerial photography

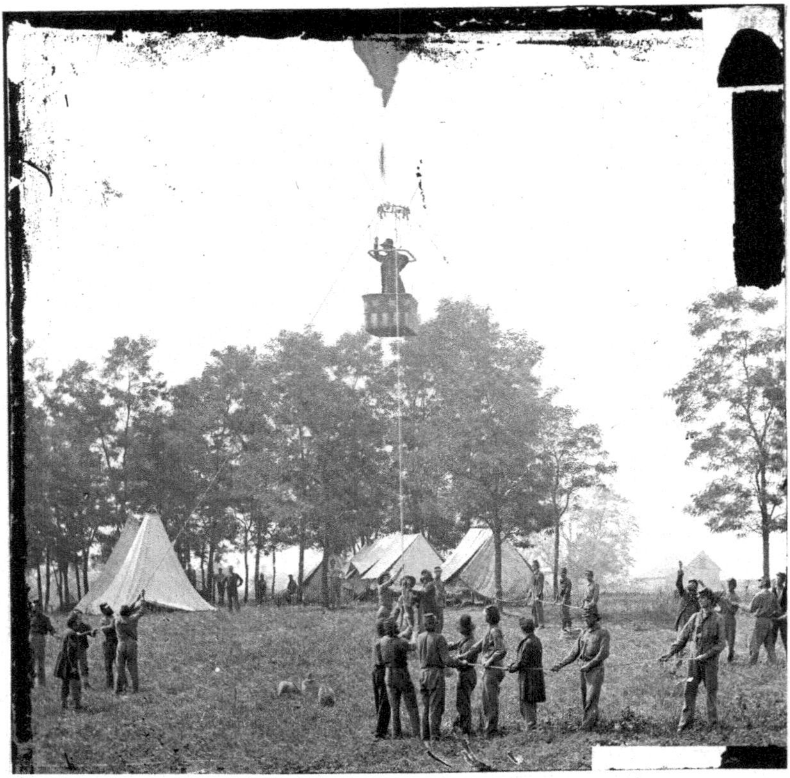

Thaddeus Lowe prepares to make aerial observations of the battlefield from the balloon Intrepid *at Fair Oaks, Virginia, May 1862. (LOC)*

a reality. Once the required exposure times were reduced to mere fractions of a second, the possibility of lofting cameras on balloons, zeppelins, kites, powered airplanes, and even strapping miniature cameras to homing pigeons became possible. By the time of the First World War, aerial photographic reconnaissance had become an essential tool of warfare. Placing cameras on powered aircraft that could maneuver at high altitudes to precise locations in the air above enemy formations enabled photography to reveal enemy movements over time.

Of course, if photographs could be taken from airplanes flying high above enemy positions, so too could bombs be dropped from them, and this was to become one of the great horrors of the twentieth century.

Before his historic flight to the Moon in Apollo 11, Neil Armstrong talked about the importance of space exploration as a way of gaining a better understanding of our proper place in the cosmos by taking yet another step back:

> It would be presumptuous for me to pick out a single thing that history will identify as the result of this mission. But I would say that it will enlighten the human race and help us all to comprehend that we are an important part of a much bigger universe than we can normally see from the front porch. I would hope that it will help individuals, the world over, to think in a proper perspective about the various endeavors of mankind as a whole. Perhaps going to the Moon and back in itself isn't all that important. But it is a big enough step to give people a new dimension in their thinking—a sort of enlightenment.
>
> After all, the earth itself is a spacecraft. It's an odd kind of spacecraft, since it carries its crew on the outside instead of inside. But it's pretty small. And it's cruising in an orbit around the sun. It's cruising in an orbit around the center of the galaxy that's cruising in some unknown orbit, in some unknown direction and at some unspecified velocity, but with a tremendous rate of change, position and environment. It's hard for us to get far enough away from this scene to see what's happening. If you're in the middle of a crowd, the crowd appears to extend in every direction as far as you can see. You have to step back and look down from the Washington Monument or something like that to see that you're really pretty close to the edge of the crowd, and that the whole picture is quite a bit different from the way it looks when you

> are in the middle of all those people. From our position on the earth it is difficult to observe where the earth is and where it's going, or what its future course might be. Hopefully by getting a little farther away, both in the real sense and the figurative sense, we'll be able to make some people step back and reconsider their mission in the universe, to think of themselves as a group of people who constitute the crew of a spaceship going through the universe. If you're going to run a spaceship you've got to be pretty cautious about how you use your resources, how you use your crew, and how you treat your spacecraft. (Armstrong, pp. 337-338.)

Many of the other Apollo astronauts expressed similar ideas about gaining perspective through the traversal of space and time, as though the keys to enlightenment were somehow coded in installments scattered throughout a vast imagined Cartesian coordinate system of the universe, and that we would eventually be compelled to go chasing after all of them before we could hope to fully grasp the true meaning of life.

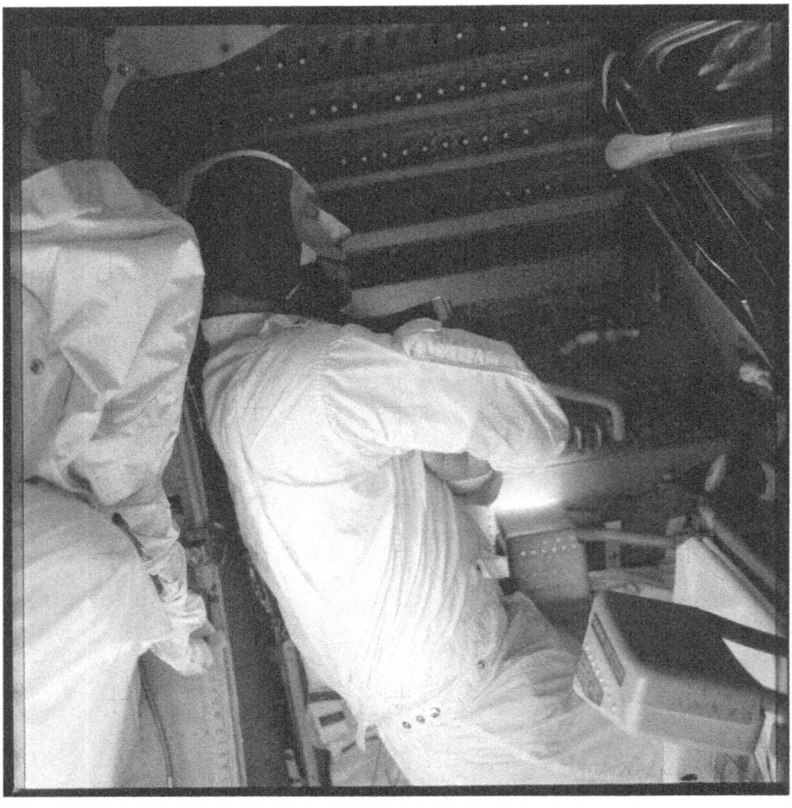

After a catastrophic failure of the life support system on the Apollo 13 Command Module, the astronauts used the Lunar Module as a lifeboat. The temperature fell to near freezing levels for the last days of their return flight from the Moon. (NASA)

13

When the U.S. first decided to put humans into capsules atop ballistic missiles to counter the challenge the Soviets had presented with their early successes in space, the "Mercury" program was launched. NASA's initial plan was to seal up the men in a capsule with no windows. The men chosen to be astronauts in the Mercury program were extraordinary people, all military pilots who had proven their courage by enduring an excruciating program of physical tests that NASA put them through in the selection process. They were men who could be spun in centrifuges, tossed around inside diving airplane cabins, and exposed to the severest heat and cold. They could remain stoic when various probes were inserted into every orifice in their bodies. They were the least likely humans on earth to retreat from physical danger or panic, or vomit up their lunch when shaken violently. Tom Wolfe wrote the definitive and immensely entertaining book on the subject, *The Right Stuff.*

But these men objected strongly to not having a window, even though they were aware that their jobs as the first astronauts would not require them to actually see out the window. The only significant difference between Enos, the last chimpanzee astronaut, and Alan Shepard, the first human one, was that Enos did not know what he was getting into before being blasted into space. According to one account of Enos's flight, he expressed his extreme displeasure with what had been done to him by behaving disgracefully in a naughty chimpanzee sort of way at his post-flight press conference. (Degroot, p. 157) It is unlikely that a window would have helped calm his outrage.

The first two Mercury flights, by Shepard and then Gus Grissom, were suborbital: they went up and traced a huge arc over the western Atlantic and then returned, landing not far, in space terms, from where they had taken off. The only view the astronauts had outside was through a periscope.

It was on the third orbital flight by John Glenn that a tiny window was added. He took photographs of the Earth using a modified Ansco camera he had purchased in a drug store in Cocoa Beach and a Leica camera provided by NASA. Both cameras had been modified by NASA engineers for convenient use in space. Thus Glenn became the first photographer in space. Commenting on the experience

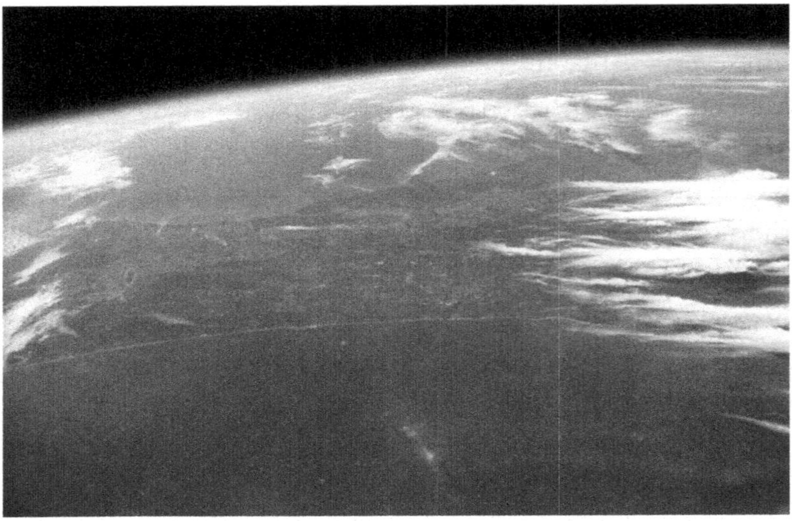

The first published photograph of earth from space taken by John Glenn showed the curvature of the earth and the blackness of space. (NASA)

of seeing Earth from orbit for the first time, he wrote, "It was surprising how much of the earth's surface was covered by clouds ... The different types of clouds—vertical developments, stratus clouds, and cumulus clouds—are readily distinguished ... Only a few land areas were visible during the flight because of the cloud cover ..." (Glenn)

Glenn's picture of Earth from orbit, mostly blue with white swirls below and black void above, was the first of thousands of similar pictures that would reveal patterns and features of the planet that could only be seen from orbit. Glenn's picture showed the entire width of the Florida peninsula, with the Atlantic Ocean in the foreground and the Gulf of Mexico in the background, something that had never been seen in the same frame before. It allowed us to step back from our current picture of the world to see ourselves from a higher level. Over the next few years, we would see the entire Earth as a globe rising above the lunar horizon, first from images sent back to Earth by a robot called the Lunar Orbiter 1, and later from photographs taken by the Apollo Astronauts.

In 1992, humanity took its final step back on its quest to gain higher perspective when NASA's Galileo probe, on its way to Jupiter, captured an image of Earth and Moon together floating in the blackness of space. The desire to make this picture, the ultimate selfie, was essentially the same desire that motivated the earliest cave painters—to step back and reframe our understanding of ourselves.

During these years of space selfies, NASA also turned the cameras outward to explore the cosmos. The first celestial object of attention was the Moon itself, and a number of probes were sent to photograph and test its surface to make

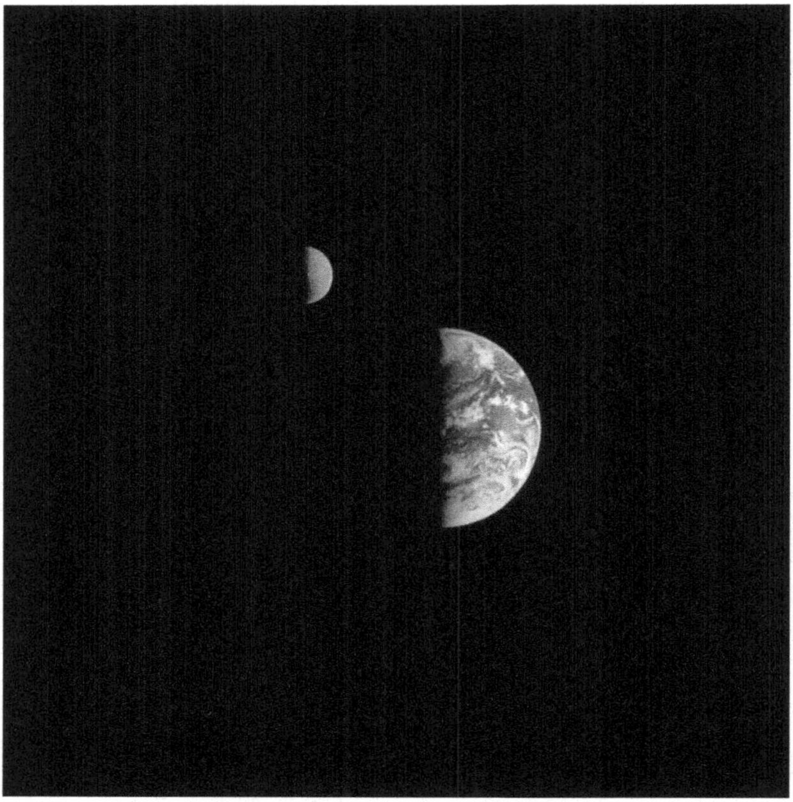

Photograph of the Earth and Moon together taken by the Galileo spacecraft on its way to Jupiter. (NASA)

sure it would support a landing. The first probes were a series of missions called "Ranger." The Ranger rockets were designed to fly directly toward the Moon, transmitting back images until the rockets crashed into the lunar surface. The first six Rangers failed to produce any pictures, but Rangers 7, 8 and 9 sent back detailed images, the closest ones revealing features on the surface as small as half a meter across. This gave the first close-up views of the surface of the Moon at a resolution high enough to show whether landing a small machine containing people would be practical.

After the Ranger program, five "Lunar Orbiter" missions produced a library of high-resolution photographs that mapped almost the entire surface of the Moon at resolutions of a few meters. The technology combined chemical photography with electronic scanning, ultimately transmitting the scanned images back to Earth. The Lunar Orbiter camera exposed photographic film which was chemically developed on board in an automated process engineered by Eastman Kodak. Then the developed film was electronically scanned on board in narrow strips and converted into analog radio signals transmitted back to Earth, where they were reconstructed to make final printed photographs. The light-sensitive silver salts and wet development chemistry used in the Lunar Orbiter spacecraft were direct descendants of the wet-plate collodion process used by Nadar to make the first aerial photograph from a balloon more than century before.

All of the high-resolution photographs taken by the Apollo astronauts were on photographic film that was brought back home and developed by similar chemical processes. Until the astronauts finally landed and walked on the Moon, most of the photographs they took were of the Moon

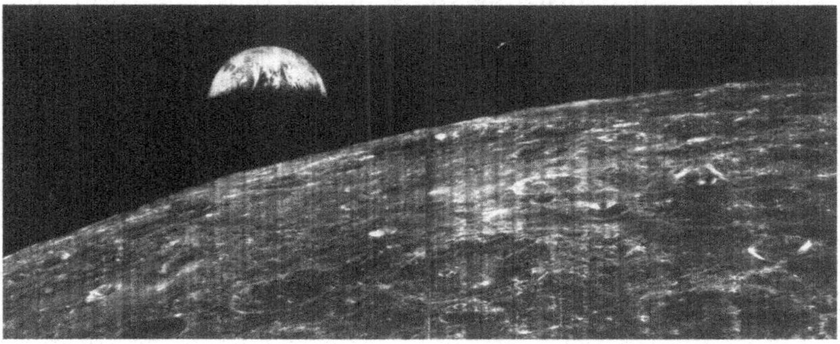

The first photographic view of the earth from lunar orbit. (NASA)

itself. Once they began to walk around on the Moon, they started taking pictures of each other doing various tasks. On the third Moon landing (Apollo 14), Alan Shepard demonstrated the clear fact that walking on the Moon had become almost routine by pulling out some golf balls and hitting them with an improvised six-iron. The first American to fly into space a decade earlier was now the first (and so far the only) Moon golfer.

The thousands of photographs made by the Apollo astronauts are in the public domain and most are accessible in digital form on the Internet. My personal favorites are the relatively few that the astronauts took of themselves on board the Apollo command and lunar modules during ordinary moments of everyday life, especially one of Eugene Cernan after he had come inside the lunar module from his last walk on the Moon at the end of the Apollo 17 landing. Cernan has taken off his astronaut suit and is grimy with sweat and Moon dirt. He wears an expression of both exhaustion and elation. Here was one of the perfect champions of our species at the end of an epic adventure only twelve men would ever get to experience, now finally returned to his full humanity among the rest of us. I can never know what it felt like to be Neil Armstrong stepping out onto the Moon for the first time, but I can imagine how Eugene Cernan felt, exhausted at the end of a grueling physical workout.

When Neil Armstrong first stepped onto the Moon, his famous words, “That’s one small step for a man, one giant leap for mankind,” made a connection back through all the generations who had looked up into the heavens wondering and philosophizing about what was out there. He had followed the arc of human inquiry upward, from the time

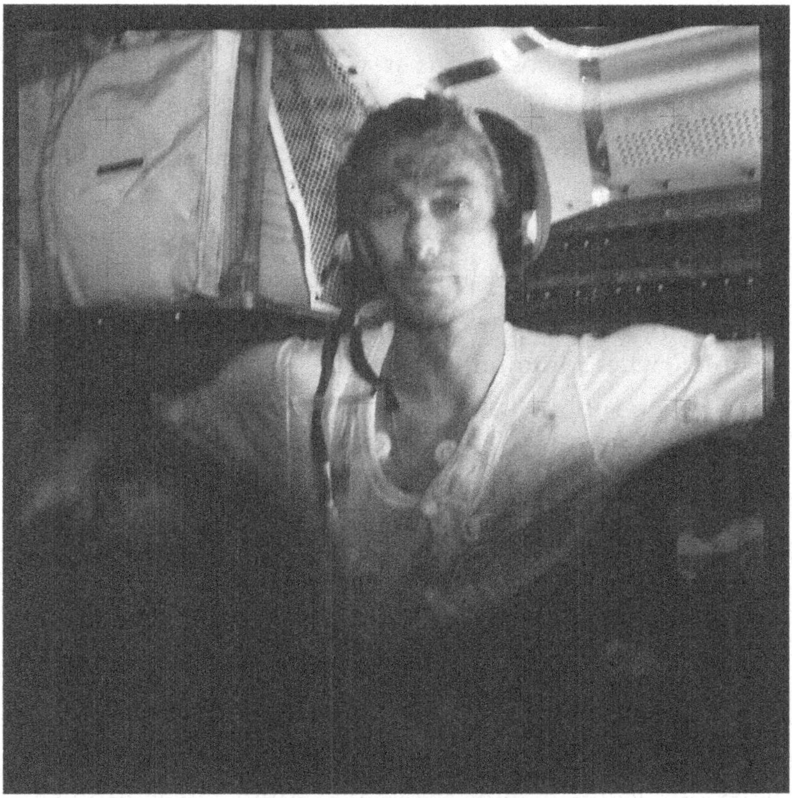

Eugene Cernan inside the Lunar Module after his last excursion on the Moon. (NASA)

of the Tower of Babel, through to the Trylon of the 1939 World's Fair and all the mighty rockets of the space program, and was implying that we had finally arrived at the zenith of our aspiration. What we actually found there was revealed a few minutes later when his partner Edwin Aldrin stepped onto the Moon ground and spoke his first two words: "Magnificent desolation."

Since that moment we have seen pictures in breathtaking detail taken by robotic probes visiting every planet in our solar system. We've seen images taken from orbiting space telescopes of the cosmos as it was and has been evolving since almost the beginning of cosmic time. Thus far, Aldrin's two words still apply. Beyond our planet, the universe still appears both magnificent and desolate. Every few months we are treated by NASA scientists to a new glimmer of possibility that life may exist somewhere out there. But how could there be a place with life more splendidly diverse than this one, where hummingbirds and sperm whales co-exist with lawyers and ballerinas and millions of other species of plants and animals in a system that has been evolving for billions of years? If there is a more interesting place in the universe, I feel no particular need to upgrade my ticket.

In his last taped interview six months before his death in the summer of 1998, Alan Shepard, the first American in space and the fifth man on the Moon, spoke of the experience of standing on the lunar surface for the first time and looking up at the Earth. He spoke of a "tremendous sense of accomplishment" and "self-satisfaction." He continued,

> But then that went away because we had a lot of work to do. But I'll never forget that moment.
>
> Another moment I will never forget is after Ed [lunar module pilot Edgar Mitchell] had followed me down and we had set out some of our equipment, taken the emergency samples, we had a few moments to look around, to look up in the black sky—a totally black sky, even though the Sun is shining on the surface it's not reflected, there's no diffusion, no reflection—a totally black sky and seeing another planet: planet Earth. Now planet Earth is only four times as large as the Moon, so you can really still put your thumb and your forefinger

> around it at that distance. So it makes it look beautiful; it makes it look lonely; it makes it look fragile. You think to yourself, just imagine that millions of people are living on that planet and don't realize how fragile it is. I think this is a feeling everyone has had and expressed it in one fashion or another. That was an overwhelming feeling in seeing the beauty of the planet on the one hand but the fragility of it on the other. (Shepard)

Perhaps the memory of sensing the fragility of Earth as it floated in the blackness of space was amplified in Shepard's mind by his knowledge that he was suffering from leukemia, battling for his own fragile life. Perhaps the impression of fragility is inevitable when Apollonian man finally takes his last step outward into the cosmos, and begins the return voyage back to the only part of reality that is not desolate.

Edwin Aldrin described the encroachment of his own sense of fragility after walking on the Moon in *Return to Earth*.

> It soon emerged that my life was highly structured and that there had always existed a major goal of one sort or another. I had excelled academically, being at the top of the schools and classes I had attended during my life. Finally there had been the most important goal of all, and it had been realized—I had gone to the Moon. What to do next? What possible goal could I add now? There simply wasn't one, and without a goal I was like an inert ping-pong ball being batted about by the whims and motivations of others. I was suffering from what poets have described as the melancholy of all things done. (Aldrin, p. 300)

Aldrin's life came undone once he returned from the Moon. He struggled with depression and divorce before beginning a slow recovery toward a tolerable earthly life. Eventually he found his way back to the familiar ground of Apollonian striving, becoming a major advocate, along with Neil Armstrong and other former astronauts, for manned missions to Mars. His ultimate recommendation of a cure for our melancholy: more magnificent desolation.

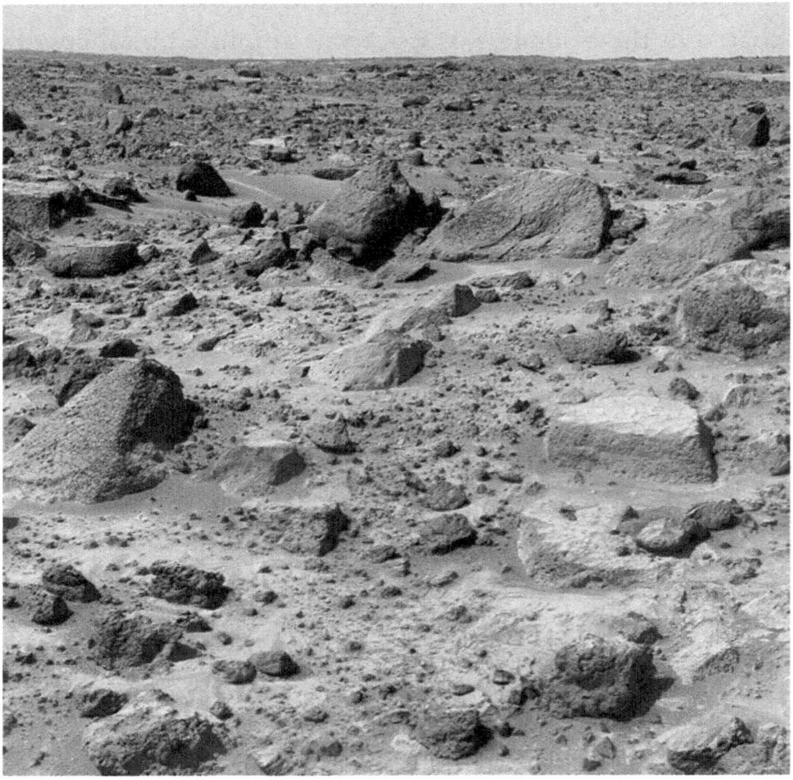

A boulder field on Mars. (NASA)

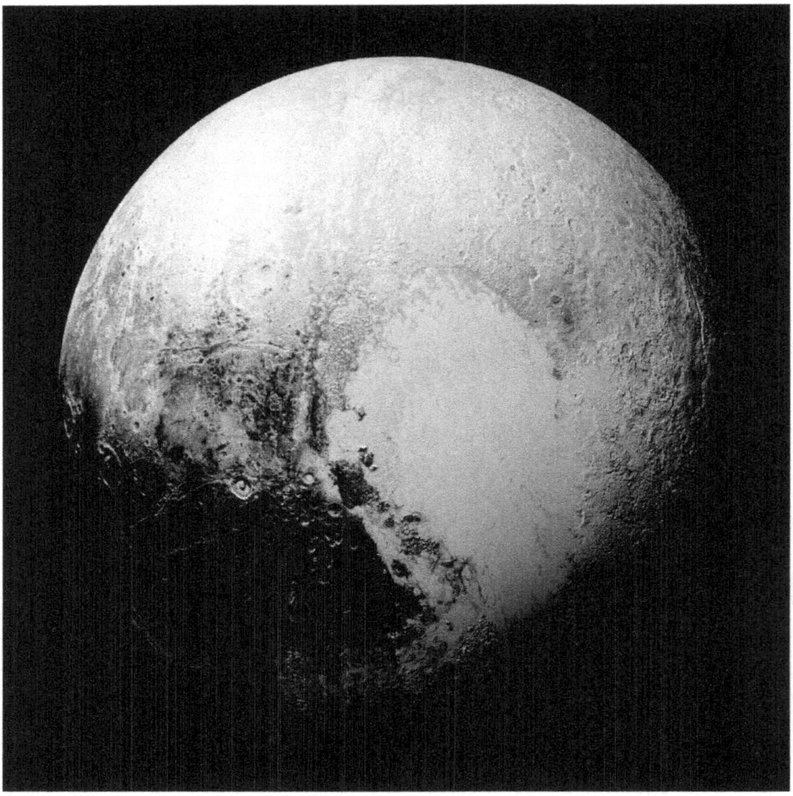

NASA's New Horizons spacecraft captured this high-resolution enhanced color view of Pluto on July 14, 2015. (NASA)

14

From the moment of birth our world begins to expand. Through all the years of growing up, we venture outward, trying to understand the universe and our place in it. The trick is to realize when we have reached the limits of what we can discover out there, and make the conscious decision to begin the return journey. This move may be more difficult for astronomers and planetary geologists than for others. But in academia, it is acceptable to stay on the outbound path of discovery forever, never ceasing the quest for new knowledge. This quest may satisfy Apollo, but it leaves the other gods unhappy. And it is unlikely that anyone has ever been saved by Apollo alone.

In my own outbound journey, I found myself cast in the role of a college professor in an institution dedicated to being and staying at the forefront of applied science, technology and art. Faculty members are expected to keep current with and contribute to the creation of new knowledge. There is not a lot of time in such a place for reflecting on the past.

During the academic year of 2011–12, I was fortunate to be granted a sabbatical leave after serving as a dean for the previous fourteen years. This was my first opportunity to temporarily step off the academic treadmill after thirty years of constant forward movement. After initially thinking I would try to spend the year abroad exploring some new avenue of academic inquiry, I began to realize that what

I really wanted was to stay close to home. In the twenty years we had lived in our house, I had seen very little of the neighborhoods immediately surrounding my street. I drew a circle on the map with a radius of one mile around our house and resolved to walk every street and alley, observing and photographing as much of the life inside the circle as I could. The circle became my world during that year.

During the same sabbatical year, I returned to my earlier passion of flying model sailplanes, which had lapsed since I

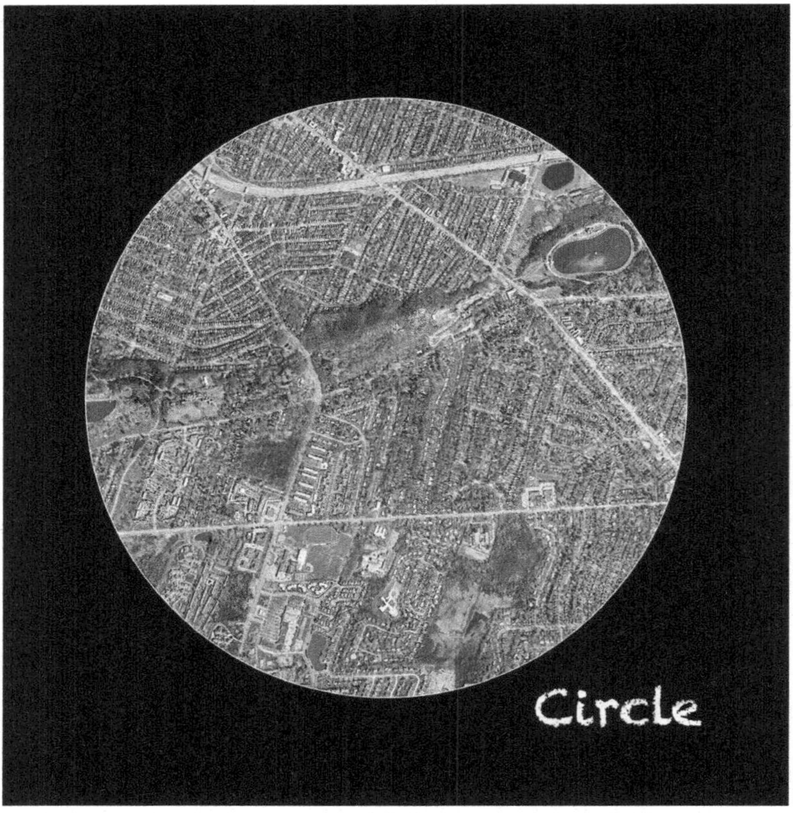

The variety of life within a mile radius of our house provided the subject matter for this book.

had finished passing on the family aviation traditions to my children. The technology of model airplanes had evolved significantly since those days: radio-control systems were now computerized, and new, high-efficiency motors and batteries had vastly improved reliability and performance. Getting into the air had never been so easy. I began to launch my new sailplane from a large campus field used by the aeronautical engineering club students to test their new designs. One day, after gaining some confidence in the technology and my flying skills, I tried to capture some aerial video footage by taping my new iPhone to the side of the glider. The resulting video was better than anything I had been able to produce in the past, and the aerial photography bug that had lain dormant in my system for many years came alive.

Félix Nadar and James Wallace Black had endured significant physical discomforts to make their first aerial photographs from balloons in the 1860s, and soon thereafter the possibility of sending a camera aloft without having to accompany it bodily presented an appealing prospect. The first patents were issued in that same decade for systems that would allow photographs to be made remotely from tethered balloons. At the time these ideas were not practical, but by the beginning of the twentieth century dry photographic plates and film were sensitive enough to be exposed remotely from the air, producing stunning aerial photographs from balloons and kites.

One of the most successful images during this period was a panoramic photograph of San Francisco shortly after the 1906 earthquake, made by the American photographer George R. Lawrence with a massive camera suspended

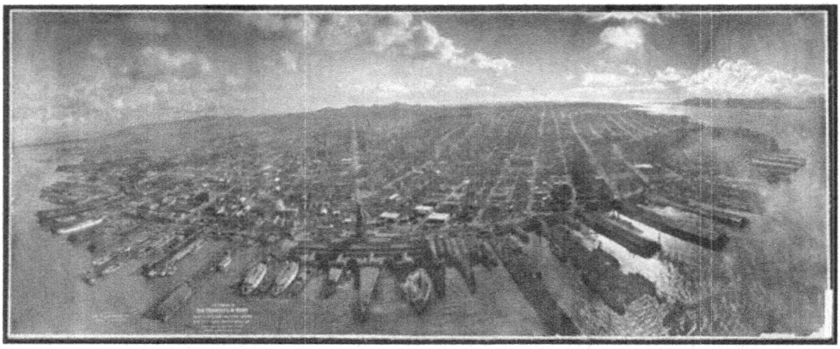

Panoramic view of San Francisco shortly after the 1906 earthquake taken from a camera suspended from a string of seventeen kites by George Lawrence. (LOC)

from a string of seventeen kites flown 2,000 feet above the San Francisco Bay. The photographic negative was four feet across and contact prints made from it were sold in such great numbers that Lawrence made a fortune.

Kites and balloons depend upon the wind, which can quickly change velocity and direction without warning. Maneuvering a kite or tethered balloon into the desired position for an aerial photograph is challenging, especially if moving the anchor point on the ground is difficult. But kites and balloons were the only options for remote-controlled aerial cameras until reliable radio-control systems made it possible to mount a camera on a fixed-wing airplane or helicopter. And even with the ability to fly a remote-controlled aircraft to a desired point in the air, it remained a difficult challenge to visualize what the camera would record. Good framing and composition were more a result of luck than photographic skill. To control these variables the photographer still needed to ascend into the air with the camera.

Then at the beginning of the present decade a breakthrough in technology initiated a new aerial photography revolution. This was the multi-rotor drone, with four or more rotors, capable of carrying a camera and flying with a precision never before imaginable. The precision is made possible by the incorporation of a GPS (global positioning system) that can lock onto several GPS satellites simultaneously to determine precise location in three-dimensional space relative to the ground, coupled with a digital flight computer that can control each motor independently, to maintain a hovering position or fly through a pre-programmed path.

Multi-rotor drones have opened up new zones of airspace for photographic exploration that no previous technology had allowed. A fixed-wing aircraft must always be moving forward to maintain lift, so it requires massive volumes of open atmosphere in which to operate. Its flight is always in relation to the body of air through which it flies, so it will drift with wind currents as it flies forward. The deities to which we pray when flying fixed-wing aircraft are the gods of the winds: fickle and complex, and mostly invisible. During the drive to a flying field with one of my model airplanes, I've always been chiefly concerned with the moods of the wind gods. Improved control technology has helped us gain a better footing when facing the winds, but they are still our masters, and we bow our heads in respect whenever we are about to fly.

Multi-rotor drones do not need to be as respectful of the winds. Their gods are the geosynchronous satellites that orbit the Earth in exact coordination with the Earth's rotation to maintain a fixed position in space relative to the ground. Once locked onto a number of these satellites, a drone can ignore the winds as long as they remain temperate. Only when the winds become agitated or enraged does a drone need to pay its proper respects and keep its feet on the ground.

Their obedience to celestial gods and disrespect for earthly ones detach drones from the long traditions of aviation and aerial seeing that came before. This gives them an aura of menace, which may be one reason why they have caused so much controversy. In form, they seem to be unrelated to any previous earthly flying machines, but instead the descendants of the Apollo lunar modules and other machines designed to explore the airless reaches of interplanetary space. Their shadows, sometimes captured by their onboard cameras when landing, mimic the enlarging shadow of the Apollo 11 Lunar Module on the dark gray rubble of the Sea of Tranquility observed by Neil Armstrong as he groped for his famous landing spot on the Moon.

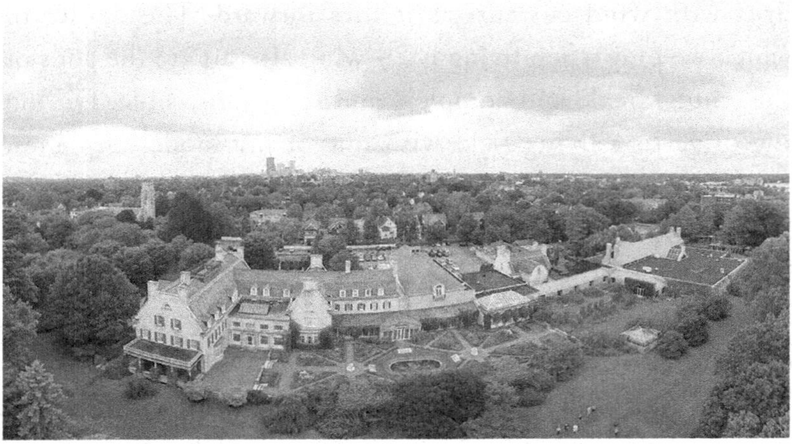

This 2014 panoramic view of the George Eastman Museum was assembled from multiple photographs taken from a drone hovering at an altitude of 100 feet in a neighborhood full of trees. Such an image would have been impossible to make with previous aerial imaging technologies.

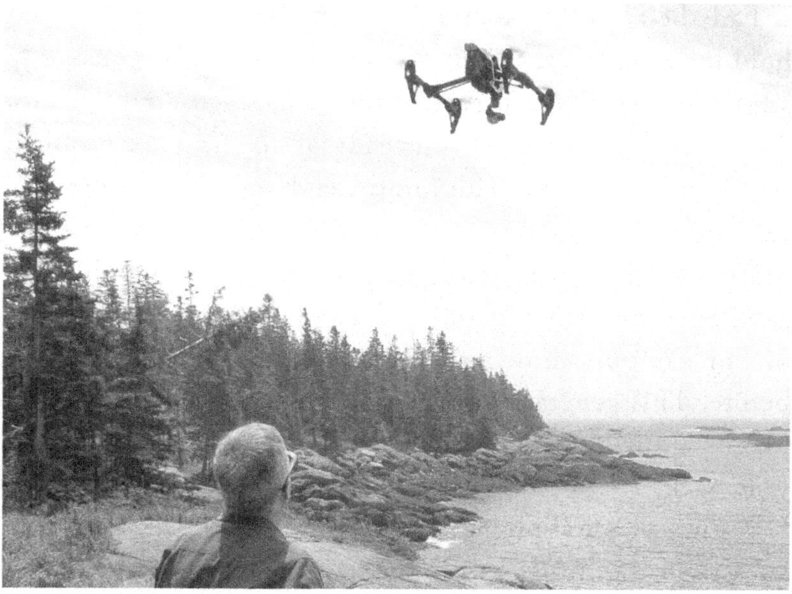

Multi-rotor drone with camera.

The ability of multi-rotor drones to fly with extreme precision relative to the ground makes it possible to position aerial cameras in locations never before accessible. For the first time, we can place our eyes and cameras remotely at any point in the aerial zone that lies between the ground and the altitude where conventional model airplanes and helicopters safely fly. Before the advent of multi-rotors, this drone zone was not accessible. Multi-rotor camera drones have brought us a new way of seeing our world.

When I returned to the classroom in the fall of 2012 after my sabbatical leave, I purchased one of the first generation multi-rotor drones to experiment with this new platform for aerial photography. The drone was small, NASA white, and had a fixed mount on the bottom for a camera.

It had the ability to lock onto multiple GPS satellites and hold its hovering position to within a few feet by constantly adjusting the speed of each rotor to compensate for wind. The resulting video was unsteady at times. This problem has since been solved with improved designs that mount the camera on a device called a "gimbal" that counteracts the motion of the drone as it steadies itself in the wind. With my new drone I began to produce photographs and videos of our campus, showing images that had never been seen before. This generated a lot of excitement and interest and led to a growing demand for more. By the spring of that first year back, I was enjoying an early local monopoly on this new kind of aerial photography.

I used the drone to produce a series of aerial videos of

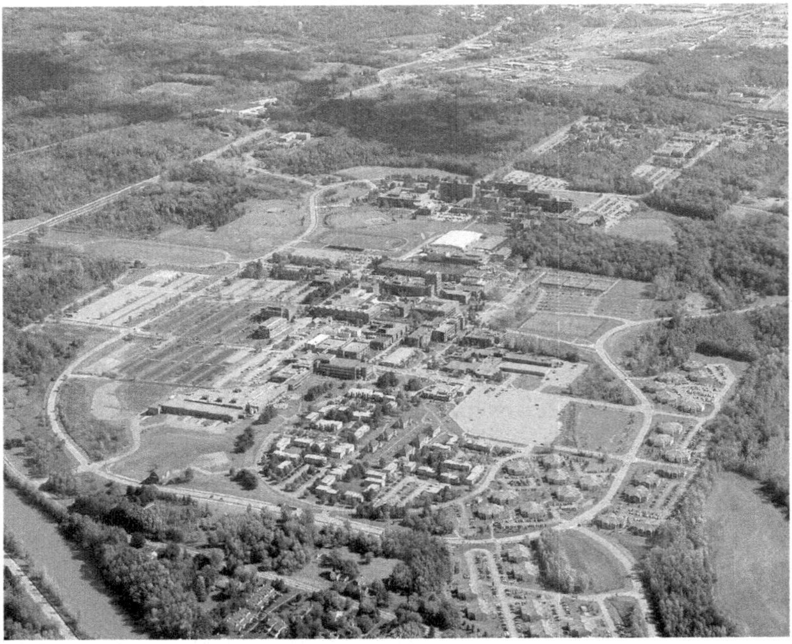

The RIT campus from the window of a commercial airliner in 2009.

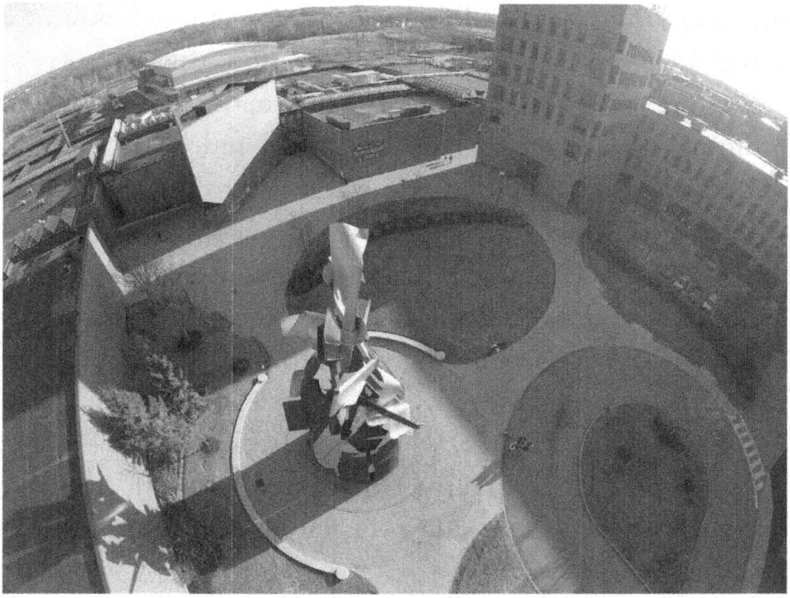

Albert Paley's Sentinel *monument on the RIT campus photographed from a multi-rotor drone (photo by Sarah Sampson and Andrea K. Edwards).*

the campus to be included in a time capsule marking the transition of our academic calendar from quarters to semesters. An all-campus ceremony was planned to bury the time capsule. The committee responsible for deciding what went into it thought that aerial videos would provide the best overview of the physical campus for future generations.

The founder and chair of our software engineering program, Fernando Naveda, had been recruited by the administration to manage the three-year process of calendar conversion, a morass of political and logistical complexity. For some recreational relief from this difficult job, Fernando had an idea to include a bit of classic slapstick video comedy along with the serious videos that would be sealed up in the time capsule. Playing on the theme of the rise of menacing drones, he recruited our provost for the lead role in a short video production. In the video, the sinister shadow of the drone creeps up the side of RIT's main administration building until it reaches the provost's window on the seventh floor. He is working at his computer desk. He slowly turns his head toward the hovering drone outside the window, does a classic double take, then jumps up and runs away, disappearing into the shadowed interior of his office. We had a lot of fun shooting the video, and everyone on the time capsule committee loved it except for the people from University News Service, who felt that drones had become too controversial and scary to be made light of in this way. So the video was never shown in public, and never made it into the time capsule.

Despite the undercurrent of worry about the dark side of drones, excitement was mounting about the pictures and videos we could obtain with them. It was clear that a new chapter in the evolution of aerial photography had begun. And because multi-rotor drones were much easier to fly than any previous model aircraft, it became feasible for the first time to contemplate offering a new course in aerial photography. Previous generations of radio-controlled flying models had required many hours of practice to learn how to fly, and failure to continuously control the aircraft would almost always result in a crash. Multi-rotor drones are different. Their default flight behavior is to remain hovering in a stationary position until a command is transmitted by the pilot. If you take your hands off the controls, instead of crashing, the multi-rotor drone will just stop in its tracks and hover. When the battery voltage drops below a certain

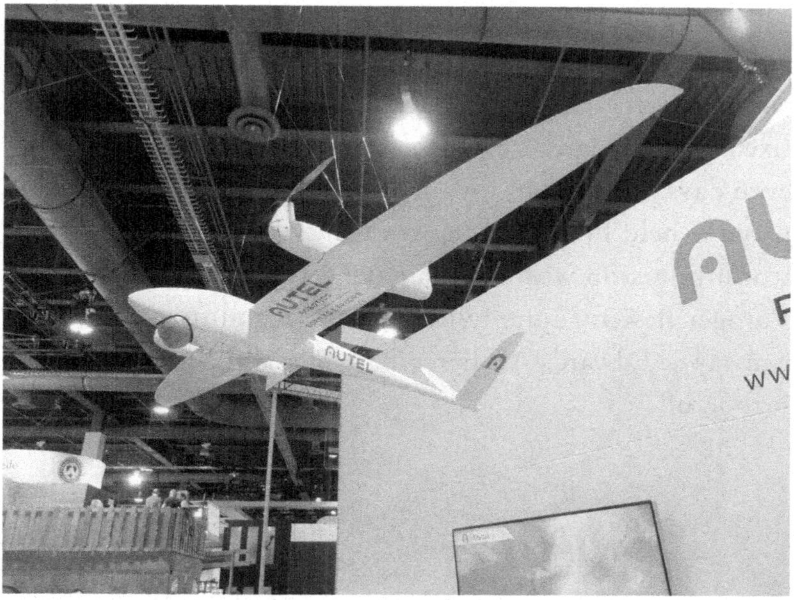

This commercial drone shown at the 2015 Consumer Electronics Show in Las Vegas combines the advantages of a multirotor drone for vertical ascent and descent with the efficiency of a sailplane wing for long duration flights.

safe threshold, the drone will land itself automatically, almost exactly at the point where its flight began. This takes away the panic factor, and allows novice pilots to gain flight experience much more easily than with older technology.

The one disadvantage of multi-rotor designs when compared with fixed-wing designs is in the much greater amount of energy required to stay aloft. A model sailplane can sometimes fly for hours without any power at all. A multi-rotor drone without power to the rotors will fall from the air like a stone. (The glide ratio of a drone without power is 0.) So multi-rotors only became feasible when battery and motor technology had become efficient enough to do the job.

For applications where flight times must be longer than an hour at altitudes higher than a few hundred feet, fixed wing aircraft will continue to dominate. The most efficient fixed-wing designs are capable of staying aloft for hours or even days. The record for a manned fixed-wing powered airplane is held by the Rutan Voyager, which flew around the world non-stop without refueling in December, 1986. The Voyager flew for nine full days before landing on the same runway at Edwards Air Force Base in California from which it took off.

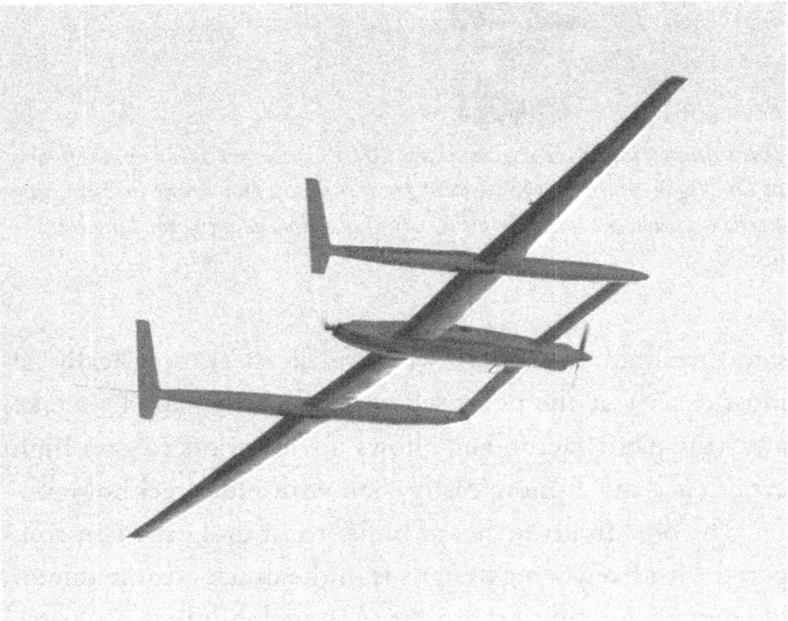

The Rutan Voyager was the first powered airplane to fly all the way around the world nonstop in December, 1986. The high efficiency of the large wing and lightweight composite construction enabled the feat. Within a generation of this flight, commercial airliners employing many of the same construction methods were routinely flying nonstop halfway around the world.

On June 28, 2015, an airplane called the Solar Impulse, driven by electric motors powered by solar panels, took off from Nagoya, Japan and flew more than 5,000 miles to Hawaii in 117 hours.

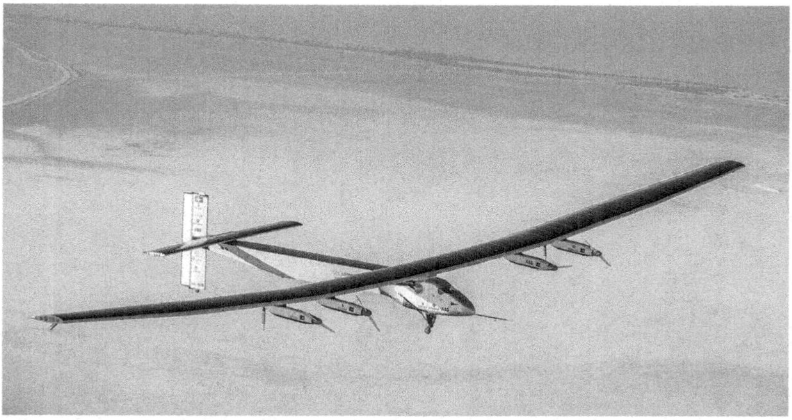

The Solar Impulse solar-powered electric airplane.

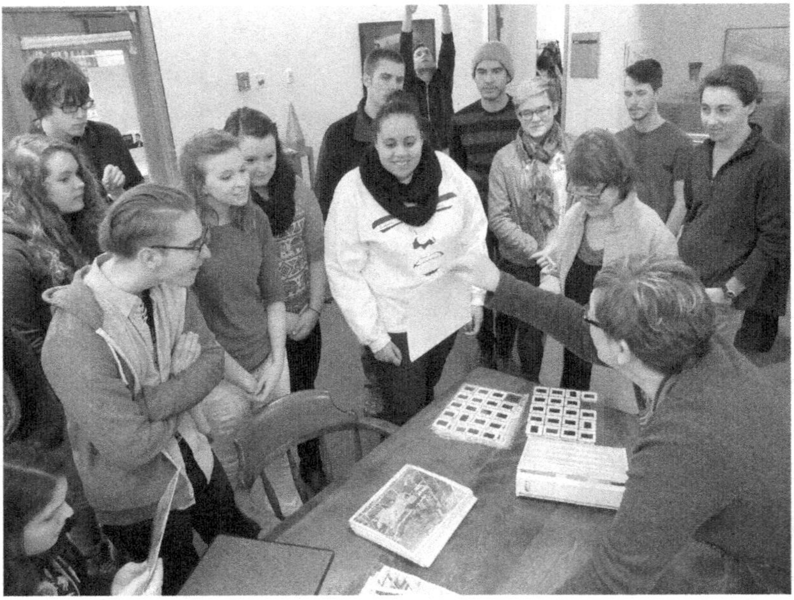

During the first week of the new aerial photography course, we visited the RIT archives to view a collection of aerial photographs taken of the campus during its original construction in the mid 1960s.

15

After experimenting with two generations of multi-rotor drones from the spring of 2013 through the summer of 2014 I decided to offer a new course in aerial photography during the spring semester of 2015. The first half of the semester would be too cold and snowy to do much flying, but this would give the students a chance to read and think about the history of aerial seeing and aerial photography, beginning with the first wet-plate collodion pictures made from hydrogen balloons by Félix Nadar and Jame Wallace Black in the 1860s, and progressing through the various technologies and techniques from that time until the present day. The students would learn about the history of photography from balloons, kites, airplanes, spacecraft, and even homing pigeons. They would have time to develop an imagination about what the world must look like from the perspectives made possible by drones, before actually taking to the air.

This would be the first course in aerial photography offered by the School of Photographic Arts and Sciences at RIT, a school that traces its institutional lineage back to 1902, one year before the Wright Brothers made their first flight. Since that time the school has prepared many graduates who have made important contributions to the advancement of the science, technology and art of aerial photography. But the high cost of aircraft rental had previously prevented the school from offering formal coursework in the field. Now, the rapid advance of drone technology was making it possible. The course would also serve as a kind of Trojan horse, appearing on the outside to be entirely focused on the technological and aesthetic revolution in aerial photography, but harboring within its belly my ulterior purpose of smuggling a lifelong passion for flying into my workplace and sharing it with my students. Although I didn't realize it at the time, in retrospect it's obvious that I stole this page directly from my father's playbook.

Of all the many courses I have created during my teaching years, the aerial photography course generated by far the most excitement in the larger community. It is the only sub-

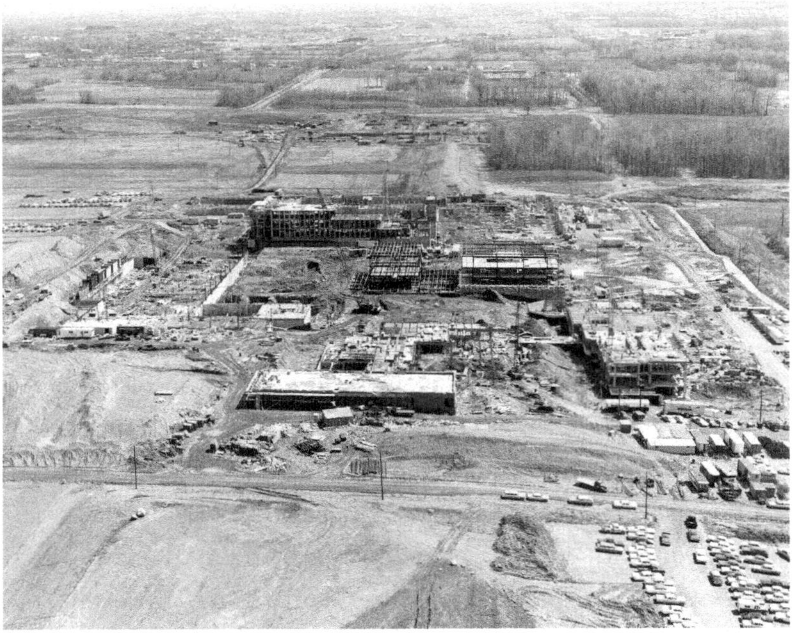

Aerial photograph taken by Martin R. Wahl in 1966 during the construction of the RIT campus on a tract of farmland in Henrietta, New York. (RIT Archives)

ject I have ever taught that held the possibility of universal appeal, perhaps because it allows us to do the most fundamental thing that defines what it means to be human—to step back and reframe our view of the world in order to gain perspective on our existence. Drone photography represents an important departure from the long march of aerial photography, from the time of Félix Nadar to the latest high-resolution images of the surface of distant planets sent back to Earth, because drones have allowed us to begin to reframe that part of our world we skipped over on our voyage out to the stars. Drones give us aerial views of the world at a scale that keeps our bodies, and not just our tracings, clearly in the picture. They allow us to reframe reality in small steps rather than giant leaps, and show us realities we have the greatest opportunities to affect.

When Alan Shepard stood on the Moon and pinched his view of the tiny Earth between his thumb and forefinger, he used one word, "fragile," to sum up our entire world. This must be a powerful temptation for the space traveler. And there is no doubt that from a certain perspective, the Earth is properly described as tiny, fragile, lonely, and even insignificant. From far enough away, everything becomes insignificant. Although it's a common oversimplification, we can't help thinking of the territory between New York and Los Angeles as "fly-over" country when we are flying over it. It's inevitable. From 35,000 feet, the Earth begins to lend itself to concise descriptions. From a jet plane, the Earth is mostly blue and brown with white swirls. From the Moon it's a marble. From Mars it's a speck of light. From Pluto it's a celestial coordinate toward which to point a high-gain antenna.

Drones bring us back down to an altitude that the Wright brothers themselves whizzed past within a few short years of their famous Kitty Hawk flights. A few decades after their first flights, airplanes were flying thousands of feet above the ground, and the view from the airspace between the ground and 500 feet up was only seen briefly by people on their way up or down from cruising altitude. (During my father's experimentation with his aileron-less ultra-light airplane, he flew around in this proximate airspace quite a bit, but he had his hands full trying not to crash, and probably didn't have much opportunity to enjoy the visual experience.) Drones are now filling in a critical void in our aerial understanding of our world.

There are many practical benefits to this new aerial perspective. In short, drones, or UAVs as they are coming to be called, have significant potential to save money and lives. This is why the FAA has felt pressure to quickly develop regulations that will allow for the safe use of UAVs by civilians across a wide range of applications. Japan is leading the way with the use of UAVs for crop dusting, with thousands in use to spray rice fields. Every year in the U.S., a number of crop dusting pilots have been injured or killed in the line of duty, and thousands of farm workers are exposed to dangerous levels of agricultural chemicals. The use of UAVs will help mitigate both of these risks. The FAA approved the use of UAVs for agricultural spraying in the U.S. in 2015.

Another non-visual use of UAVs, demonstrated by companies like Amazon, will be for transporting and delivering parcels. With GPS guidance and the ongoing development of effective collision avoidance technology, it is likely that we will witness a dramatic increase in UAV traffic in the skies above our heads in the coming years. We will inevitably learn to co-exist with them and eventually to ignore them, once they are in abundance. When the Wrights first flew their airplane in public, thousands of people would gather to watch a single flight. Now, we hardly notice flying machines carrying hundreds of souls streaking across the sky every few minutes.

With few exceptions, the work of UAVs involves photographic imaging of some kind. In agriculture, the ability to see an entire field of crops from an aerial perspective can help a farmer optimize irrigation and chemical treatment plans. In the building trades, UAVs are fast becoming indispensable tools. Félix Nadar's first money-making idea for his wet-plate collodion balloon photographs had been to replace land-based surveying with aerial techniques. Now his predictions have come true, with UAV systems that can fly over large geographic areas, and then construct accurate three-dimensional digital models from the data collected.

Much of the current speculation about the future of UAVs is colored by their growing use as weapons of war. Unlike all previous generations of military aircraft, UAVs can be flown and used to dispense lethal firepower by pilots sitting in suburban office buildings thousands of miles away from the theatre of conflict. The ethical issues surrounding these new remote warfighting capabilities are the subject of much of our current discourse about war, and beyond the scope of this book. However, the most benign use of any kind of UAV is still often overshadowed by the work of military UAVs with frightening names like Predator and Reaper. Perhaps in time, as the technology advances and becomes more common, we will come to see civilian UAVs as essen-

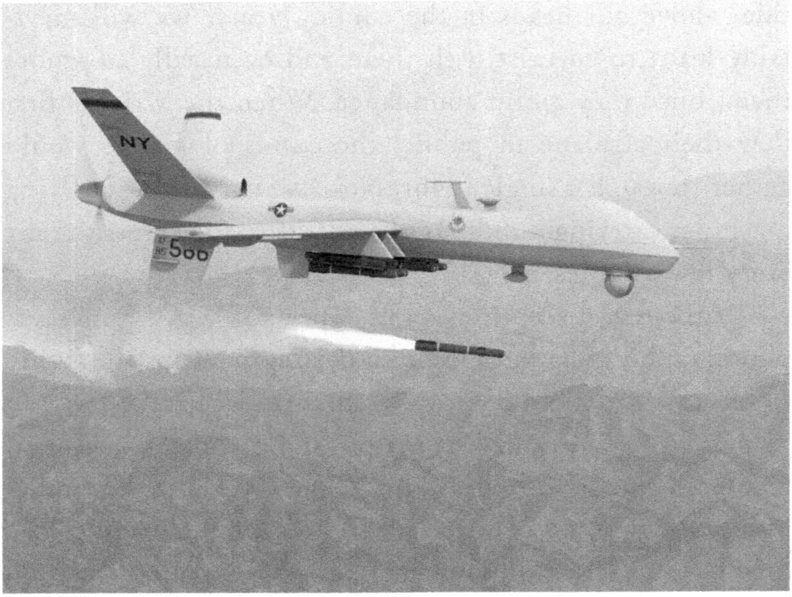

The Reaper military drone. The bulge at the front has the profile of a manned fighter plane canopy, but is opaque, allowing the drone to perform its deadly work without direct human witness of the resulting destruction.

tial tools of everyday life.

As I began preparing to teach my course in aerial photography, teams of space scientists and engineers were vastly extending the reach of our vision into the cosmos. On Nov. 12, 2014, the European Space Agency successfully landed a probe, named Philae, on the surface of Comet 67P/Churyumov-Gerasimenko, more than ten years after it had departed from Earth. The lander was part of a larger orbiting spacecraft called Rosetta. Both of these names refer to places in Egypt. A Mediterranean port city on the mouth of the Nile River, Rosetta (Rashid in Arabic) is where the famous Rosetta Stone was discovered in 1799. Philae was originally the southernmost island and temple complex in the Nile River in ancient Egypt. The word itself is from the ancient Greek meaning "the end."

On July 15, 2015, NASA's New Horizon spacecraft flew within 8,000 miles of the surface of the planet Pluto, taking a series of spectacular photographs of the planet and of its Moon, Charon. The photographs from Pluto and the surface of Comet Churyumov-Gerasimenko are similar to photographs from all the other terrestrial planets and Moons,

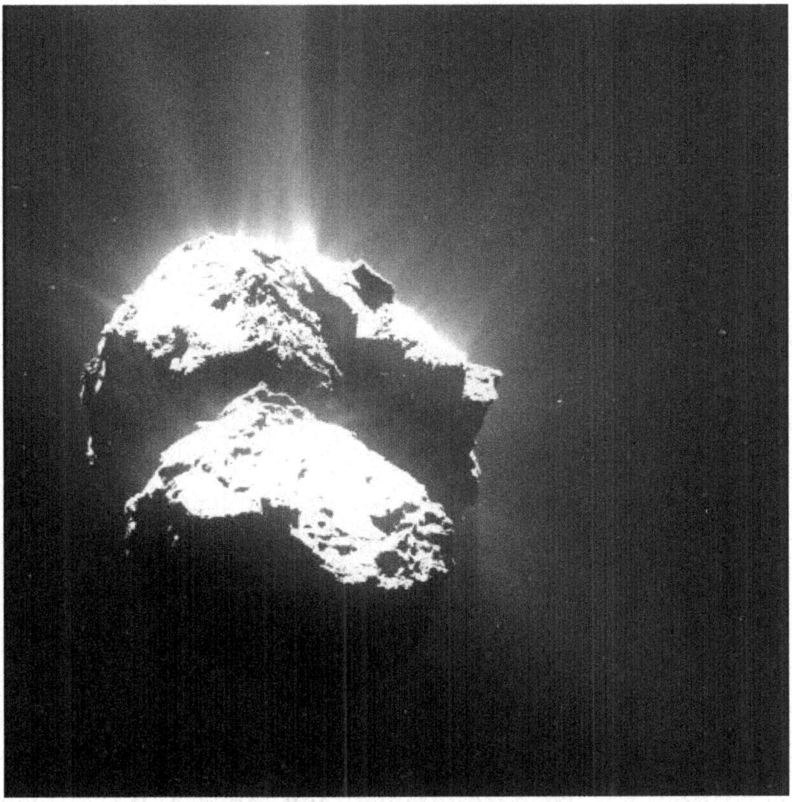

This image of Comet 67P/Churyumov–Gerasimenko was captured by Rosetta's OSIRIS narrow-angle camera on 26 July 2015 at 15:13 GMT from a distance of about 170 km.

which themselves appear similar to any random pictures one would take in the remotest deserts of the earth where no evidence of life is visible. Whether our aspirations for space probes are to unlock ancient mysteries, or reveal new horizons, thus far they have all taken us back to the same place: the cold, stony, lifeless void that existed before life began.

With the Pluto fly-by, we have reached the edge of our solar system and run out of planets to photograph and analyze up close. It has been a most amazing ride, but our long history of trying to understand ourselves better by stepping back and reframing the world from a higher perspective is coming to an end. Where else can we go? Unless NASA finds life "out there" soon, or can convince enough people that they would rather take a one-way death trip to Mars than a long weekend camping trip to the Mojave Desert (where scientists have been simulating the exploration of Mars), our willingness to continue funding the outbound voyage will also come to an end.

This places us at the threshold of a new age of exploration. If we understand that life is the only thing we truly care about, and that all of the known life in the cosmos exists within a few miles of the surface of our own planet, we can turn our full attention to the real work at hand, in our neighborhoods, workplaces, classrooms, and households. Now, and in the future, our greatest adventures will be the ones closest to home.

Like technology itself, the entire world of higher education has changed dramatically since I first began teaching more than three decades ago. Back then, knowledge resided either in people's heads, research labs, or books. The job of a teacher was to transfer a body of relevant knowledge to a classroom full of students who would sit quietly taking notes and occasionally asking questions for clarification of the material being presented. Professors had a uniform expectation of all students in any particular class. A single metric in the form of an examination was given to students to determine individual levels of comprehension, and grades were determined objectively. In disciplines like science, technology, engineering and math (the so-called STEM disciplines), this model still largely prevails.

An aerospace company vying for a contract to design and manufacture components for a new NASA interplanetary space probe endeavors to hire engineers capable of working with people who all possess a certain standard knowledge and vocabulary in engineering. So they seek new employees each year from an international pool of college graduates, and judge the relative quality of each person by grade-point-average. When I first came to Rochester, Eastman Kodak Company was considered one of the leading technology companies in the world, routinely hiring only the top engineering students from top ranked universities across America. Now companies like Google and Facebook enjoy their pick of each litter.

Teaching a required course in a discipline that prepares students for these types of jobs is relatively straight-forward. There is a well-defined curriculum and there are clear ways to measure student command of the material. Exams can be objective and uniform. One size fits all. The assumption that every student can be measured on the same objective scale is conventional wisdom. In recent years some accommodations have been made for students who have been identified with various kinds of learning disabilities, but in the engineering disciplines this has mostly taken the form of offering special tutoring and extending the time allotted for exams. Students with learning disabilities are still expected to master the same common body of material in any given course.

The aerial photography course I was designing was entirely different, at the opposite end of the spectrum from a required course in an engineering discipline. The course would be an upper level elective in an art school for students from a variety of disciplines. It would not be a pre-requisite for any subsequent courses, so I was free to design the curriculum without constraint. The course would be my first opportunity to share a lifetime of experience of aerial imagination and aerial photography with a group of students who had come voluntarily into my classroom.

In courses like this, students arrive on the first day from all points of the compass. The only thing they have in common is that they are all on the final stage of their ascent into orbit after having spent most of their lives in school, their formal education nearly complete. They are each following a unique trajectory, the result of their own particular years of experience. An elective course is an island where they all land temporarily to share a common experience before continuing on their separate voyages. This metaphor is complicated by the fact that students are typically enrolled in three or four other courses at the same time, so they only live on any one island part time.

When we design courses, the goal is to provide a set of common experiences for all students to share, but this goal is elusive. With an elective subject as specific as aerial photography, it is natural to assume a certain common level of interest, but each student brings a different set of eyes. For this first time offering the course, I set the enrollment limit at fourteen students. With my available budget, I purchased four complete multi-rotor drone/camera kits. I planned to teach the students how to operate the drones during the first month of the course, and then certify them to check out the drone kits from the school to complete their assignments. I required the students to work in pairs when they were flying the drones.

Of the fourteen students in the class, five (Lizz, Elisabeth, Megan, Nick, and Max) were from my program and had been in at least one previous class with me, so we had already worked together. Five of the students (Jace, Justin, Giles, Tori, and Zach) were from the Photographic Sciences bachelors program, and brought their strong technological interests to the class. Two students (Andrea and Sarah) were from the fine art photography program. Sandra was an advertising photography major, and Rob had just transferred into RIT from another college. With such a small class, students quickly begin to differentiate. Justin, Elisabeth, and Giles made it clear from the start that they were interested in learning about the technology. Everyone else seemed to be primarily interested in using the technology to make beautiful pictures. Only one of the fourteen students (Justin) had previous experience flying a drone or radio-controlled model airplane of any kind.

Students of this generation have grown up spending much of their playtime in virtual worlds, where there are no physical consequences to failure. So they approached the drones with a certain fearful respect. I reinforced this by showing them some videos of drones crashing, a rapidly proliferating genre on the Internet. To give them the opportunity for low-risk practice, I purchased some small, inexpensive quad-rotor drones with built-in video cameras that could be flown inside. The students took turns borrowing these practice drones for the first several weeks of class, bringing back entertaining videos captured by the drones mostly crashing into things inside their apartments.

Mastery of these small indoor drones is more difficult than the larger drones they would ultimately use for aerial photography—the indoor drones respond to the controls much quicker, and lack the stability provided by the GPS systems of the larger outdoor drones. I reasoned that if the students could learn to fly the small ones with confidence, they would have no problems flying the larger ones. I scheduled an indoor flying contest for the first week of March. The students would fly the small drones through an obstacle course we would set up in the classroom, competing for prizes. This would give them an incentive to practice and gain confidence with the controls.

Unfortunately, the winter was turning out to be one of the coldest on record, with temperatures during the first several weeks of the semester remaining in the single digits—much too cold to think about flying drones outside. I told the students we would be able to start flight training with the camera drones outside once the daily temperature reached about 25 degrees, still well below freezing, but tolerable. In about the third week of the semester we had a few days warm enough for an outdoor flight, and I was able to demonstrate the operation of one of the drones for the class. But then the temperature plummeted again, and the

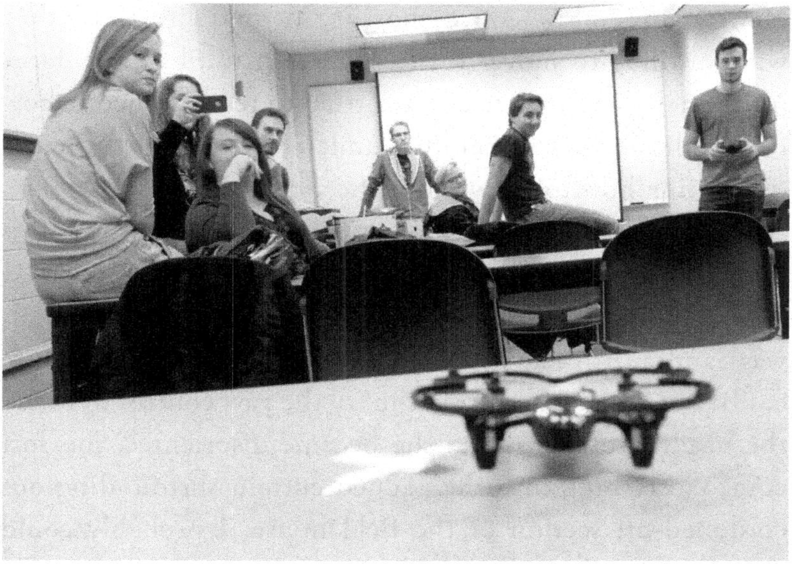

Students developed their flying skills with small multi-rotor drones, far more difficult to fly than the large ones they would use for photography.

forecast for the next couple of weeks looked bleak. The students were beginning to get impatient. One of them, Max, commented with dry humor, "You sure picked a good time to offer a course in aerial photography." Everyone laughed, including me.

With no relief from the bitter cold in the forecast, I made arrangements with the management of the campus field house to hold some indoor flight training sessions there to begin to give students some experience flying. Even though the space was adequate for the purpose, we would lose one huge advantage to flying the drones outside—within an enclosed space covered by a roof, there is no way to connect to the GPS satellites. Without GPS, the drones do not automatically hold their position when you take your hands off the controls. They behave more like familiar

Newtonian bodies—once moving in any direction, they will continue to move in that direction until the operator intervenes. Because I had never tried to teach someone how to fly a drone indoors before, I underestimated the difficulty of learning how to fly without the aid of GPS.

The first flight training session in the field house was on Monday, February 16. Four students (Jace, Zach, Max, and Sandra) signed up. The first student to try the controls was Sandra. At first, she was able to control the drone quite easily, but when I suggested she try the yaw control to rotate the heading of the drone she became disoriented and lost control, crashing into the padded curtain surrounding our cordoned-off section of the field house. I probably could have prevented the crash if I had aggressively taken the controls out of her hands. But I hesitated just long enough

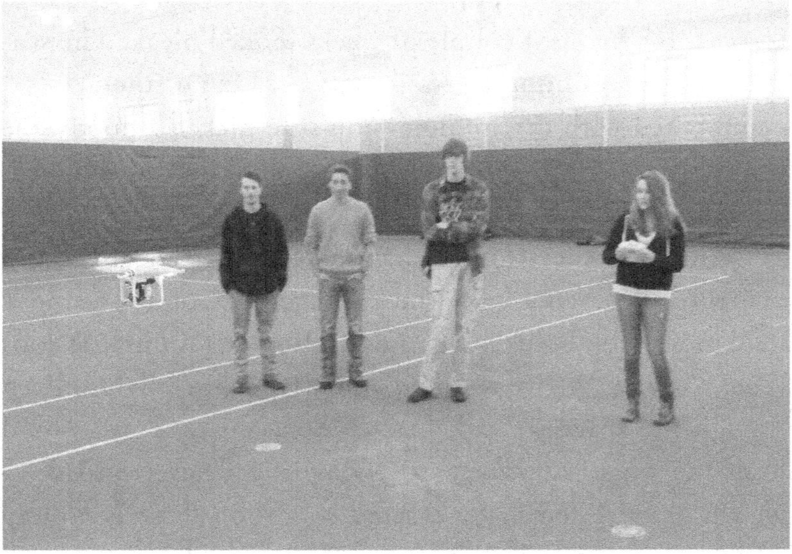

The first group of students to try flying the drones indoors included Jace, Zach, Max and Sandra. Sandra lost control of the drone shortly after this photograph was taken and crashed.

to fail to avert the accident. The drone suffered some minor damage, and we were all shaken a bit. Max declared, with a tone of finality that seemed to leave no room for argument, "I'm not going to be able to learn how to fly that thing."

I assured him and the other students that flying outside would be much easier, that the primary cause of the accident was my own inexperience in teaching, and that I would not let it happen again.

Still the weather report remained bleak, with no foreseeable break in the frigid temperatures. So with great caution I continued offering the indoor training sessions that week in the field house, and with what we had learned from the first failed session, the students began to gain experience flying the drones. The following week was the fifth week of the semester, and the forecast was worsening. The temperatures the previous weekend had dipped below zero, and there was no relief in sight. On the morning of Tuesday, February 24, 2015, I had to cover my face from the bitter cold as I walked from the parking lot into work. I felt the first stirrings of despair at the hands of the relentless winter.

When I got to my office, I was met by Rodney Lezette, an investigator from RIT Public Safety. He informed me that one of my students, Max, had gone missing on Sunday, February 22. He had been last seen that evening at the Charlotte Pier on Lake Ontario, walking away from his parked car toward the frozen lake. Someone had called 911. Mr. Lezette asked to accompany me to class, to see if Max would show up. I told him that Max had never missed a class during this semester, or the previous semester. When Max did not show up for class, and after Mr. Lezette asked the students to report to Public Safety if they had any information about Max, I was filled with dread. As I looked into the eyes of each student, I saw the same emotion.

Lake Ontario does not freeze over completely in the winter because, though it is the smallest of the Great Lakes in area, it is very deep. During the coldest months of the coldest winters, ice forms along the shore, sometimes reaching out into the lake for a few miles, but there is always open water beyond the ice. The only place to reach the water without walking far out onto the ice is at the mouth of the Genesee River, bordered on one side by the Charlotte Pier.

Max had spent summers at a family cottage near the Charlotte Pier, and he enjoyed going to the Pier to walk out into the midst of the water, so there was some early speculation by the police that he may have fallen into the Lake by accident. But the fact that he had left his wallet and phone at home, and driven himself alone to the Lake on a frigid Sunday night argued against such an accident.

Now formerly hidden clues to the impeding tragedy began to fall into place before my eyes. The college years can be a time of great stress in a family. A child grows from infancy to the threshold of adulthood under watchful eyes and above a safety net of support during the years of preparation. Parents guide their children in their ascent from Earth toward the moment of staging where they will drop away like a spent booster rocket and trust others to finish the job of accelerating them into a sustainable orbit. The years of college can feel for parents like a communications blackout with a spacecraft circling around the back side of the Moon. When a faint voice comes crackling through the static after long periods of silence, the sense of relief can be overwhelming.

These blackout years can be trying in the best of cases, where the child has soared through the early years of school with success, and embraces the college experience enthusiastically. But they are especially difficult for the parents of students who have struggled to get a footing in school and in life. In many ways the far side of the Moon is also the dark side for those of us entrusted with their care. The only indication I ever receive about a student who has suffered from a learning disability is a notification at the start of the semester that the student needs some special accommodation such as untimed exams or extra help outside of class. The notification says nothing about the nature of the disability or the pain it has caused. So there is no way to avoid inflicting more pain, if certain requirements of a course are the cause.

Even among students who have not been identified with disabilities, there are great differences in learning modes. At the start of every class in recent years, I've done a quick survey to get a sense of the diversity of the students who will be with me for the semester. One question I ask is simple: Do you enjoy reading? The truth is that a significant percentage of my students admit they do not read, and that reading is something they find difficult and unpleasant. In a literature course, this would be a major impediment to learning. But the visual arts attract a broader range of students with different aptitudes and preferred ways of learning. Some read with the ease of literature students, and others do not. Some think clearly in mathematical terms, and others decide long before they reach college that math is not something they can do. Over the years I have learned to build in optional approaches to learning to accommodate this diversity.

One of the objectives of the new aerial photography course was to provide an historical survey of aerial seeing and image-making. I chose two books to assign as texts, knowing that some of the students would have a harder time with them than others. One was a classic illustrated history by Beaumont Newhall entitled *Airborne Camera*. The other was a more recent book by Denis Cosgrove and William L. Fox entitled *Photography and Flight*. I placed both books on reserve in the library and informed the students that the second book was also available as an e-book accessible through the library website. Since the grade for the course would be based entirely on aerial photographic work, the purpose of the readings was to give the students background for classroom discussions and historical context for the presentation of their work at the end of the semester. There would be no closed book quizzes or exams, so the reading was supplementary to the assigned work.

During the first few weeks of class, when the weather was too cold to contemplate any kind of outdoor flying, I gave a series of lectures about the history of aerial photography, covering the important content from both texts. Because both books were on reserve in the library and I covered the important history in class, I did not expect any of the students to buy their own copies of the books. So I was surprised after the semester ended to receive a package in the mail from Max's mother containing copies of both books that Max had purchased. This would be one of many things I would learn about Max from his family over the next several months.

From the time Max went missing on February 22, nearly

two months passed before his body was discovered floating in the lake by a fisherman. The police had called off the search after the first week, and his family members had returned to their home in Connecticut with the presumption that he had drowned, but with no definitive proof. They held a memorial service for him at Congregation B'nai Israel in Bridgeport, where his father, Ivan, delivered a eulogy for his son. Nine hundred people attended the service, and many asked afterwards for copies of the eulogy. In response to these requests Max's father published the text on the Internet. Max's family also sent me a DVD recording of the memorial service. From his father's eulogy I learned many things about Max that I wish I had known when he was alive.

Max's father said,

> Max always marched to his own beat. As a toddler, he didn't like loud noises, new foods or itchy tags. He was on his own planet and happy to be there. By age two, though, we realized he was different in ways that were stunting him and we intervened with every available resource: Special pre-school, speech therapy, OT, PT, psychologists, specialists—we spent the GNP of several small countries having him tested, all to find out he is "somewhere on the learning disorder spectrum."
>
> ... Max was a rule follower, rarely varying from routine. He loved structure. He did well when told what to do. That may be due to birth order, or it may just have been his personality. He feared getting into trouble. He feared a lot of things. If something proved difficult, he got anxious. Rather than work harder, he tended to shut down. But when Max decided to do something—once he

> moved past the anxiety—he did it very well. We regularly reminded him that once he faced up to the fact that he had no choice about becoming a bar mitzvah, he aced his Torah portion. Once we told him he had no choice about getting his driver's license, he passed the test. And if you ever drove behind him, you know he drove the speed limit.

In a previous course Max had taken with me, I had witnessed both his impulse to shut down when he became anxious as well as his ability to rally and triumph once he determined to move past his anxiety. Helping students like Max overcome their anxieties and resist the temptation to shut down is one of the most important missions of teaching. Because Max had ultimately conquered his fear and triumphed in the earlier class, I was not alarmed when Max declared he did not think he would be able to learn how to fly the drones. I should have been. I reassured him that it was not as difficult as he imagined, and that I was confident he would succeed as he had before. I was wrong. I wish I could go back to that moment and change the way I responded to Max's declaration. I can't.

A motto for all college teaching could be borrowed directly from the Latin of the British Royal Air Force, *Per ardua ad astra*, Through struggle to the stars. This is the promise we make to our students and their families. But we are also aware that with thousands of young people reaching for the stars, there will be casualties along the way. So all universities offer a range of services for students who have trouble during their ascent. We have counseling centers and armies of specialists whose job it is to help students find their way back to their proper ascendant trajectory.

When I began teaching, still on my own upward ascent, it was easy to sign onto the mission with great single-mindedness. But age and decades of experience have revealed other, more important, aspects of the mission.

If we are fortunate to live long enough, the place we will ultimately discover at the farthest reaches of our outbound adventure will suddenly shed all of its exotic newness to reveal itself to be exactly the same place our journey began. This happened to me several times before I began to lose interest in continuing the outbound journey. It happened at the end of a hike up China's Great Wall when, during a moment of repose, the interpreter looked at me with sad eyes and told me she wished she didn't have to work so many hours so she could see more of her young daughter. It happened again in a restaurant in Red Square when the young balalaika player dressed head to toe in shining gold and playing serenely at the end of our table yawned and glanced at her watch. It happened every time I saw a child doing something that reminded me of my own child doing the same thing. I'm sure it's what I would have felt had I been Alan Shepard after hitting golf balls on the Moon, or Dorothy at the end of *The Wizard of Oz*. Time to go home.

This recalls the dialog between the goddess Kalypso and Odysseus at the point where Odysseus has decided that he must leave Kalypso's island paradise and return home. Kalypso begins the dialog.

> "Son of Laërtês, versatile Odysseus,
> after these years with me, you still desire
> your old home? Even so, I wish you well.

If you could see it all, before you go—
All the adversity you face at sea—
you would stay here, and guard this house, and be
immortal—though you wanted her forever,
that bride for whom you pine each day.
Can I be less desirable than she is?
Less interesting? Less beautiful? Can mortals
compare with goddesses in grace and form?"

To this the strategist Odysseus answered:

"My lady goddess, here is no cause for anger.
My quiet Penélopê—how well I know—
would seem a shade before your majesty,
death and old age being unknown to you,
while she must die. Yet, it is true, each day
I long for home, long for the sight of home.
If any god has marked me out again
for shipwreck, my tough heart can undergo it.
What hardship have I not long since endured
at sea, in battle! Let the trial come."
(*Odyssey*, Book 5, lines 212–233)

At this moment Odysseus abandons one idea of progress, replacing it with another. The first is rooted in our desire to escape our human destiny and shed our mortal bodies once and for all. It drives us in the direction of what some contemporary Platonists have called the "singularity," where our minds will finally be liberated from their material dependence on our bodies, and we will live forever in the circuitry of evolving computer systems. It drives us in the direction of signing up for one-way tickets to Mars. Ultimately it may drive us in the direction of giving up our struggle, allowing ourselves to fall.

Odysseus chooses a different path, leading back to his mortal existence in the embrace of family and home, there to establish his own form of progress. Thus Odysseus finds himself at the threshold of a new future, and a different pathway to progress. Instead of going farther and farther from home seeking adventure in the exotic unknown, he will find his adventure slowly welcoming the rest of the world to join his household, one traveling stranger at a time.

Although teachers spend most of their energy helping students prepare for the outbound journey, I've realized that it's also very important to drop markers for them as they head into life's labyrinths, so they will eventually be able to find their way back out. These markers may only become meaningful later in life; they largely go unnoticed by the students at the time they are offered.

The markers sometimes take the form of stories about times in my own life when I reached a limit of my capabilities or interests, or faced defeat or failure, and had to change direction or retreat from an intended mission. I've often told students that quitting can be a good thing, opening new doorways while closing others. More often the markers are in the form of photographs from the family album which I have appropriated as illustrations in lectures and books throughout my years of teaching, allowing me to include an ongoing family narrative as a side story in almost all of my classes. For several years I recruited a portrait of my grandfather Odysseus to illustrate some basic principles about photographic reproduction that were relevant to a technical course I was teaching. Other members of my extended family have played similar roles. When my son Gus was six or seven years old, he enjoyed such celebrity in one of my

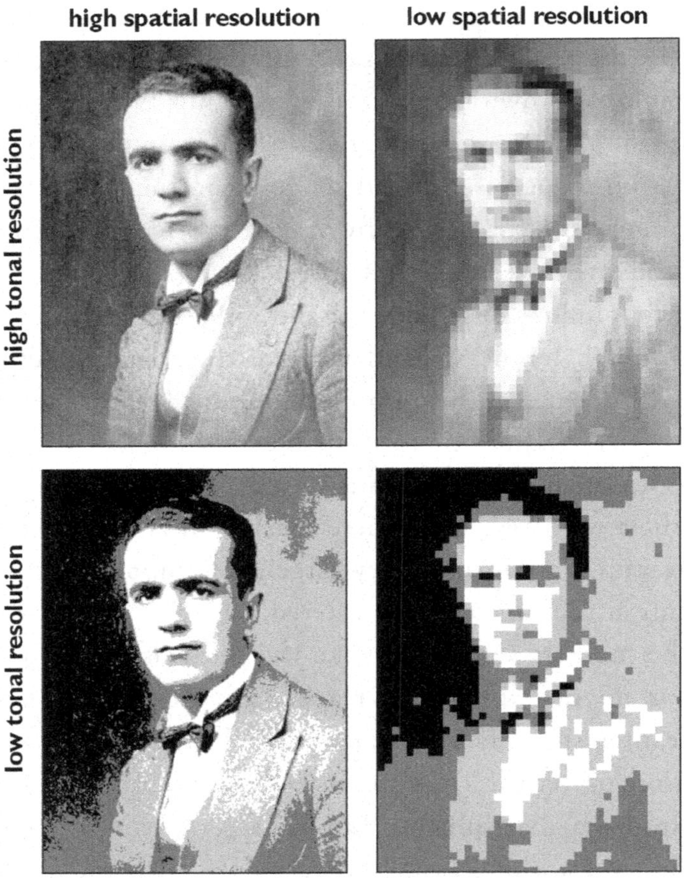

My grandfather James (Odysseus) appeared in this illustration of a basic photographic concept I used for several years. Often students would come up after the lecture in which this illustration appeared, and ask whether the person depicted was related to me. I would tell them that he was my grandfather, that he had died many years before I was born, and that it made me happy to know my students saw a resemblance.

classes that for years afterward, former students would ask, "How's Gus doing?"

To have a chance for these things to work, the student must survive the college years, and Max did not. But I cannot stop wanting to reach out to Max, and he, in turn, continues to speak to me.

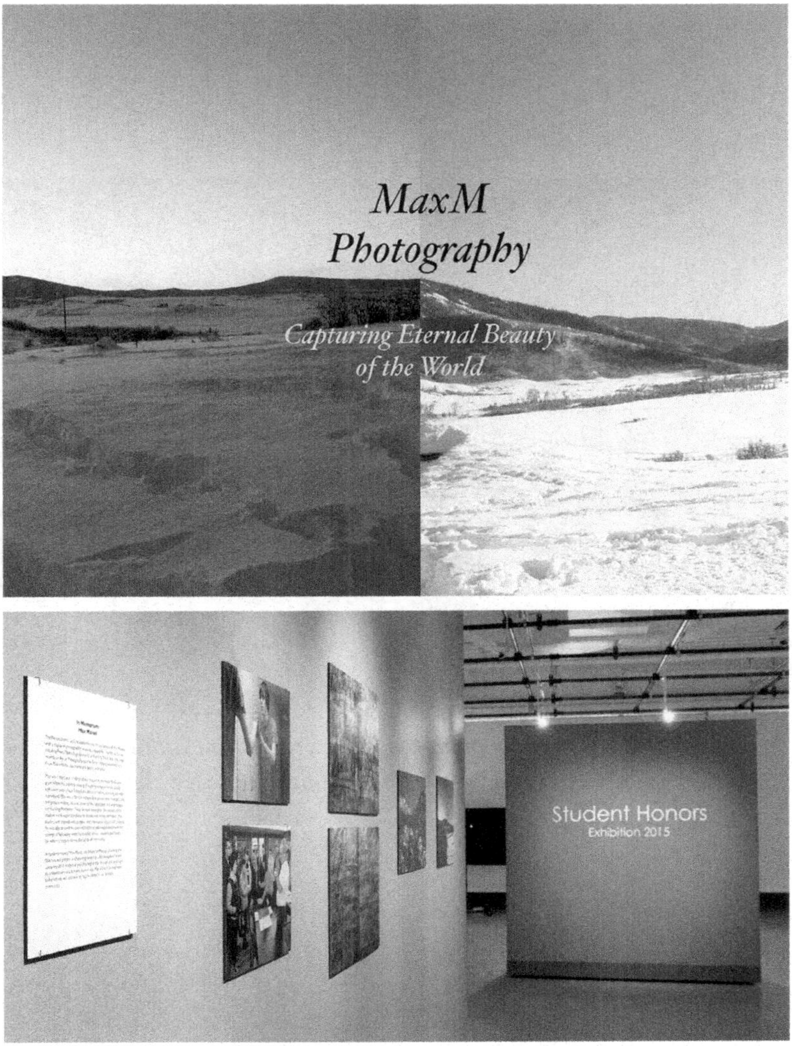

Max was memorialized with a display of his work at the entrance to the 2015 School of Photographic Arts & Sciences Student Honors Show. Above is a poster Max created for an earlier class with me.

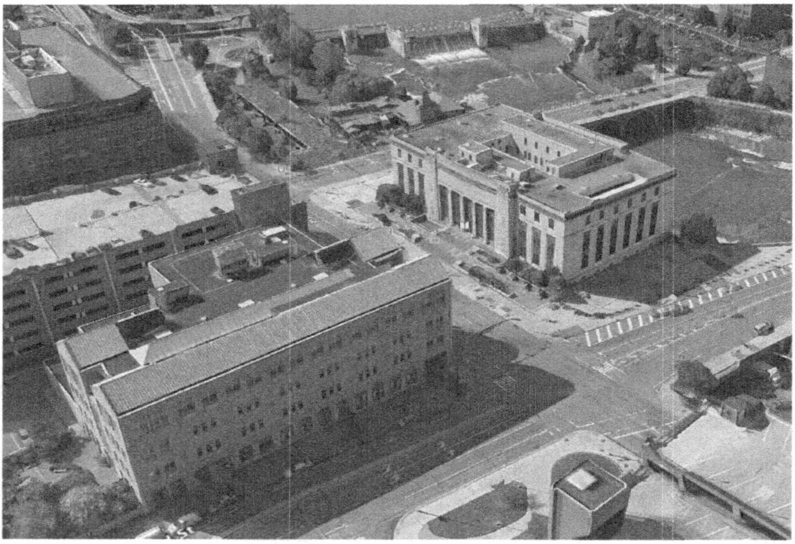

Max had intended to photograph the Rochester Central Library, and showed this Google Earth projection of the building to the class.

16

After Max's disappearance, the aerial photography class continued to meet every Tuesday and Thursday morning at 9:30 a.m. for the remainder of the semester. Max would never know how profoundly his absence would be felt.

One of the assigned projects was to research a possible subject for a series of aerial photographs in the Rochester region. I showed the students how to use Google Earth to explore possible vantage points for their photographs before investing the time and taking the necessary risks to fly the drones. Max had shown the class some views of his proposed subject, the Rochester Central Library. The week after Max went missing, one of his fellow students, Rob, asked me whether it would be OK to change his plans and do Max's project instead, as a way of honoring his memory.

The first formal assignment in the course had been to produce a stereo aerial view of some part of the RIT campus. This assignment grew out of the experiment we had made the first day we were able to fly the drone outside, on February 12. By moving the drone laterally while snapping still images, it is possible to obtain two images that, when viewed through a stereoscope, produce the illusion of 3D. After our experiment I made a sample stereo print from our first set of images and brought it to class with a special viewer. I mounted the print on the wall and invited the students to look through the viewer. Everyone was excited to see the stereo effect. However, Max had not been able to see it when he tried. He abruptly declared it would not be possible for him to see it, and gave up.

Two months later, the day after Max's body had been identified by the police, William Destler, the president of RIT, visited our class to give a short demonstration of his own new drone. When I offered to let him look through the stereo viewer at our test prints, he told us he had never been able to see stereo because he lacked depth perception. He humored me by trying, but then declared, much as Max had, that he would not be successful. We learned that a small percentage of people, despite having good vision in both eyes, are simply incapable of seeing stereo. Max and the president of our university shared this disability. I wish Max had known that.

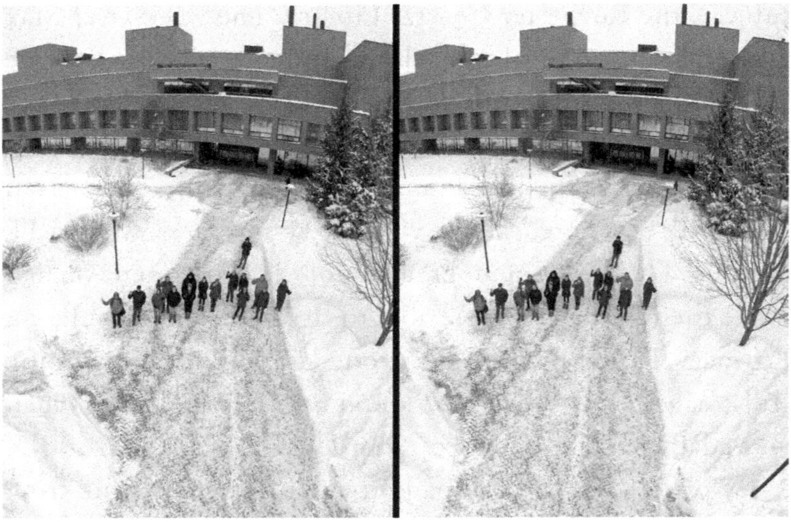

A stereo image pair of our class standing in the quad outside our building. The two images were made sequentially as the drone moved from left to right.

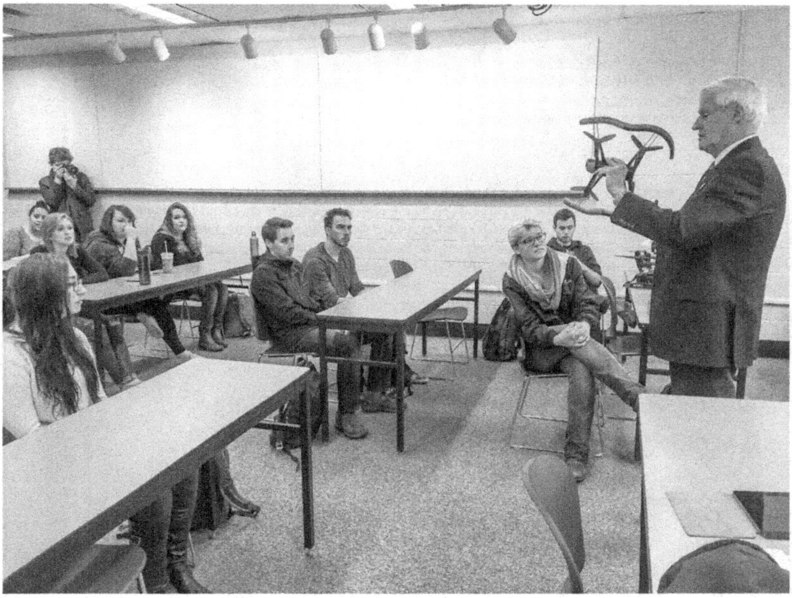

On April 21, the day after Max's body was identified, RIT President Bill Destler came to our class to demonstrate his newest drone. I had asked him a few weeks before whether I could borrow it to show the students, and, to my surprise and delight, he had offered to come and talk to the students himself. Because President Destler did not know that Max had been a member of our class, we waited until after he departed before observing a moment of silence in Max's remembrance.

In his eulogy Max's father had said, "Max had a wonderfully dry sense of humor," something I witnessed many times in class as Max delivered his perfectly-timed comments whenever things did not go as I had planned. I wish Max could have lived to see the comedy of errors that happened to our class not long after his death. On April 16, I received a note from Kelly Redder, of RIT Development and Alumni Relations, asking whether I would be willing to do some aerial photography of a newly-acquired "alumni house" on the west side of campus. Kelly wanted to start

From: Kelly Redder <karrar@rit.edu>
Date: Thursday, April 16, 2015 at 10:13 AM
To: Frank Cost <ficppr@rit.edu>
Subject: Drones and the Alumni House

Hi Frank -

Thank you so much for being interested in the Alumni House and some drone activity. I saw what you've been doing and thought it might be a nice mix. Would you be interested in coming to check out the House before renovations (which will occur somewhere over the next year), so you can get a sense of what we'll be thinking about? You're the expert, so any recommendations you have would be most helpful. I can give you a tour of the interior as is and we can walk the grounds and see what you think.

Is your Outlook updated? Is that the best way to get on your calendar, or do you have preference for time/date?
Thank you so much! Kell

Kelly Redder
Assistant Vice President, *RIT for Life* and Director of the RIT Alumni House
Development and Alumni Relations
P 585.475.7412 C585.261.4351 F 585.261.5308

R·I·T **Rochester Institute of Technology**
116 Lomb Memorial Drive, USC 03401/Rochester, NY 14623

Give every year—make an impact every day. See how.

Connect with us:

CONFIDENTIALITY NOTE: The information transmitted, including attachments, is intended only for the person(s) or entity to which it is addressed and may contain confidential and/or privileged material. Any review, retransmission, dissemination or other use of, or taking of any action in reliance upon this information by persons or entities other than the intended recipient is prohibited. If you received this in error, please contact the sender and destroy any copies of this information.

R·I·T Rochester Institute of Technology Directories RIT Home RIT Search

To: RIT faculty, staff and students

From: Dr. Sandra Johnson, Dr. Jeremy Haefner, Dr. James Watters

Date: May 27, 2015

Subject: Unmanned Aircraft Systems (a.k.a drones)

The local inspector of the Federal Aviation Administration and the Director of Aviation at the Greater Rochester International Airport have informed the administration of RIT that flying any Unmanned Aircraft Systems (UAS) outdoors, regardless of the UAS's size or weight, at any elevation on campus is prohibited. This prohibition applies to all faculty, staff and students.

Your assistance is appreciated as always.

documenting the transformation of the house into a new alumni center for the campus with a series of aerial photographs and videos that she could use for fund-raising. I agreed to do the work, and Kelly sent out a notification to Campus Public Safety to alert them to the fact that a camera drone might start flying in the vicinity of the alumni house. Kelly's memo opened up Pandora's Box.

Little did we know at the time that officials from the FAA had visited RIT the previous November, and at that time had announced they were imposing a ban on all drone flying activities on the campus, since the entire campus falls within a five-mile radius of the Rochester International Airport. Notification of this ban had not yet been disseminated to the wider campus community. Had they sent out a campus-wide memo, I would not have been able to offer the aerial photography class at all, and no one would have had to learn how to fly a drone.

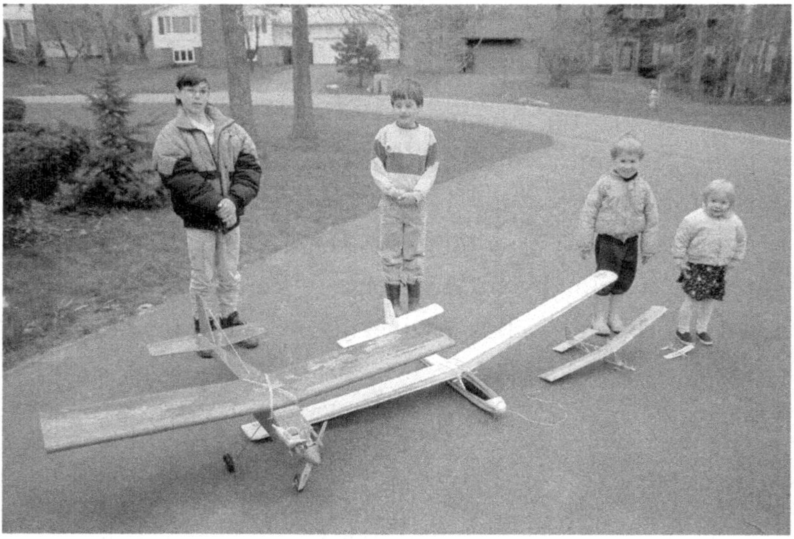

David Marmarosh, an older kid from down the street, gravitated toward our family when he wanted to learn how to build and fly remote-controlled model airplanes. Here he joined Roger, Gus and Elaine Cost on our driveway to pose with their models.

17

On many occasions during the years my children were on the steepest parts of their rocket ascents to the stars, I wished I could capture some of their spilled energy and store it for a later time, when gravity would begin to assert its authority and their trajectories would begin to arc back toward Earth. I knew, as all people eventually know, that the transition from childhood to adulthood would bring great challenges, and that a stored reserve of power might be helpful during some future crisis of confidence. But spilled energy is a libation we are obliged to make when we are raising children. There is no way to capture it, so it has to be enjoyed while it is being poured out onto the ground, or lost.

During those years, model aviation and the pursuit of the vicarious experience of flight was my primary teaching laboratory. It was far easier to let a fragile balsa wood model teach its non-verbal lessons about the true nature of reality than to try to explain it in parental language that would almost always fall on deaf or highly resistant ears. Each crashed airplane, with its accompanying outburst of tearful anger, felt like a vaccination against potential future spiritual disappointments. It was especially heartening to see one of the kids explaining to another some limitation of reality based on a shared failure.

This old-fashioned analog approach to teaching works well in the material realm of life governed by gravity and

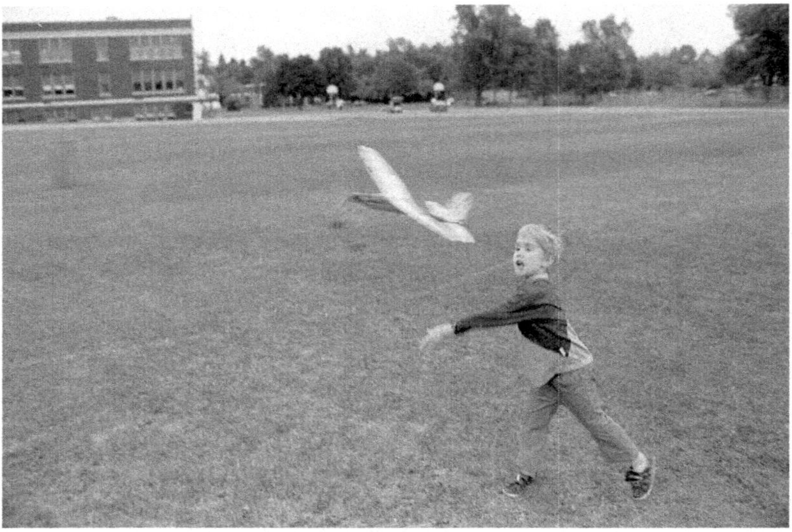

Gus launches a rubber-powered model.

other fundamental realities of nature. But ever more fantastic virtual worlds beckon, promising complete escape from natural forces. Once a person is lured through a portal into one of these alternative universes, all the lessons that broken model airplanes can teach are rendered as annoying as the voice of one's father saying, "Be careful not to fly too close to the Sun."

When my own children went wandering through those portals to explore worlds where gravity could be ignored, where anything could happen, and where death could be erased with a reset button, I knew it was impossible to go chasing after them into the labyrinth. On the few occasions I tried, I found myself transformed into a helpless creature without a sense of how to navigate in the new world. I could only wait outside, hoping they would at some point catch a glimpse of something infinitely more splendid than all the pixels in the universe could simulate, and try to find their way back through the door.

But this is the hope of a person who does not understand the terrible pain that reality inflicts upon some individuals, and their need for escape. It's a hope rooted in a naïve belief that it is possible for something to have universal appeal. It's a hope that makes it possible to write a book, to present an idea to an unknown audience, to design a new course and then try to teach it. The belief is naïve because there is so much evidence to the contrary. For several years I kept a pair of course evaluations from a required course I had taught tacked to my bulletin board above my desk. In the comments box, one student's evaluation read, "This was the best course I ever had. I loved it. Thank you!" On the other evaluation, the student had written, "This course sucked!" These were their realities.

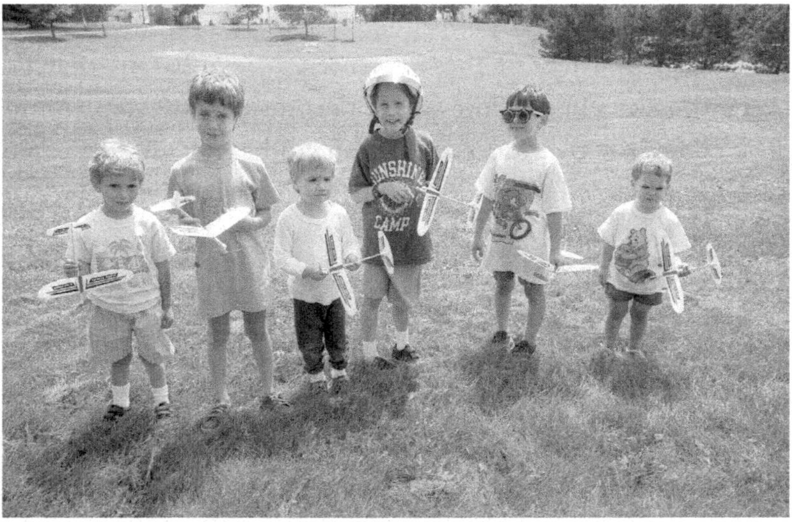

Roger (in the helmet) started a model airplane club, intending to teach his friends about the principles of aerodynamics.

In my role as Daedalus at the start of the aerial photography course, I had instructed my students to never fly the drones alone, and to always refrain from flying them over water. Every student complied with this request except for one. Zach was a quiet student who always had a smile on his face. He politely accepted every assignment without objection, and never petitioned for exemptions from the rules. Yet Zach had desires to make images that could only be made if he disregarded my rules completely.

One morning in April, before first light, Zach drove by himself with one of the drones to Chimney Bluffs on the shore of Lake Ontario, about an hour east of Rochester, and waited for the Sun to appear in the Eastern sky. The bluffs are at the intersection of one of the large glacial hills and the Lake. From the air it looks like the lakeshore slices through the middle of the hill, exposing the bluffs.

Standing on the edge of the cliff, Zach flew the drone out over the water to photograph the first sunlight striking the bluffs. In a few of these pictures, it is apparent that he is standing so close to the bluffs that one wrong step would have taken him over the edge. But he didn't fall, and he came back with some of the most beautiful and evocative images of the entire semester.

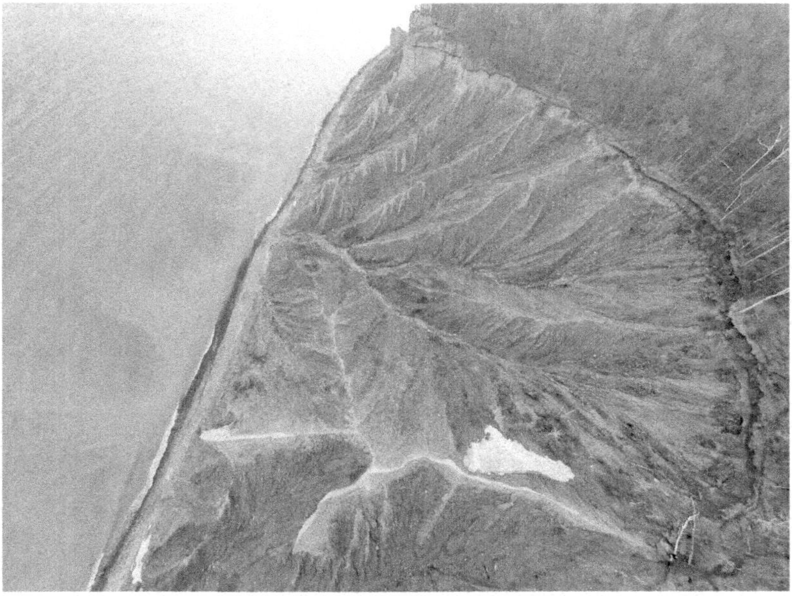

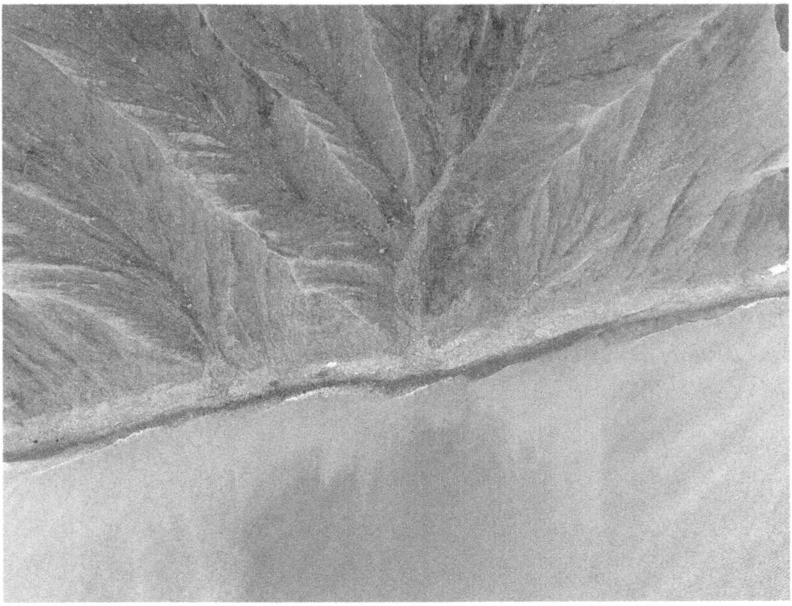

Chimney Bluffs on the southern shore of Lake Ontario, photographed from the air by Zach Pezzillo.

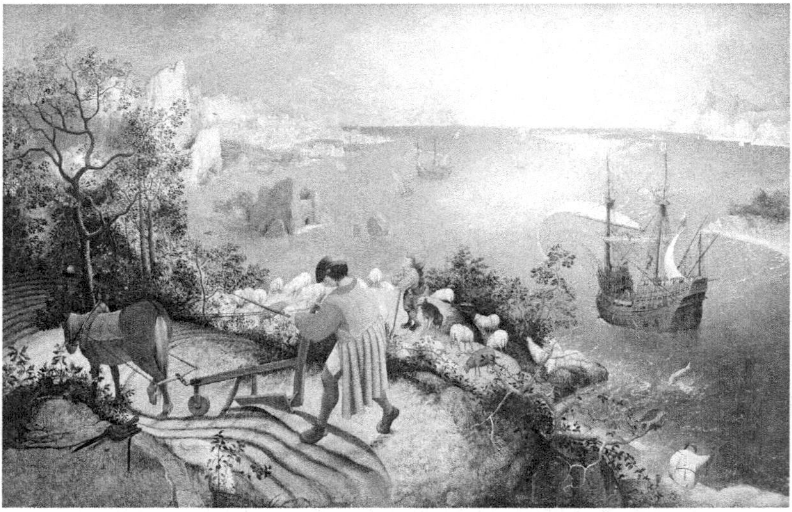

Landscape with the Fall of Icarus, long thought to be by Pieter Breugel, but possibly a copy of the original, which may have been lost. (Prado Museum)

18

Max's disappearance into the Lake brought back a rush of early childhood memories of the contemplation of my father's twin brother's drowning. I remembered replaying the scenario of a boat overturning on a lake and a person trying to swim to shore but not making it. I remembered details of my interactions with Max recurrently, almost obsessively at times, thinking, "if only..."

For the first week after his disappearance, we held out hope that Max would show up and tell us that he had just taken a break from school and gone off to hide somewhere. On several occasions during that week my heart skipped a beat when I saw someone at a distance who resembled Max. But eventually this hope dwindled and the long vigil for news of a found body began.

During that time Max was with me almost constantly, and regularly reminded me of others in my life who had tragically departed. Max sent me on a search through boxes of old family photographs for renewed information that would bring my father's lost twin brother closer. This quest served as a form of palliative in the absence of any information about Max's fate.

What I found were a dozen or so photographs of my drowned uncle, including a United States Navy identification card with his thumb print on the back. One of the photographs had a brief note to my grandmother in his handwriting. These few objects were all the physical evidence remaining of him, and they became precious as I awaited news about Max.

In searching for my uncle, I discovered a handful of studio portraits of a young woman I did not recognize, some alone and some with people who resembled teenage versions of my grandmother Dimitra and her older brother, George. When I asked my father about them, he said they depicted my grandmother's youngest sister, who had never emigrated from Europe, and had died as a young adult from influenza. He was not sure of her name. She had never been mentioned by anyone in the family. One of the photographs had a handwritten note in Greek on the back. A Greek-speaking friend helped me decode the writing. It was a note to my grandmother in the U.S. from her younger sister, Eleni. She had been my great aunt. She had lived her life in the neighborhood of ancient Troy. She had been beautiful. She, as my mother, had been named after Helen. And she would have been lost to all memory had I not gone looking for pictures of her nephew, my father's twin.

Max, my father's lost brother and my newly discovered aunt formed a company of friends in my mind. When I imagined one, I could see the others. One I knew personally and two indirectly through family connections.

What can these people, who departed this world so

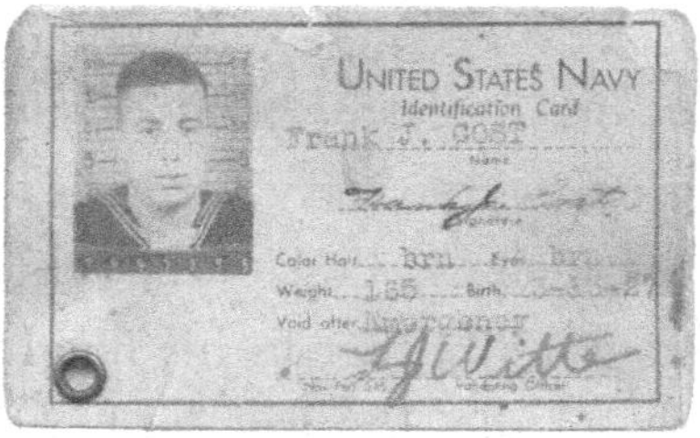

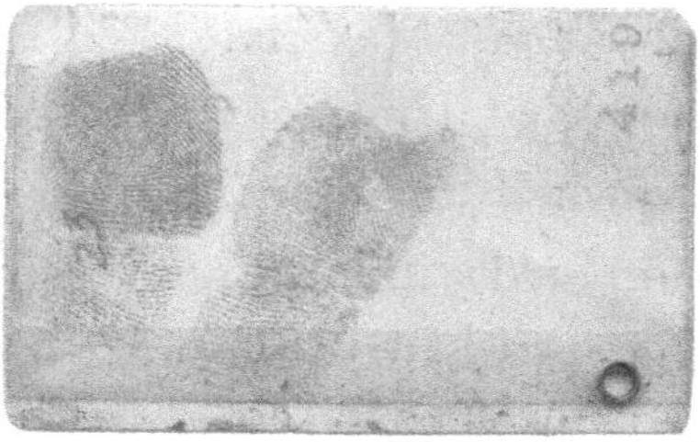

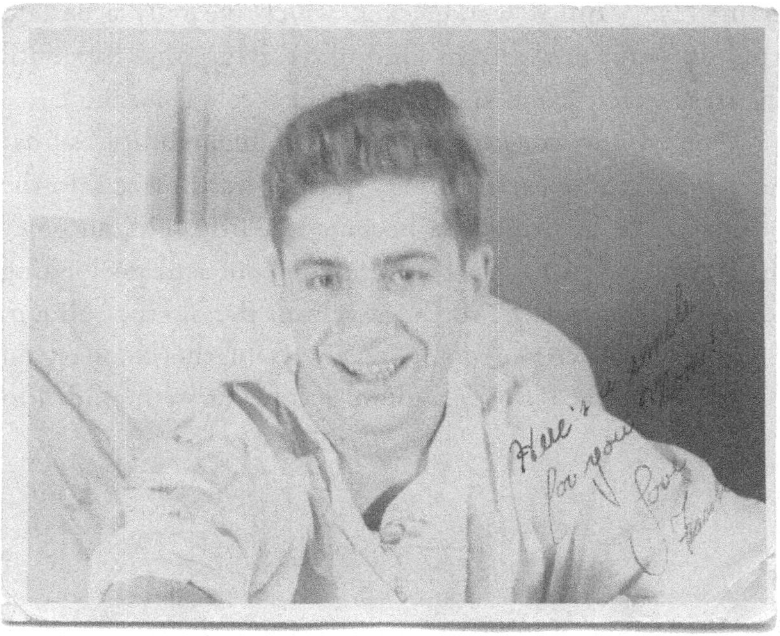

A photograph sent home by Frank while serving in the Navy. His brief note to his mother is the only sample of his handwriting that survives.

young, before they had a chance to see what their lives could become, teach from their places of repose beyond the curtain of mortality? How can they help open our eyes?

Our greatest asset as humans is our ability to adapt to changing situations, and improvise accordingly. Among all the known creatures of the universe, we do this better than any others. We do it so well that, however radical any change in the environment, we only require a short time to adjust and establish a "new normal." This makes it possible for humans to survive in almost any climate, under any kind of political regime, absorbing almost any imaginable gain, or sustaining almost any imaginable loss. It places us at the extreme end of the spectrum of life from such creatures as the extinct ivory-billed woodpecker, which ate only a certain kind of worm in a certain kind of decaying pine tree until the trees were cleared and the woodpecker was no more.

One of the consequences of our adaptability is that nearly everything extraordinary quickly transforms into the ordinary. The here and now becomes the prison of our boredom and restlessness and we are compelled to go looking for something new. Until the advent of the hot air balloon, this quest was confined to the points of the compass on the earth's surface. But regardless of how far we intended to

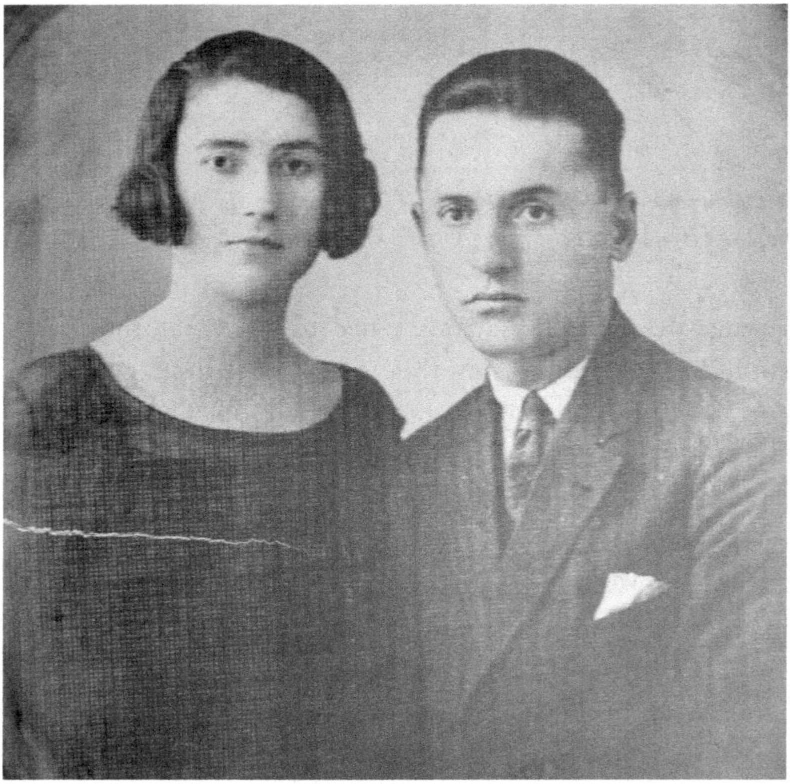

My grandmother's younger sister Eleni with her elder brother George some time in the early 1920s.

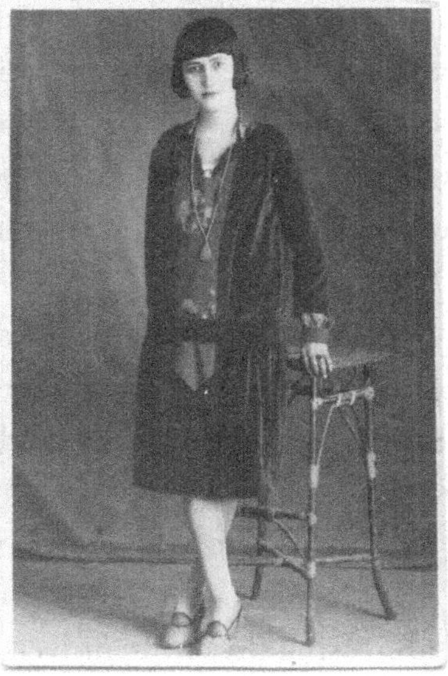

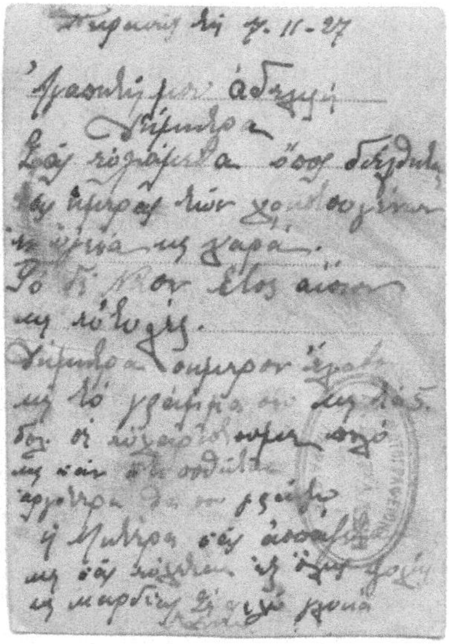

"My dear sister Dimitra, We wish you spend the Christmas days with health and joy. And may the New Year be auspicious and happy. Dimitra, today I received your letter with 5 dollars. We thank you very much and wish for you everything you desire. I will write to you later. Mother is kissing you and wishing for you from all her heart and soul. Kissing you sweetly." dated November 7, 1927.

wander in our search for novelty, the planet, being a sphere, eventually sent us back in the direction of wherever we started. Our flight up into the sky opened up a new frontier of experience that satisfied the craving for a while. Then space seemed to offer the possibility of a frontier that would never close. By pointing our rockets out into the heavens we thought we had found a permanent solution to our chronic wanderlust.

But space travel also quickly transforms the places we visit into the ordinary. Before the first rockets broke free of the atmosphere in the middle of the 20th century, our solar system held out promise of exotic possibilities of alien civilizations thriving in fantasy landscapes. Now that our cameras have visited all of the outer planets, we know that if life exists on any of them, it will be in the form of viruses or primitive organisms hiding underground or swimming in dark ice-covered oceans.

This does not dissuade those who are committed to a quest for a connection to the infinite through a never-ending crossing of space and time. But we could travel outward for thousands of years at our current pace and not get much beyond the nearest star. And what would we find there? Probably more of the same.

If, on the other hand, I imagine crossing the entire universe to the most distant and exotic galaxy, and upon arriving there happen to bump into a close friend, I am certain we would instantly recognize one another. And I am certain there could be no possibility of mistaken identity. This absolute uniqueness of the individual person in the face of the unfathomable immensity of the universe is the ultimate miracle.

But as with everything familiar and available, it is easy to look past the people who are always around. We can forget that each person is the unique result of an unbroken chain of existence that extends backward billions of years to the very beginning of life. So we need guidance.

It is in straining to see the faces and feel the bodily presence of those who have departed the world, some long before their time, that the realities they can no longer see become clear before my own eyes. I begin to see the faces and bodies of those who are alive and nearest at hand in their full splendor, and find in them the only material connection to the infinite and eternal that any of us can possibly have.

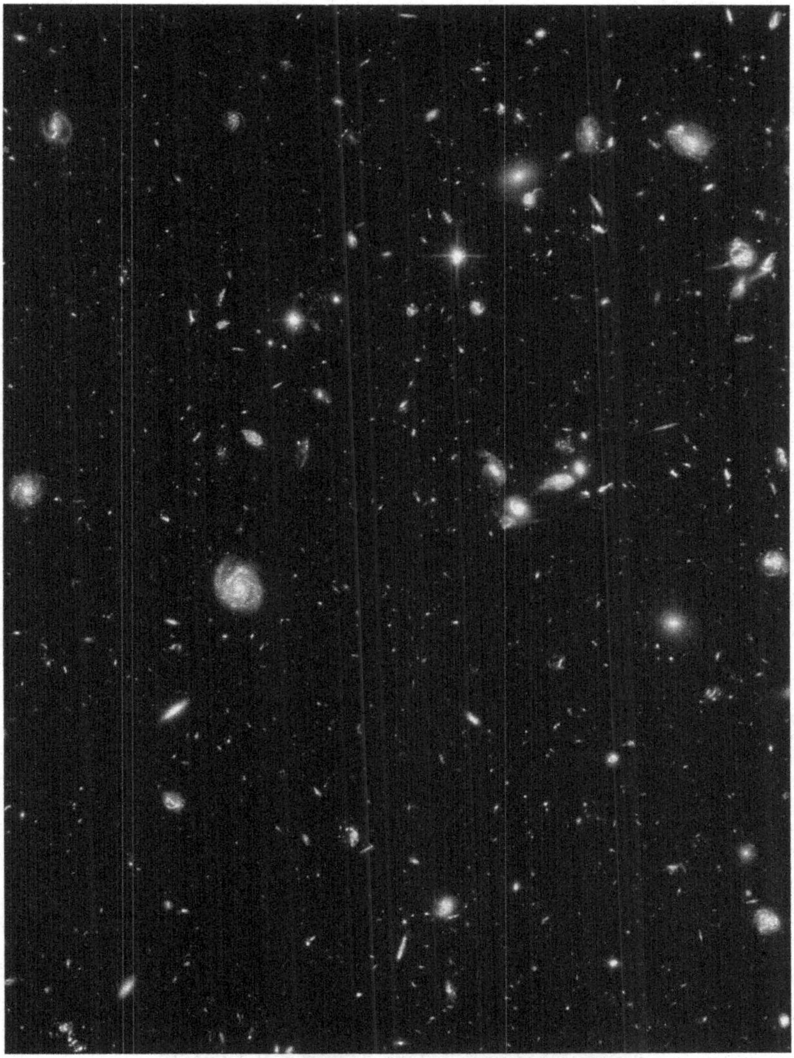

When astronomers pointed the Hubble Space Telescope at a tiny quadrant of deep space and made a series of long time-exposures, they were surprised to see thousands of new galaxies appear. The light from most of these galaxies was generated billions of years ago. According to NASA, "The image required 800 exposures taken over the course of 400 Hubble orbits around Earth. The total amount of exposure time was 11.3 days, taken between Sept. 24, 2003 and Jan. 16, 2004." (NASA)

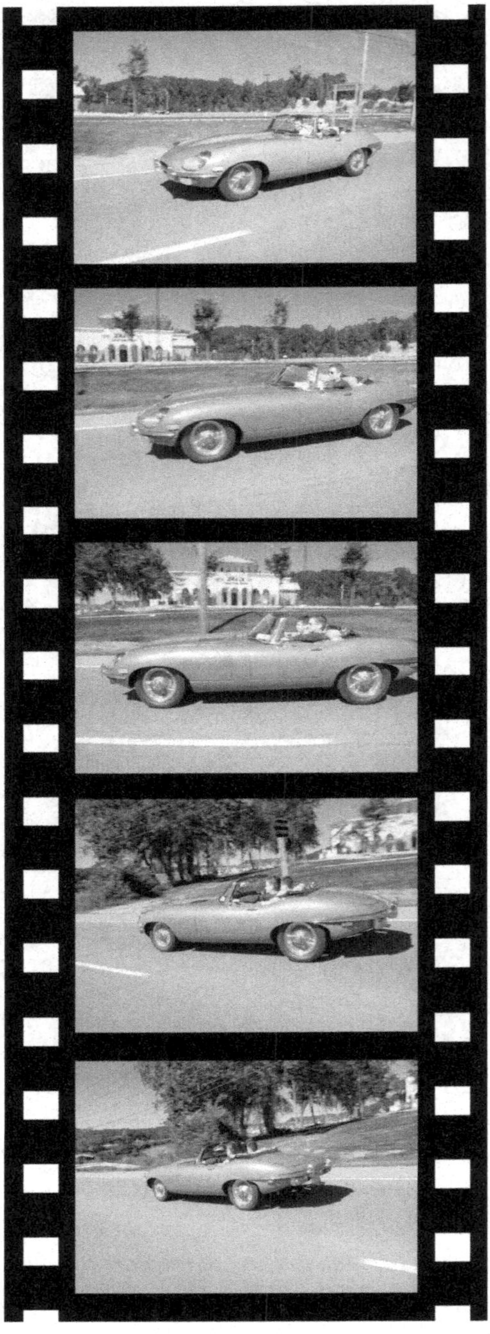

Epilogue – with gratitude for photographs

My brother Jim once purchased a 1969 E-type Jaguar sports car that had been rusting for more than thirty years in an open carport in Boston. He spent two years restoring it in his spare time. When he was nearly finished, he drove the car to an antique auto show in a nearby town to put it on display. Although the car was sparkling by comparison to what it had been, it was not flawless. The paint job was a bit lumpy and the chrome work still showed some traces of rust. He soon realized that most of the classic automobile fans attending the show were viewing his car through highly refined and critical eyes. When they looked at it they saw only where it deviated from their ideas of perfection. Several of them made it known in subtle ways that his work was not of the highest quality. In comparison to many of the other "perfect" specimens at the show, Jim realized that his car was a bit homely, and he was disappointed by the negative commentary.

Then a group of disabled adults from a local group home came walking up to his car. One of them was blind. The blind man became excited when informed by his attendant that he was standing in front of an E-type Jaguar. He told Jim this was his favorite car of all time, but that he had never actually "seen" a real one. He then asked whether he could touch it. The blind man's attendant pulled Jim aside and told him that none of the other car owners at the show would let him touch their possessions, and that it would be wonderful if he could touch this one. Jim responded, "He can get into the car and touch whatever he wants."

The blind man sat in the driver's seat and proceeded to run his fingers over every square millimeter of the interior of the car, all the while joyfully exclaiming that he couldn't believe he was sitting in a real Jaguar. One of his friends got into the passenger seat and the two pretended to be driving on a road trip together. The blind man then ran his fingers over the exterior of the car until he had touched the entire thing. When he was finished, the car was covered with his fingerprints.

Jim eventually sold the Jaguar after owning it for several years. He told me that his most cherished memory of the car is of the day he showed it to the blind man, the only person who had been able to fully appreciate it. Even Jim had not been able to see past his own idea of the perfect restoration to admire the car for what it was. The blind man liberated Jim's vision and allowed him to enjoy his own handiwork, if only for a while.

Photography too has the potential to liberate our vision, enabling us to appreciate direct experience and be utterly surprised by what we see. William Henry Fox Talbot, the English inventor of the negative-positive photographic process, described this liberation in his book *The Pencil of Nature:*

> It frequently happens, moreover—and this is one of the charms of photography—that the operator himself discovers on examination, perhaps long afterwards, that he has depicted many things he had no notion of at the time. Sometimes inscriptions and dates are found upon the buildings, or printed placards most irrelevant, are dis-

> covered upon their walls: sometimes a distant dial-plate is seen, and upon it—unconsciously recorded—the hour of the day at which the view was taken (Fox Talbot).

Fox Talbot was surprised by the unedited view of reality that came from the camera, and he and his contemporaries were thrilled by it. From the time of Fox Talbot to the present day, photography has provided us a way of seeing the world through the agency of what he called "nature's hand." But almost from the beginning we have been compelled to reintroduce the hand of the human creator into the process; to turn Fox Talbot's "pencil of nature" back into a pencil. We naturally want to say things about the world through photography. Yet unlike any previous pictorial medium, the world can also say things about itself to us through photographs. But if we are too distracted by our efforts to speak through the medium, it is easy to overlook some of the simplest, yet most important messages the world is trying to send back.

Each photograph captures a tiny reflection from a unique viewpoint of the vast and infinite world. By the time Fox Talbot had taken his first photographs, he already knew that no matter how many more would be taken from that time onward, no two would ever be the same. The absolute uniqueness of each photograph is a testament to the infinite splendor of the natural world. Photographs give evidence that each moment, witnessed from a variety of viewpoints, happens only once in the history of the world, and will never happen again. Photographs prove that if we miss a particular moment while it is unfolding, we can never recapture it. This gift of unique moments can become a burden if we become greedy, desiring to be in more than one place at a time or to live a life (or multiple lives) other than the one we are living. The ubiquity of photographs can lead to utter distraction if we think we ought to take in as much simultaneous reality as possible. This notion, reinforced by the ready availability of mediated experience everywhere we look, can drain us of the capacity to graciously receive the simple gift of a unique moment. To fully appreciate this gift requires turning off all other channels, overcoming the fear that we may miss something important if we do that.

Our expulsion from Paradise at the beginning of our mythical history must have happened when we were tricked into thinking that by seeing and knowing what we ourselves could not perceive with our own powers, we would ascend to ever higher planes of consciousness, reducing the gap between our mortal selves and the infinite with each upward movement. The proliferation of cameras and recorded views that are not our own seems to promise to take us eventually to the top of the highest mountain, and offer us intellectual dominion over all of nature. But this is a delusion.

As a child I was filled with anxiety for a past I wanted to change, and a future I could not possibly know. I spent much time wishing that my father's twin brother had not drowned, and that I would have been able to touch him and know him as I could touch and know the members of my family who were still alive. I worried about keeping myself out of danger so that I wouldn't risk losing my own life. I believed that such a loss would be something my father could not endure, and I wanted to protect him from such a terrible thing. Thus I became cautious about my physical existence, suppressing the desire to seek thrills or take bodily risks. While I watched others take to the sky pursuing the thrill of flight, I sought a different kind of adventure, fervently studying everything within my field of vision and trying to describe what I saw, first in words and then in pictures.

The arc of that adventure, from my first childhood contemplation of the Dürer woodcut of Icarus falling into the sea, to this moment of writing this sentence in this book, becomes ever clearer. The first part of the journey was a quest to see more clearly into the past as a means of gaining command of the present and control of the future. If only the past had been different, the present and future might somehow be better. If only we could learn from the past, we could avoid the same mistakes in the present, and bring about a better future. If only we could make all the right decisions, our future would be as good as it could possibly be. If only there were no tragedy.

This kind of proto-utopian thinking eventually yielded to a growing sense that the present, in every aspect, rests upon a framework of the past that cannot be altered, that the future cannot be protected from tragedy, and that the only way to live in freedom, and therefore with some chance of happiness, is with reconciliation for everything that happened in the past, and hope for everything that might happen in the future. Photographs have the potential to bear witness to this truth, if we will only see them for what they are. Therein lies their ultimate value.

References

(Aldrin) Aldrin, Edwin E., *Return to Earth* (New York: Random House, 1973).

(Armstrong) Farmer, Gene, and Dora Jane Hamblin, *First on the Moon* (New York, Little Brown & Company, 1970).

(Barthes) Barthes, Roland, *Camera Lucida: Reflections on Photography* (New York, Farrar, Straus and Giroux, 1981).

(Civil Rights) Commission on Civil Rights, Washington, D.C., *Process of Change: The Story of School Desegregation in Syracuse, New York* (June 1968).

(Cosgrove) Cosgrove, Denis, and William L. Fox, *Photography and Flight* (London, Reaktion Books, 2010).

(Cost) Cost, Frank. *Pocket Guide to Digital Printing* (New York, Delmar, 1997).

(Degroot) Degroot, Gerard J., *Dark Side of the Moon: The Magnificent Madness of the American Lunar Quest* (New York, New York University Press, 2006).

(Fox) Fox, William L., *Aereality: Essays from the World Above* (Berkeley, Counterpoint, 2009).

(Fox Talbot) Fox Talbot, William Henry, *The Pencil of Nature* (New York: Da Capo Press, 1969).

(Glenn) http://earthobservatory.nasa.gov/IOTD/view.php?id=77201

(Iliad) Homer, *The Iliad.* Translated by Robert Fitzgerald (New York: Alfred A. Knopf, 1992).

(Kauffman) Kauffman, James L., *Selling Outer Space: Kennedy, the Media, and Funding for Project Apollo, 1961–1963* (Tuscaloosa, The University of Alabama Press, 1994).

(LOC) Library of Congress website.

(Mailer) Mailer, Norman, *Of a Fire on the Moon* (Boston, Little, Brown and Company, 1969).

(Nadar) Nadar, Félix, *When I Was a Photographer* (Cambridge, The MIT Press, 2015).

(NASA) National Aeronautics and Space Adminstration https://www.nasa.gov/ and https://www.spacetelescope.org/images/heic0611b/

(Newhall) Newhall, Beaumont, *Airborne Camera: The World from the Air and Outer Space* (New York, Hastings House, Publishers, 1969).

(Odyssey) Homer, *The Odyssey.* Translated by Robert Fitzgerald (New York: Alfred A. Knopf, 1992).

(Peabody) Peabody, Josephine Preston, *Old Greek Folk Stories Told Anew* (New York, Houghton Mifflin, 1897).

(Shepard) last interview, http://www.jsc.nasa.gov/history/oral_histories/ShepardAB/ShepardAB_2-20-98.htm

(Wolfe) Wolfe, Tom, *The Right Stuff* (New York: Farrar, Straus and Giroux, 1979).

Acknowledgments

This book grew out of an invited presentation I made on July 13, 2015 at the Fabrica Communication Research Centre in Treviso, Italy (http://www.fabrica.it). That presentation was recorded and can be viewed here:

https://vimeo.com/138757286

The Fabrica presentation was also published as an illustrated book, *Pilot Flight Record and Log Book.* The enthusiastic response of students and staff at Fabrica to both the presentation and accompanying book provided the initial fuel for this larger writing project.

Several colleagues read early versions of this text and gave valuable feedback, leading to substantive improvements.

Skip (Carl) Battaglia, Professor Emeritus, School of Film and Animation, Rochester Institute of Technology

David Branca, class of 2005, School of Media Sciences, Rochester Institute of Technology

Owen Butler, Professor Emeritus, School of Photographic Arts & Sciences, Rochester Institute of Technology

Meredith Davenport, Associate Professor, School of Photographic Arts & Sciences, Rochester Institute of Technology

Willie Osterman, Professor, School of Photographic Arts & Sciences, Rochester Institute of Technology

David Pankow, Curator Emeritus, Melbert B. Cary Jr. Graphic Arts Collection, Rochester Institute of Technology

Rebeca Posadas-Nava, class of 2020, School of Photographic Arts & Sciences, Rochester Institute of Technology

Peter Riva, International Transactions literary agency, manager of the 1985 Voyager around-the-world flight.

Special thanks to RIT Professor Angela Kelly and Boston University Professor Toni Pepe for invitations to give lectures based on this book to their classes, and to Professor Willie Osterman for the invitation to present to the faculty of the RIT College of Imaging Arts & Sciences during his 2016–17 faculty lunchtime lecture series.

My heartfelt thanks to Ivan Maisel and Meg Murray, parents of Max Maisel, for their gracious willingness to allow me to tell my experience of their son's tragic death.

My greatest thanks to Patricia Cost for her superb and tireless editing and creative guidance throughout this and all of my projects.

Frank Cost
frank.cost@rit.edu
James E. McGhee Distinguished Professor
School of Photographic Arts & Sciences
Rochester Institute of Technology

Supplementary videos

The first aerial drone video of the George Eastman Museum. This video was part of an exhibition of innovative imaging technologies at the Eastman Museum in Winter 2014.

RIT photo arts students perform some "human typography" in September 2014.

The "world's first pinhole photo captured by drone," March 2015.

Aerial footage of the "Big Shot" number 30 on the RIT campus in September 2014.

The author's children attempt to fly their homebuilt "hang glider" in 1995.

Emil J. Cost flies a control-line model of a Nieuport 28 biplane in Syracuse in the 1950s.

Fossil
Press

88451210R00137

Made in the USA
Columbia, SC
05 February 2018